A Translation of the Choice Tang Quatrains

中英文版

唐人绝句精粹

上卷
Volume One

献给共和国七十华诞

周方珠 编译
By Zhou Fangzhu

北京师范大学出版集团
BEIJING NORMAL UNIVERSITY PUBLISHING GROUP
安徽大学出版社

图书在版编目(CIP)数据

唐人绝句精粹:中英文版:上、中、下卷/周方珠编译. —合肥:安徽大学出版社,2020.1
ISBN 978-7-5664-0613-2

Ⅰ. ①唐… Ⅱ. ①周… Ⅲ. ①绝句－诗集－中国－唐代－汉、英 Ⅳ. ①I222.742

中国版本图书馆 CIP 数据核字(2019)第 287186 号

唐人绝句精粹(中英文版)
Tangren Jueju Jingcui

周方珠 编译

出版发行:	北京师范大学出版集团 安徽大学出版社 (安徽省合肥市肥西路 3 号 邮编 230039) www.bnupg.com.cn www.ahupress.com.cn
印　　刷:	安徽昶颉包装印务有限责任公司
经　　销:	全国新华书店
开　　本:	170mm×240mm
印　　张:	69.25
字　　数:	709 千字
版　　次:	2020 年 1 月第 1 版
印　　次:	2020 年 1 月第 1 次印刷
定　　价:	229.00 元
ISBN 978-7-5664-0613-2	

策划编辑:李 梅 李 雪		装帧设计:李 雪 李 军	
责任编辑:李 雪 高婷婷		美术编辑:李 军	
责任印制:赵明炎			

版权所有　侵权必究

反盗版、侵权举报电话:0551-65106311
外埠邮购电话:0551-65107716
本书如有印装质量问题,请与印制管理部联系调换。
印制管理部电话:0551-65106311

总目
General Catalogue

前言

Preface

上卷（Volume One）

中卷（Volume Two）

下卷（Volume Three）

译后记（Postword）

前言
Preface

  中国是诗的国度。中文是诗性的语言。

  诗歌在中国享有极高的文学地位。如果说文学是精神食粮,诗歌便是以其酿造的美酒,而绝句则是其中的琼浆玉液。

  绝句源于六朝,发展至唐代已臻于完美。绝句有五绝、六绝和七绝三种。唐人为绝句者,上自帝王公卿,下至普通百姓,佳作累累,脍炙人口。在近五万首唐诗中绝句约占五分之一,其内容浩繁:大千世界、奇妙景象、古今史实、宇宙星空,无所不及。诗歌或伤春悲秋、悲天悯人,或怀古咏史、警世叹事,或吟诵爱情、感伤离别,或归隐山林、赞叹自然。绝句将大自然之崇山巍岳、诗人之喜怒哀乐纳入区区二十余字之中,其蕴含的巨大能量和信息量其他文体难以比拟。其幽远的意境,余音绕梁,常常使读者掩卷之后,被引入言有尽而意无穷的想象空间。这就是诗歌的功能与作用。

  子曰:"诗可以兴,可以观,可以群,可以怨。"(《论语·阳货》)"兴、观、群、怨"是孔子对诗歌社会功能的概述。

所谓"兴",与诗歌创作手法"赋、比、兴"中的"兴"不同。这里的"兴"读平声,表达的是"起"的意思,是指对道德情感的激活,使人格臻于成熟完善。在所有的艺术创作中,诗歌与音乐是最需要激情的。因此,诗人和音乐家往往会在其作品中唤起曾经体验过的情感,并将其幻化成诗句和旋律,使读者和听众也能体验到相同的情感。这便是移情(empathy),艺术上也称共鸣。"故正得失,动天地,感鬼神,莫近于诗。"(《毛诗序》)这便是"诗可以兴"的内涵。

所谓"观",即了解诗人的个人之志,并进而窥察国家政治、外交等方面的治世盛衰。在孔子看来,诗歌不仅能展示诗人的心理情感,也能反映当时社会群体的心理变化,社会风俗盛衰。这与《礼记·王制》中所说的天子"命大师陈诗,以观民风",和《汉书·艺文志》所云"古有采诗之官,王者之所以观风俗,知得失,自考正也"完全一致。自然界的气候时令变化决定何种生物在何时出现,精神文明的产物和动植物一样受其所处的政治生态环境制约。

"诗可以群"中的"群"是动词,表"合群,会合"。孔子言"诗可以群",指的是人可以通过赋诗来交流与沟通彼此的想法,从而协调人际关系,使国家内部团结起来,国与国联合起来。例如,《荀子·非十二子》有"壹统类,而群天下之英杰"之说。王维的《送元二使安西》、李白的《赠汪伦》《黄鹤楼送孟浩然之广陵》、杜甫的《赠李白》等均有同声相应、同气相求之意。一句"举头望明月,低头思故乡"不知唤起多少远在异国他乡同胞的浓浓乡情;一首《义勇军进行曲》谱上曲之后,曾激起无数华夏儿女的爱国之情,凝聚了中华民族的向心之力。"诗可以群"意在此。

"诗可以怨"意指诗歌可以用来发泄怨恨、排解忧愁。孔安国将"怨"解释为"刺上政也",意指诗可以用来针砭时弊,确认了诗的批判作用。汉代学者何休在《春秋公羊传·宣公十五年》里指出:"男女有所怨恨,相从而歌,饥者歌其食,劳者歌其事。"社会的不公需要批判,民众的忧烦必须舒散,否则会积淀成不稳定因素。"诗可以怨"一方面是给当政者的警示,而另一方面不失为一种统治策略,让不稳定因素在诗歌等文学艺术中得以释放、化解。古往今来,不乏其例:古有唐人杜甫的《登高》《茅屋为秋风所破歌》、白居易的《琵琶行》《长恨歌》;今有《天安门诗抄》,其中《扬眉剑出鞘》最为典型。所谓"愤怒出诗人"即对"诗可以怨"的最好诠释。

总之,孔子的"兴、观、群、怨"较为全面地概括了诗歌的社会功能与作用。笔者以为,诗歌的功能与作用可以概括为:抒发诗人之情,言明骚人之志,教化平民百姓,体现世事民情,反映民众意愿,怡悦读者身心。

诗歌的功能与作用能否在译文中予以体现,取决于译者能否将原文信息全面地传递给译文读者。翻译难,译诗更难,绝句翻译尤难。绝句的语言特征是:结构独特,语言凝练,情节跳跃,节奏明快,音韵和谐,意境幽远。对任何译者而言,这些特征都是挑战。故此,对于诗歌翻译,学者们持两种截然不同的观点:不可译者如美国诗人 Robert Frost 认为"诗就是在翻译中失去的东西";持另一种观点的如 William Trask 则认为"诗不可译,正是因为不可译,我才翻译"。笔者认为,在经济与文化全球化的今天,译者所要面对的不是可译不可译的问题,而是如何译。

笔者在绝句翻译时所遵循的是"保留'空白',意蕴忠实,形式对应,韵律相近"的原则。

同英文及印欧语系的大多数语言相比,中文属于强信息语境语言(high-context language),是非常诗性化的语言。汉语诗歌向来强调"不着一字,尽得风流"(司空图《二十四诗品·含蓄》)。"言外之意,象外之旨"永远是诗人追求的终极目标。故此,中国诗词文本中留有大量"空白",其中包括主题空白、语用空白、语义空白和结构空白。"空白"具有不确定性,它是联结创作意识和接受意识的桥梁,是前者向后者转换的必不可少的条件。它促使读者和译者(译者首先必须是读者)去寻找、品味诗歌的意义,从而赋予他们参与作品意义构成的权力。正如法国象征派诗人保尔·瓦莱里所言:"我诗歌中的意义是读者赋予的。"正是空白和意义的不确定性才构成了诗歌的基础结构,即"召唤结构"。"召唤结构"把诗歌与读者自身的经历以及对外部世界的想象联系起来,产生意义反思,使其沿着通幽的曲径(空白)进入洞天桃源,进而产生"天地入胸臆,吁嗟生风雷;文章得其微,物象由我裁"(孟郊《赠郑夫子鲂》)的感觉。这一过程便是诗歌空白的审美价值所在。距离产生美,要体现诗歌的神韵,就要在译诗中适当地保留原诗的空白。保留原诗中的空白,一是对原作者的尊重,二是让"召唤结构"激活读者的审美想象,从而完成品味、寻味、体味、玩味、回味之后仍有余味的审美体验。请看译例:

寻隐者不遇

贾岛

松下问童子,
言师采药去。
只在此山中,
云深不知处。

A Vain Visit to a Recluse

By Jia Dao

Under the pine tree I asked the lad,
"My master is out for herbs," he said.
Somewhere in the mountains he told me,
But deep in clouds nobody could see.

"松下问童子",所问何事,诗人并未说明,为读者留下了语用空白,读者只能从童子的回复中去领悟。根据第三、四行的内容可知"言师采药去"之后也有空白,即"何处采药"。此类空白在原作与读者之间形成审美距离,可让读者自由想象。为了保留这种审美距离,译者保留了原作的空白,从而让译文读者也享受距离产生的美感。

诗歌空白的审美价值是以接受美学和接受理论为基础的,每位读者借此而产生的想象空间虽然有重叠部分,但不可能完全相同,因此可以说诗歌文本的意蕴是多元的。诗歌意蕴的多元性往往会导致误读,进而产生误译或曲解原意,从而使译文读者接受错误信息。请看以下译例:

凉州词

王之涣

黄河远上白云间*,

一片孤城万仞山。

羌笛何须怨杨柳,

春风不度玉门关。

Out of the Great Wall

By Wang Zhihuan

The yellow sand uprises as high as white cloud,
The lonely town is lost amid the mountains proud.
Why should the Mongol flute complain no willows grow?
Beyond the Gate of Jade no vernal wind will blow. (许渊冲译)

依据《辞海》的解释,《凉州词》亦名《凉州歌》是乐府曲名,原是凉州(今甘肃武威)一带的歌曲。唐代诗人多用此调作歌词,描写西北的塞上风光和战争情景,其中以王翰和王之涣所作最为著名。由此可见,凉州为真实地名,《凉州词》也确有其曲,且有特定的文化内涵。显然,《凉州词》译为 Out of Great Wall 所指太泛,语义内涵流失太多。其次,"羌笛"译为 the Mongol flute 也不妥,羌笛是流行于我国甘肃、青海和川北地区的一种乐器,将其译为"蒙古的

---

* 一作"黄沙直上白云间"。

笛子"与原意相去甚远。最后,"玉门关"位于今甘肃省敦煌西北,是汉武帝时设置的重要关隘,距今天的玉门市千里之遥,绝非今日玉门市的城门。因此,将"玉门关"直译为"the Gate of Jade"过于牵强,基本语义和文化内涵流失太多。为尽量保留原文的基本意蕴,笔者试译如下:

Song of Liangzhou

Winding up to white clouds the Yellow River licks the sky,
Atop the soaring peaks lonely is the fort rising high.
The Qiang flute you need not bewail for weeping willows,
Beyond the Yumen Pass the vernal breeze never blows.

意蕴忠实是诗歌翻译的基础,原文信息在译文中流失过多势必造成读者的误读。如此,翻译也就失去了意义。

结构独特是诗歌与其他艺术形式的最显著区别,绝句的形式更是独一无二。英语中的 quatrain 是指四行诗,尤其是隔行押韵的四行诗,与汉语中的绝句基本对应。因此,将绝句译为英文四行诗是可行的。如:

池上双凫

薛涛

双栖绿池上,
朝暮共飞还。
更忆将雏日,
同心莲叶间。

Double Wild Ducks on the Pond

By Xue Tao

A pair of wild ducks dwell on the green pond,
Side by side they come and go day and night.
Feeding their ducklings well is their strong bond,
Looking after their young with all their might.

有的学者将绝句译为六句,甚至八句,虽然形式上看似诗歌,但原诗结构已经走样。有的学者甚至将诗歌译为散文,原文结构已不复存在。皮之不存,毛将焉附?故此,笔者认为,保留绝句的结构形式是诗歌翻译的最基本要求。

　　所谓"韵律相近"而非"相同",是基于表意文字和表音文字存在很大差异,尤其在节奏和韵律方面不同而提出的。汉语是声调语言,一字一个音节,并无明显的重音。因此,主要以平仄音调组成诗句。英语是拼音文字,凡是两个音节以上的单词都有明显的重音,格律诗以轻重(或重轻)音节相间的排列方式形成节奏,以音步为单位。汉语中的平仄无法移入英诗。同样,英语诗歌的抑扬、扬抑也无法照搬入中文诗。因此,翻译中取得完全相同的效果几乎不可能。所谓的"音美"系指译诗与原诗在节奏与押韵方面虽有所不同,但相似度较高。如:

送友人

薛涛

水国蒹葭夜有霜,
月寒山色共苍苍。
谁言千里自今夕,
离梦杳如关塞长。

To a Friend

By Xue Tao

Along the waterside reeds are dyed with rime at night,
In the cold moonlight mountains and hills turn greyish white.
From this date, it's said we'll be thousand miles apart,
Far beyond the Great Wall on my dream it casts a blight.

　　原诗是七言绝句,一、二、四尾韵,译诗为七音步(heptameter),aaba 尾韵,节奏相似,韵式相同。两者相似度较高,效果与功能基本一致。译文较为全面得传递了原文的信息。故此,译文读者便可获得与原文读者基本相同的信息和审美体验。

中国传统文化源远流长、博大精深,是中华民族5,000年文明的民族之魂。在经济与文化全球化的今天,中华民族的伟大复兴是一种文化传统的复兴。要增强中华民族的文化自信,就要从传统的文化原乡中汲取力量,就要让中国传统文化走向世界,融入其中,与世界文化交流互鉴。诗歌是中国传统文化中的瑰宝,其中蕴涵着慰藉人生的精神给养,滋润一代又一代华夏儿女。"胸藏文墨怀若谷,腹有诗书气自华",当下世人的心灵依然渴望古典诗词的甘霖。"今人不见古时月,今月曾经照古人。"让传统文化的精髓流入今人的心灵,让先贤的智慧发挥"观乎人文,以化成天下"的力量,成为复兴中华民族的精神动力。民族的才是世界的,让中国诗歌走向世界,让异域读者感受中华文化的无穷魅力,使其在多元文化大拼盘中熠熠生辉。

2018年于巴黎

Preface
前言

China is a land of poetry. And Chinese is a language of poetic quality.

Poetry is of great importance in Chinese literature. If literature is taken as the intellectual staple, poetry is the good wine made out of the staple, and quatrains are the top-quality nectar.

Originated in the Six Dynasties (222~589), quatrains were gradually attaining to perfection, which are classified to the quatrain of five characters per line, that of six characters per line, and seven characters per line. In the Tang Dynasty, people of all descriptions, from emperors to the common plebs, were greatly interested in poetry, which resulted in lots of excellent poems of great popularity. Of nearly fifty thousand poems in the Tang Dynasty, quatrains make up 20%, which cover a wide range of topics. Some of them are sentimental about the spring or autumn, or full of deep concerns for the people and the country; some meditating on the past or reflecting on ancient events to admonish the current conditions; some singing the praises of love or expressing the parting sorrows; some praising highly the great nature and the life in seclusion. A quatrain is composed of only around twenty characters, yet it contains the various aspects of the great nature and complex emotions of the poet. The great volume of the information is condensed into a little poem with the artistic mood of profound implication that leaves a vast imagination space for readers. This is what poetry functions.

Confucius summarized the social roles of poetry as follows (*The Analects of Confucius*):

To thrive the readers' emotions

To observe the reality of a country

To assemble the like-minded people

To vent resentment

To thrive the readers' emotions means that readers' emotions are aroused by reading poems through which their personality is attaining to perfection. It is known to all that of all the artistic works poems and music demand enthusiasm to the greatest degree. So poets and musicians usually evoke the emotions of the past and turn them into poems and music works to make their readers and audience feel empathy with themselves, which can distinguish right from wrong, and even move the heaven and earth as it is pointed out in *The Preface to the Book of Poetry*. This is why we say poetry can thrive the readers' emotions.

To observe the reality of a country here means to make a survey of the aspiration of the poet through which the system of government of the country and its diplomatic relations with other countries can thus be learned. Poems, in Confucius's opinion, can not only reflect the mental state of the poet, but also that of the social community then, and in the meanwhile the prosperity or decline of the social morals and customs then, which is in conformity with the classical doctrine of ancient sage in *The Book of Rites* and *The History of Han*. Animals and plants in the world are very much conditioned by climatic variation; the same is true of the mental fruit that is conditioned by the political ecological environment.

To assemble the like-minded people implies that by composing poems poets can have an exchange of views with each other, and to gather the social elite all over the world just as is pointed out in *The Book of Xunzi*, thus a better coordination between the like-minded people can be facilitated and solidarity among different ethnic groups can be achieved. The famous poems, such as "Farewell to My Friend Yuan Er on His Mission to Anxi" by Wang Wei, "To Wang Lun" and "Sending Meng Haoran off to Guangling at Yellow Crane Tower" by Li Bai, and "To Li Bai" by Du Fu, all share the implication that "Like attracts like". The two poem lines from Li Bai's poem "Homesickness at Dead of Night" "Raising my head I see the moon so bright, Bowing down I become homesick at night" have evoked the homesickness of innumerable overseas Chinese. The national anthem of the PRC "March of the Volunteers" has aroused the patriotic sentiments of so many sons and daughters of the Chinese nation, and thus the powerful cohesiveness is formed. The above-mentioned examples are the best explanation to that "poetry can assemble the like-minded people".

To vent resentment means to air one's discontent or assuage one's grief by composing poems. Some scholars believe that poetry can be used to criticize the social evils of the day and to remove malpractices of the time. He Xiu, a famous scholar in the Han Dynastry pointed out in *The Spring and Autumn Annals with Commentaries by Gongyang* that, " When resentment is harbored, people sing together, starving people praise their food, and laborers eulogize their achievements. " To vent resentment by means of composing poems is on the one hand a warning to those in power and on the other a tactic for governing, through which the discontent can be eliminated and the destabilizing factor can be resolved effectively. There is no lack of precedents since time immemorial: "On the Height" and "My Cottage Unroofed by Autumn Gales" by Du Fu; "The Everlasting Regret" and "Song of a Pipa Player" by Bai Juyi; especially "A Hero with His Sword Drawn" from the *Anthology of Poems in Memory of Premier Zhou Enlai*. The proverb "indignation makes a poet" is the best paraphrase to the saying "Poetry can be used to vent resentment".

The above-mentioned four points by Confucius, in a word, have summarized the overall aspects of the social function of poetry. The author believes that the function of poetry can be summed up as: expressing the poet's feelings, conveying the writer's emotion, cultivating the common people, observing the mundane affairs of the world, manifesting the opinions at the grassroots and pleasing the readers.

The function of poetry can whether or not be manifested in the translated text is determined to what degree the information of the source text is conveyed to the readers of the target text. Translation is difficult, even more difficult is that of poetry, and quatrains in particular. The characteristic features of quatrains are as follows: unique in structure, terse in language, flexible in plot, sprightful in rhythm, melodious in rhyme and profound in implication and artistic mood. These features present a great challenge to the translator whoever he is. With regard to translation of poetry therefore there are two totally different opinions: "translatable" and "untranslatable". Robert Frost believes that "Poetry is what gets lost in translation"; William Trask holds that "I translate poems just because some people think they are untranslatable". The author thinks that the problem we confront at present is by no means that of "translatable or not", but that of "how to translate" with the advance of economic and cultural globalization.

The following principles are strictly adhered to for the translation of this book:

>To have the original gaps reserved
>
>Be faithful to the original in meaning
>
>Be true to the original in structure
>
>Be similar to the original in rhyme and rhythm

Different from most of the Indo-European Languages, Chinese language is a high-context language of poetic quality. The special emphasis of Chinese poetry is placed on brevity in diction and grace in style. The implied meaning between the lines, behind the lines and beyond the lines, is always the final goal of poets. There are therefore a lot of gaps in Chinese poetry, including the thematic gaps, pragmatic gaps, semantic gaps and syntactic gaps. Indeterminacy is characteristic of these gaps, which is the bridge between the awareness of the poet and that of the readers, and help the readers (A translator first of all is a reader) seek and ponder on the subtle meaning of a poem, which is the process of constituting the meaning of a poem. Paul Valery, a French symbolist poet, pointed out that the meaning of the poems resulted from the reading of readers. Gaps and indeterminacy of meaning of a poem form the basic structure—appealing structure that serves as a bridge between the poem and the readers' experience and his imagination based on his reading the poem and experience, which give free rein to his imagination. This process totally reflects the true value of aesthetic appreciation of poetry. Distance helps generate the awareness of beauty. In order to highlight the charm of a poem, a translator is supposed to keep its gaps well preserved in the translated text, which is the proper respect to the writer of the original on the one hand, and causes the appealing structure to bring the readers' aesthetic imagination into full play on the other, and then the aesthetic experience of tasting, chewing, pondering and appreciating can be accomplished. See the following example, please.

寻隐者不遇

贾岛

松下问童子，

言师采药去。

只在此山中，

云深不知处。

A Vain Visit to a Recluse

By Jia Dao

Under the pine tree I asked the lad,

"My master is out for herbs," he said.

Somewhere in the mountains he told me,

But deep in clouds nobody could see.

What is the concrete question after the first line, the poet failed to tell readers, which turns out to be a pragmatic gap that can be realized only from the answer "My master is out for herbs" in the second line of the poem. From the third line and the last line, we can see that there is also a gap immediately after the second line of the poem, which may be "Where is your master out for". These gaps form the aesthetic distance between the original and readers, which help give them free rein to their imagination. In order to let the readers of the translated text enjoy the same aesthetic experience the translator has these gaps well preserved in the target text.

The aesthetic value of gaps in poetry is based on acceptance aesthetics and aesthetic theory. The imagination space of a reader may possibly overlap that of another reader to certain extent, but the complete overlap is extremely rare. It is thus believed that the implied meaning of a poem is diversified, which sometimes leads to translator's misunderstanding or even misinterpreting the meaning of the original text and then conveying the wrong information to readers of the translated text. See the following example, please.

凉州词

王之涣

黄河远上白云间，

一片孤城万仞山。

羌笛何须怨杨柳，

春风不度玉门关。

Out of the Great Wall

By Wang Zhihuan

The yellow sand uprises as high as white cloud,

The lonely town is lost and the mountains proud.

Why should the Mongol flute complain no willows grow?

Beyond the Gate of Jade no vernal wind will blow.

(Translated by Xu Yuanchong)

The title of this quatrain, according to an authoritative Chinese dictionary, is the name of a *qu* tune popular among the ordinary folk in Liangzhou (Wuwei City, Gansu Province today). This title was often used by the poets in the Tang Dynasty for portray of scenery and wartime conditions in the northwest border area, of which the most famous are poems by Wang Zhihuan and Wang Han. It is thus clear that Liangzhou is the name of a specific place and the title of the quatrain is indeed the name of a tune with certain cultural connotation. Evidently the translation of the title "Out of the Great Wall" is not faithful to the original as too much of its cultural connotation is lost. And what is more, "羌笛" is translated into "the Mongol flute" which is not proper as the translation and the original are far apart in meaning. Finally, "玉门关" in the original was a real pass in the northwest of Dunhuang City, Gansu Province. The pass was set up in the Han Dynasty, which is far away from today's Yumen City. It is thus clear that the translation "the Gate of Jade" is a word-for-word translation with no regard for its cultural connotation. In order to have the basic meaning and the cultural connotation well preserved in translation, the author translates the quatrain as follows:

Song of Liangzhou

Winding up to white clouds the Yellow River licks the sky,
Atop the soaring peaks lonely is the fort rising high.
The Qiang flute you need not bewail for weeping willows,
Beyond the Yumen Pass the vernal breeze never blows.

The real value of translation lies in fidelity to the original meaning, which is of first importance. Leaching out too much of the original information in translation will certainly result in misunderstanding of the readers of the translated text. If this is the case, translation will be of little value.

Unique structure is characteristic of poetry, which is remarkably different from all other literary forms, and quatrain in particular. Quatrains in English are more or less the same with those in Chinese. It is thus feasible to translate Chinese quatrains into English quatrains. See the following example, please.

池上双凫

薛涛

双栖绿池上,
朝暮共飞还。
更忆将雏日,
同心莲叶间。

Double Wild Ducks on the Pond

By Xue Tao

A pair of wild ducks dwell on the green pond,
Side by side they come and go day and night.
Feeding their ducklings well is their strong bond,
Looking after their young with all their might.

Some scholars have Chinese quatrains translated into poems of six lines, eight lines, some scholars even have poems translated into prose. It is known to all that the structure of a Chinese poem is of great importance to its meaning. If the structure is spoiled, its meaning will certainly be affected. To have the structural shape of the original poem well preserved is the primary demand for a translator.

The translation principle of being similar to the original in rhyme and rhythm instead of being identical to the original is based on the great difference between Chinese and English in rhyme and rhythm. The tonal patterns in classical Chinese poetry are formed by the level and oblique tones in Chinese prosody which can be hardly transferred to English poetry, and the rise and fall of the English tonal patterns cannot be transferred to Chinese poetry either. It is thus clear that the identical tonal effect can be hardly produced in translation between Chinese and English poetry. The standard of so-called "beauty in sound" means the translated verse and the original poem enjoy great degree of similarity in rhyme and rhythm, but far from being identical. See the following example, please.

送友人

薛涛

水国蒹葭夜有霜，

月寒山色共苍苍。

谁言千里自今日，

离梦杳如关路长。

To a Friend

By Xue Tao

Along the waterside reeds are dyed with rime at night,
In the cold moonlight mountains and hills turn greyish white.
From this date, it's said we'll be thousand miles apart,
Far beyond the Great Wall on my dream it casts a blight.

The original poem is a quatrain with seven characters per line in the rhyme scheme of "aaba", which is translated into a poem of heptameter in the rhyme scheme and rhythm correspondent to the original. The information of the original poem is conveyed to the great degree to the readers of the translated text. The readers of the translated text can therefore gain almost the equivalent information and have nearly the same aesthetic experience as the readers of the original poem do.

The extensive and profound Chinese culture has a long history of five thousand years which is the spirit of Chinese nation. At present, the economic and cultural globalization is on the upswing. The national rejuvenation means the rejuvenation of Chinese cultural heritage. In order to strengthen the confidence in culture of Chinese nation, it is of great importance to derive nourishment from the source of traditional culture and let it go out of our country and merge with the world culture to promote the exchange and mutual learning between them. Poetry is the precious treasure of traditional Chinese culture, which is rich in nourishment for mind, nourishes the Chinese people from generation to generation. "Extensive reading makes a super mind, reciting great poems renders you graceful." People of the world at present are still thirsty for the sweet dew of classical poems. "People at present have no chance to enjoy the moonlight of the ancient past, but the present moon did shine overhead the ancients." Let the quintessence of the traditional culture flow into the heart of the present people and turn into great power for rejuvenation of Chinese nation. The culture with distinct national identity is usually more acceptable to the world people. Let Chinese poetry melt into the world culture, and the charm of traditional Chinese culture display in the palette of the world culture.

2018, in Paris

上卷目录
Catalogue of Volume One

虞世南	……	1	张　说	……	56
孔德绍	……	3	苏　颋	……	67
王　绩	……	5	张九龄	……	69
上官仪	……	8	崔国辅	……	73
卢照邻	……	10	王　翰	……	82
韦承庆	……	12	王之涣	……	85
骆宾王	……	16	孟浩然	……	89
李　峤	……	21	刘方平	……	100
杜审言	……	25	王昌龄	……	104
王　勃	……	27	王　维	……	123
宋之问	……	40	李　白	……	157
郭　震	……	45	崔　颢	……	198
贺知章	……	50	高　适	……	200
陈子昂	……	54	储光羲	……	206

刘长卿	210	贾　至	273
杜　甫	227	钱　起	277
岑　参	254	韩　翃	294
金昌绪	263	顾　况	298
张　继	264	戴叔伦	316
裴　迪	266	韦应物	331
皇甫冉	269	司空曙	348

虞世南

虞世南(558～638),字伯施,越州余姚(今浙江慈溪)人。曾在朝为官,能文辞,工书法,是初唐四大书法家之一。《全唐诗》存其诗一卷。

Yu Shinan(558～638) styled Boshi, was born in Yuyao, Yuezhou County (Cixi City, Zhejiang Province today). Once served as a government official, Yu was well versed in writing and calligraphy, well known among the four calligraphers in the early Tang Dynasty. There is one volume of his poems collected in *The Complete Collection of the Tang Poetry*.

春夜

春苑月裴回,
竹堂侵夜开。
惊鸟排林度,
风花隔水来。

Spring Night

Over the spring garden is the moon in the sky,
Night is deep and the bamboo hall open wide.
Back to the woods the birds are startled to fly,
Wafted with wind is the scent from the riverside.

蝉

垂緌饮清露,
流响出疏桐。
居高声自远,
非是藉秋风。

To Cicadas

Hanging your feelers you drink nothing but dew,
Your singing flows from the sparse phoenix trees.
Atop the trees far and wide your chirps issue,
Your high-pitch voice needs no help of autumn breeze.

孔德绍

孔德绍(？～621)，会稽(今浙江绍兴)人。孔子第三十四世孙。其诗朴实无华，风格清新。《全唐诗》存其诗十二首。

Kong Deshao(？～621)，born in Kuaiji(Shaoxing City，Zhejiang Province today) was a 34th generation descendant of Confucius. His poems are simple in language but fresh in style，of which twelve are collected in *The Complete Collection of the Tang Poetry*.

落叶

早秋惊叶落，
飘零似客心。
翻飞未肯下。
犹言惜故林。

To Fallen Leaves

Early autumn sees leaves falling，I'm so sad，
Homeless tramps they seem motherless children mad.
Twirling up and down reluctant to go away，
It seems they cry，"with mother tree we like to stay."

清　王翚　《秋树昏鸦图》

王　绩

王绩(585~644),字无功,号东皋子,绛州龙门(今山西万荣)人。初唐为官,后弃官还乡。王绩是初唐著名诗人,诗作平淡疏野。《全唐诗》存其诗一卷。

Wang Ji(585~644), styled Wugong, also known as Dong Gaozi, was born in Longmen, Jiangzhou(Wanrong County, Shanxi Province today). Wang was a government official in the early Tang Dynasty, but he resigned from his post later. As a famous poet in the early Tang Dynasty, Wang's poems were plain but unconventional in style, of which one volume is collected in *The Complete Collection of the Tang Poetry*.

初春

春来日渐长,
醉客喜年光。
稍觉池亭好,
偏宜酒瓮香。

In Early Spring

Longer and longer are the spring days,
As spring comes I am happy always.
It's pleasant to walk around the pond,
But sweet smell of wine wafts around.

秋夜喜遇王处士

北场芸藿罢,
东皋刈黍归。
相逢秋月满,
更值夜萤飞。

A Chance Meeting with Mr. Wang at Autumn Night

Hoeing is over in the northern garden,
Back from mowing I am home free from burden.
A chance meeting with my friend in the moon light,
Fireflies glow with green light in the autumn night.

独酌

浮生知几日,
无状逐空名。
不如多酿酒,
时向竹林倾。

Drinking Alone

Life is nothing but a fleeting dream,
Fame's vain glory vanishing like steam.
It would be better to make more wine,
Drinking in bamboo grove is so fine.

上官仪

上官仪(608~664),字游韶,陕州陕县(今河南三门峡)人。贞观进士,唐高宗时为相。麟德初,被告与废太子通谋,下狱死。其诗被士大夫们纷纷效仿,称为"上官体",对律诗的形成颇有影响。《全唐诗》存其诗一卷。

Shangguan Yi(608~664), styled Youshao, was born in Shan County, Shanzhou(Sanmenxia City, Henan Province today). Having passed the highest imperial examination, Shangguan was promoted the prime minister during the reign of Emperor Gaozong(Li Zhi). But in 665 he was accused of illicit relations with the dethroned crown prince, and then put into jail and died in prison. His poems, regarded as poems of "Shangguan Style" imitated by scholar-officials, exercised great influence on the development of regulated verse in China, of which one volume is collected in *The Complete Collection of the Tang Poetry*.

入朝洛堤步月

脉脉广川流,
驱马历长洲。
鹊飞山月曙,
蝉噪野风秋。

On the Way to the Emperor's Audience Hall

Smoothly the Luoshui River slowly flows,
Along the river the route my steed knows.
The moon shines at dawn and magpies fly,
Cicadas chirp in autumn and wind blows.

元　赵孟頫　《进马图》

卢照邻

卢照邻(630~680),字升之,号幽忧子,幽州范阳(今河北涿县)人。初唐四杰之一。因不堪疾病折磨,投水自尽。诗多愁苦之音。《全唐诗》存其诗两卷。

Lu Zhaolin(630~680), styled Shengzhi, also known as You Youzi, was born in Fanyang, Youzhou (Zhuozhou City, Hebei Province today). Together with Wang Bo, Yang Jiong, and Luo Binwang, Lu Zhaolin ranked among the "Four Eminent Poets in the early Tang Dynasty". Lu was tortured by a lingering illness, and killed himself by drowning. Most of his poems express sorrows and pains of his time, of which two volumes are collected in *The Complete Collection of the Tang Poetry*.

曲池荷

浮香绕曲岸,
圆影覆华池。
常恐秋风早,
飘零君不知。

Lotus of the Qu Pond

The scent of lotus flowers gently wafts around,
Lotus leaves cover clear water in the pond.
Afraid of bleak wind coming early in autumn,
Withering the flowers and falling to the ground.

九月九日登玄武山

九月九日眺山川，
归心归望积风烟。
他乡共酌金花酒，
万里同悲鸿雁天。

A Distant View on the Journey to Xuanwu Mountain

On Double Ninth Festival I gazed from a height,
Wish to have wings to fly home but it's out of sight.
Drinking chrysanthemum wine in a strange land,
No news comes to me I was in a sorry plight.

韦承庆

韦承庆(639～705),字延休,郑州阳武(今河南原阳)人。曾在朝为官,后遭贬。《全唐诗》存其诗七首。

Wei Chengqing (639～705), styled Yanxiu, was born in Yangwu, Zhengzhou (Yuanyang County, Henan Province today). Wei once served the court as a senior official for years but was demoted and banished later. There are seven poems collected in *The Complete Collection of the Tang Poetry*.

南中咏雁

万里人南去,
三春雁北飞。
不知何岁月,
得与尔同归?

To Wild Geese—Verses Composed in Exile Southwards

Banished from the court I'm heading for the south,
Late spring is the very time for geese to fly north.
The exact date for us to return I don't know,
Oh, wild geese, northward with ye I'm yearning to go.

南行别弟

澹澹长江水,
悠悠远客情。
落花相与恨,
到地一无声。

Parting from My Brother

The Yangtze River flows far away,
The sad mood grows on the parting day.
Mingled with a sense of grievance,
Fallen petals fall into silence.

江楼

独酌芳春酒,
登楼已半曛。
谁惊一行雁,
冲断过江云。

On the River Tower

Sipping good wine alone sweet as flower,
Tipsy I'm going upstairs the tower.
A flight of wild geese cry out in fright,
Flying into clouds blocking my sight.

明　仇英　《仙山楼阁图》

骆宾王

骆宾王(640~684),婺州义乌(今浙江义乌)人,初唐四杰之一。其诗多悲愤之词。《全唐诗》存其诗三卷。

Luo Binwang(640~684) was born in Yiwu, Wuzhou(Yiwu City, Zhejiang Province today). As one of the "Four Eminent Poets in the Early Tang Dynasty", Luo's poems are full of grief and indignation, of which three volumes are collected it in *The Complete Collection of the Tang Poetry*.

咏镜

写月无芳桂,
照日有花菱。
不持光谢水,
翻将影学冰。

Ode to Bronze Mirror

Like a full moon but with no laurel sweet,
With flowers reflected in the sunlight.
Like water is your gloss if let alone,
Turning back and forth like ice you shine bright.

易水送人

此地别燕丹,
壮士发冲冠。
昔时人已没,
今日水犹寒。

An Elegy to Jing Ke*

Bidding farewell to Prince Dan of the Yan State,
Your hair stood on end on high indignation.
Died a martyr our hero with failed mission,
Yet your moral fiber makes the river great.

---

* Based on historical tale, the poet expressed his esteem for Jing Ke who was engaged by Prince Dan of the Yan State as a warrior to assassinate the ruler of Qin (who later became the first emperor of China), during the Warring States period. Prince Dan gave a send-off to Jing Ke by the Yishui River, who did his utmost but failed and died a heroic martyr.

送别

寒更承夜永,
凉夕向秋澄。
离心何以赠,
自有玉壶冰。

A Send-off to a Friend

I feel chilly in the dead of night,
Cold at dusk autumn is clear and bright.
What's the state of mind at the parting?
Pure as ice in jade vase I'm all right.

忆蜀地佳人

东西吴蜀关山远,
鱼来雁去两难闻。
莫怪常有千行泪,
只为阳台一片云。

In Memory of the Belle in Kingdom Shu

Reunion between us is blocked by thousand mountains,
No news comes to each other we are kept in the dark.
You know not why I'm always in tears behind curtains,
A chance meeting indeed a bliss but it's stiff and stark.

清　石涛　《山水清音图》

李 峤

李峤(644～713),字巨山,赵州赞皇(今河北省赞皇县)人。曾在朝为官数年,后遭贬。诗多咏物之作,《全唐诗》存其诗五卷。

Li Qiao(644～713), styled Jushan, was born in Zanhuang, Zhaozhou (Zanhuang County, Hebei Province today). Li was a government official for years, but was demoted later. Most of his poems are the prescriptions of objects, of which five volumes are collected in *The Complete Collection of the Tang Poetry*.

风

解落三秋叶,
能开二月花。
过江千尺浪,
入竹万竿斜。

To Wind

Stripping the leaves off trees in late autumn,
Ushering in spring you smile at flowers growing.
Crossing the river you stir it from the bottom,
Over bamboos they've to bow with your blowing.

中秋月

盈缺青冥外，
东风万古吹。
何人种丹桂，
不长出轮枝。

To Mid-autumn Moon

Waxes and wanes the moon in the sky,
East wind blows all ages as autumn draws nigh.
Who planted the laurel in the moon?
Its branches never grow out of the balloon.

宋 马远 《月下把杯图》

送司马先生

蓬阁桃源两处分，
人间海上不相闻。
一朝琴里悲黄鹤，
何日山头望白云。

A Send-off to Mr. Sima

I'm in Penglai Palace but you're dispatched far away,
Separated by vast sea we yearn for the reunion day.
I'd like to play lute once I think of thy eminent grace,
Atop the mountain at the white clouds far away I gaze.

杜审言

杜审言(645～708),字必简,洛州巩县(今河南巩义)人。670 年举进士,曾在朝为官,后被贬,流放峰州(今越南境内)。杜审言的诗歌言语新奇,气度壮伟,对仗工整。《全唐诗》存其诗一卷。

Du Shenyan(645～708), styled Bijian, was born in Gongxian Luozhou (Gongyi City, Henan Province today). He succeeded in the highest imperial examination and was promoted to a senior official in 670, but was demoted and banished to Fengzhou(in Vietnam today). His poems are well-knit in antithesis with novel language in grand style, of which one volume is collected in *The Complete Collection of the Tang Poetry*.

渡湘江

迟日园林悲昔游,
今春花鸟作边愁。
独怜京国人南窜,
不似湘江水北流。

Crossing the River Xiang

The charm of spring reminds me of outings in the past,
Flowers and birds send me to frontier and spring fades fast.
Leaving the capital I'm sent southward into exile,
But the Xiangjiang River flows northward in former style.

赠苏绾书记

知君书记本翩翩,
为许从戎赴朔边。
红粉楼中应计日,
燕支山下莫经年。

To Secretary Su Wan

As a secretary you've a graceful manner,
Why went to the frontier waving the army banner.
Your wife at home must be pining away day and night,
Never let Yanzhi Mountain prolong her sorrow blight.

王 勃

王勃(649～676),字子安,绛州龙门(今山西河津)人。前往海南探父途中溺亡。王勃为初唐四杰之一,其诗多描写个人生活,风格清新,但不乏华艳之作,有八十余首存世。《全唐诗》存其诗两卷。

Wang Bo(649～676), styled Zi'an, was born in Longmen, Jiangzhou(Hejin County, Shanxi Province today). Wang was drowned on his way to Hainan Island for calling on his father. Wang is among the "Four Eminent Poets in the Early Tang Dynasty". Most of his poems are the pictures of his personal life in lucid style, of which some are composed of flowery words. There are about eighty of his poems extant now. Two volumes of his poems are collected in *The Complete Collection of the Tang Poetry*.

夜兴

野烟含夕渚,
山月照秋林。
还将中散兴,
来偶步兵琴。

In High Spirits at Night

In the shroud of mist is the islet at twilight,
The forest in autumn bathed in the moonlight.
Drinking and the strings are the favorites of mine*,
Playing lute with me and come to drink the choice wine.

---

* *Zhongsan*(中散) in Chinese refers Ji Kang, a famous politician and poet in East Han. *Zhongsan* was his position in the government. Drinking and playing the lute were his hobbies.

江亭月夜送别·其一

江送巴南水，
山横塞北云。
津亭秋月夜，
谁见泣离群。

Parting at the Moon-lit Pavilion（1）

The river flows from the south of the peak so high,
The mountain blocks the clouds beyond the Great Wall.
The autumn moon shines on the tower standing tall,
Too sad to think of the time when we said goodbye.

江亭月夜送别·其二

乱烟笼碧砌,
飞月向南端。
寂寞离亭掩,
江山此夜寒。

Parting at the Moon-lit Pavilion (2)

Over the green steps the thin mist is floating,
Down south the pavilion the moon is setting.
As visitors depart the night becomes still,
Over water and mountains there's a slight chill.

别人

江上风烟积,
山幽云雾多。
送君南浦外,
还望将如何。

Farewell to My Friend

Heavy is the mist over the river,
In the mountains clouds leisurely hover.
Waving farewell to thou to the waterside,
Till thy boat is out of sight away with tide.

早春野望

江旷春潮白,
山长晓岫青。
他乡临眺极,
花柳映边亭。

An Open Country View in Early Spring

The vast river in spring with water at high tide,
Rolling mountains with gliding ranges vividly green.
In the strange land calmly I'm gazing far and wide,
Flowers and willows by tall tower can be seen.

山中

长江悲已滞,
万里念将归。
况属高风晚,
山山黄叶飞。

In the Mountains

Sad is the Yangtze River reluctant to flow,
Far away in a strange land I'm longing for home.
Autumn is on the wane and the bleak winds blow,
With high winds fallen leaves here and there roam.

冬郊行望

桂密岩花白，
梨疏林叶红。
江皋寒望尽，
归念断征篷。

A Winter Outing in the Suburbs

Fair and sweet are laurel flowers on the hillside,
Sparse are the pear trees and their leaves turn red.
At a height by the river I gaze far and wide,
Yearning to return my desire's a like plant dead.

羁春

客心千里倦,
春事一朝归。
还伤北园里,
重见落花飞。

Keeping Spring Lingering

Far away from home I'm in a strange land,
Spring is on the wane that makes me strand.
Walking in the north garden I'm in sorrow,
After me closely I see petals follow.

五代 巨然 《湖山春晓图》

春庄

山中兰叶径,
城外李桃园。
岂知人事静,
不觉鸟声喧。

A Farmstead in Spring

Covered with orchid is the path to the mountain,
In the suburbs are the fruit trees in the garden.
The country farmstead remains tranquil in spring,
It seems that you can hardly hear the birds sing.

春园

山泉两处晚，
花柳一园春。
还持千日醉，
共作百年人。

To the Spring Garden

Two springs flow at dusk from the high mountain,
Willows green and flowers smile in the garden.
I'm crazy about the home-made wine so strong,
And drinking to my heart's content for life long.

秋江送别

早是他乡值早秋,
江亭明月带江流。
已觉逝川伤别念,
复看津树隐离舟。

A Riverside Parting in Autumn

At the time of early autumn I'm in the strange land,
Moving with water is the moon atop the tower bright.
As the river flows the parting pain I can hardly stand,
Trees at the ferry crossing hide the boat from my sight.

蜀中九月

九月九日望乡台，
他席他乡送客杯。
人情已厌南中苦，
鸿雁那从北地来？

Double Ninth Festival in Chengdu

On Double Ninth Festival atop the tower,
At the farewell party I'm in a strange land.
Staying in the south is indeed the bitter hour,
But no swan coming in sight I can't understand.

宋之问

宋之问(656~712),字延清,虢州弘农(今河南灵宝)人。曾在朝为官,后被贬自杀。其诗注重对仗缜密和音韵和谐,对律诗的形成和发展颇有影响。《全唐诗》存其诗三卷。

Song Zhiwen(656~712), styled Yanqing, was born in Hongnong, Guozhou (Lingbao County, Henan Province today). Song was once an official in the court, but demoted later and killed himself in 713. His poems are well-knit in antithesis with harmonious rhyme and rhythm, which is a great help to the development of regulated verse. There are three volumes of his poems collected in *The Complete Collection of the Tang Poetry*.

嵩山夜还

家住嵩山下,
好采旧山薇。
自省游泉石,
何曾不夜归。

On Way Home at Night

At the foot of Mountain Song is my abode,
Living in seclusion wild herbs are my food.
After sightseeing around the peaks and streams,
Homecoming at night I always have sweet dreams.

渡汉江

岭外音书断，
经冬复历春。
近乡情更怯，
不敢问来人。

Crossing the Han River

Awaiting for news from the mountains beyond,
Year after year I have anxiously yearned.
With every step homeward timid I grow,
Dare not ask the passers-by, why, I don't know.

宋　王希孟　《千里江山图》

在荆州重赴岭南

梦泽三秋日,
苍梧一片云。
还将鹓鹭羽,
重入鹧鸪群。

The South Ward Trip for Demotion

In a strange land flooded in late autumn,
Southward like a cloud I float in the sky.
A flight of big birds fly away from home,
Back to the flock but I can never fly.

登逍遥楼

逍遥楼上望乡关,
绿水泓澄云雾间。
北去衡阳二千里,
无因雁足系书还。

Atop Xiaoyao Tower

Atop Xiaoyao Tower I gaze fondly far away,
Out of sight is my homeland beyond green water vast.
There is a long way north to Hengyang* we've to go fast,
But no swan helps me and my message faces a long delay.

---

* Hengyang is a city in Hunan Province. It is said that wild geese and swans usually refuse to fly on southward as peaks are too high to fly over, so they stay here for the winter till the advent of spring next year, and then they resume their flying northward.

郭 震

郭震(656～713),字元振,魏州贵乡(今河北大名)人。曾在军中服役,多有战功而升官。《全唐诗》存其诗一卷。

Guo Zhen(656～713), styled Yuanzhen, was born in Guixiang, Weizhou (Daming County, Hebei Province today). Guo once served in the army and was promoted a senior officer for his honor in war. There is one volume of his poems collected in *The Complete Collection of the Tang Poetry*.

王昭君

自嫁单于国,
长衔汉掖悲。
容颜日憔悴,
有甚画图时。

To Wang Zhaojun

Since married to the Hun chieftain,
Yearning for home you're grief-stricken.
Pallid and sallow thou pine away,
No fair maiden now you're in dismay.

春歌

陌头杨柳枝,
已被春风吹。
妾心正断绝,
君怀那得知。

Song of Spring

Branches of roadside willows,
Dance as the vernal wind blows.
Lovesick I'm missing you now,
Missing me or not, God knows?

秋歌

邀欢空伫立,
望美频回顾。
何时复采菱,
江中密相遇。

Song of Autumn

Making eyes at you I'm vainly standing,
Feasting your eyes on me you're attending.
Waiting for chance to pick nut again,
Meeting on the river we wait with pain.

冬歌

帷横双翡翠，
被卷两鸳鸯。
婉态不自得，
宛转君王床。

Song of Winter

Two love birds play on the folding screen,
A pair of mandarin ducks on the quilt green.
Vivid and gentle they are so charming,
The wild mates on king's bed fondly kissing.

莲花

脸腻香薰似有情，
世间何物比轻盈。
湘妃雨后来池看，
碧玉盘中弄水晶。

To Lots Flowers

Creamy and sweet lotus flowers seem charming,
More graceful and light in the world there's nothing.
If the River Goddess appears after rain,
Pearls rolling in the green jade plates with no stain.

贺知章

贺知章(659～744),字季真,号四明狂客,越州永兴(今浙江杭州)人。工书法,少年因文词知名,其诗清新通俗。《全唐诗》存其诗一卷。

He Zhizhang (659～744), styled Jizhen, also known as a Madman in Siming Mountain, was born in Yongxing, Yuezhou (Hangzhou City, Zhejiang Province today). As a famous poet He Zhizhang was well versed in calligraphy when he was young, and his poems are lucid and plain in style, of which one volume is collected in *The Complete Collection of the Tang Poetry*.

偶游主人园

主人不相识,
偶坐为林泉。
莫谩愁沽酒,
囊中自有钱。

A Random Visit to a Garden

The owner of the garden knows me not,
My visit here is for a scenic spot.
No need to worry about money for wine,
My purse is full and money I have a lot.

回乡偶书·其一

少小离家老大回,
乡音无改鬓毛衰。
儿童相见不相识,
笑问客从何处来。

A Random Verse upon Homecoming(1)

I left home young but old upon homecoming,
My accent unchanged but sideburns are fading.
When meeting me children not know who I am,
All smiles they asked me from where I came.

回乡偶书·其二

离别家乡岁月多,
近来人事半消磨。
惟有门前镜湖水,
春风不改旧时波。

A Random Verse upon Homecoming(2)

I left home many and many years ago,
So much has faded away before I know.
Only in the Mirror Lake in front of my door,
Vernal breeze ripples the water as before.

咏柳

碧玉妆成一树高，
万条垂下绿丝绦。
不知细叶谁裁出，
二月春风似剪刀。

Ode to Willow

With slender array the tree is dressed in green,
Like fringes of jade thousand twigs droop like a screen.
By whom the slim buds are well clipped I don't know,
Thanks to the vernal breeze like scissors that blow.

陈子昂

陈子昂(661~702),字伯玉,梓州射洪(今四川射洪)人。武则天时在朝为官,后遭贬回乡。其诗高昂清峻,颇具汉魏风骨,对唐诗发展颇有影响。《全唐诗》存其诗两卷。

Chen Zi'ang (661~702), styled Boyu, was born in Shehong, Zizhou (Shehong County, Sichuan Province today). During the reign of Empress Wu Zetian, Chen was promoted to a senior official, but was demoted and dispatched home later. His poems are well-knit in structure and vigorous in style, exerting great influence on the development of the Tang poetry. Two volumes of his poems are collected in *The Complete Collection of the Tang Poetry*.

上元夜效小庾体

三五月华新,
遨游逐上春。
芳宵殊未极,
随意守灯轮。

On the Night of Lantern Festival

On the Lantern Festival night the moon shines bright,
Outing in early spring I'm in good mood tonight.
Splendid and glamorous but not yet at its height,
Watching big lanterns is indeed a great delight.

登幽州台歌

前不见古人，
后不见来者。
念天地之悠悠，
独怆然而涕下。

Sigh at the Top of Youzhou Tower

Where are you, the great sages of the past?
And where are the elite of coming years?
The heaven and earth will forever last,
I'm alone now and burst into tears.

张 说

张说(667~730),字道济,一字说之,洛阳(今河南洛阳)人。开元时任宰相,以干练著称。其诗抒情凄婉,风格清新刚健。《全唐诗》存其诗五卷。

Zhang Yue(667~730), styled Daoji, also known as Yuezhi, was born in Luoyang(Luoyang City, Henan Province today). Zhang Yue, smart and capable, was the prime minister during the reign of Emperor Xuanzong. Lyric and plaintive, his poems were composed in fresh and vigorous style, of which five volumes are collected in *The Complete Collection of the Tang Poetry*.

江中遇黄领子刘隆

危石江中起,
孤云岭上还。
相逢皆得意,
何处是乡关。

Meeting a Friend on the River

A perilous cliff on the river rises high,
A lonely cloud comes back from the sky.
Meeting on the river we are pleased,
But where is the native land I'm confused.

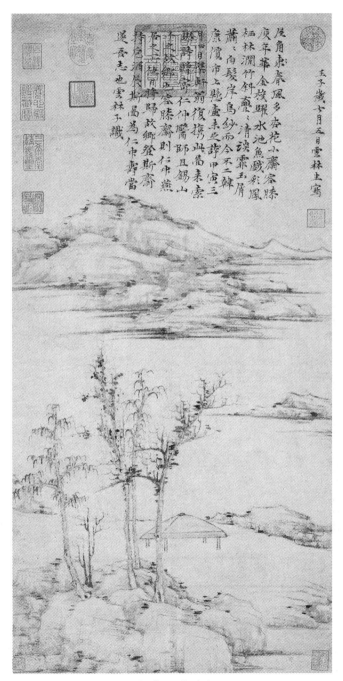

元 倪瓒 《容膝斋图》

钦州守岁

故岁今宵尽,
新年明旦来。
愁心随斗柄,
东北望春回。

A Midnight Stay on the New Year's Eve

This year comes to its end tonight,
The New Year is coming tomorrow.
Gazing at the Plough I'm in sorrow,
When its handle turns east spring comes right.

岳州看黄叶

白首看黄叶，
徂颜复几何。
空惭棠树下，
不见政成歌。

Sigh over the Yellow Leaves in Yuezhou

Grey-haired I'm gazing at leaves yellow,
Fading are trees I'm aged sad and sallow.
Under the birchleaf pear tree I'm ashamed,
With little credit to claim I'm in sorrow.

蜀道后期

客心争日月，
来往预期程。
秋风不相待，
先至洛阳城。

A Delay on the Way Home

On my way home I'm always pressed for time,
Well worked out my journey is really prime.
But autumn wind is too impatient to wait,
It arrives in Luoyang earlier and I am late.

九日进茱萸山

晚节欢重九，
高山上五千。
醉中知遇圣，
梦里见寻仙。

Double Ninth Festival in Cornel Mountain

I'm fond of Double Ninth Day in my later years,
Ascending a height into the sky I give cheers.
A drunken old man I've no company but wine,
Meeting a fairy in dreamland I feel so fine.

醉中作

醉后乐无极,
弥胜未醉时。
动容皆是舞,
出语总成诗。

Joy of Being Drunk

At the time of being drunk I'm happy and gay,
Even happier I'm than on a common day.
Behaving as if I'm singing and dancing,
Speaking like that I'm delightedly chanting.

送梁六自洞庭山作

巴陵一望洞庭秋,
日见孤峰水上浮。
闻道神仙不可接,
心随湖水共悠悠。

Farewell to Liang Zhiwei in Mount Jun

Autumn tints of Dongting Lake come into my sight,
A lone peak over the water floats with the tide.
The fairy tale on beauties makes me in sad plight,
With waves and tides my heart goes far and wide.

桃花园马上应制

林间艳色骄天马,
苑里秾华伴丽人。
愿逐南风飞帝席,
年年含笑舞青春。

Riding in the Peach Blossom Garden

In the garden bright color on the fine steed looms,
Adding to each other are beauties and peach blooms.
Sends me to the imperial banquet the south breeze,
Year after year we sing and dance in our prime and bliss.

同赵侍御望归舟

山庭迥迥面长川，
江树重重极远烟。
形影相追高翥鸟，
心肠并断北风船。

Yearning for the Homeward Boat

Facing the long river is the tower far away,
Trees along the river banks stretch into mist gray.
Birds and their shadows across the sky in flight,
Broken is my heart with the boat out of sight.

和尹从事懋泛洞庭

平湖一望上连天，
林景千寻下洞泉。
忽惊水上光华满，
疑是乘舟到日边。

Going Boating on Dongting Lake with Yin

The calm lake stretches far and wide to the sky,
Mirrored on the water is the scene of woods high.
Suddenly spoiled is the brilliance so bright,
As if my boat is sailing to the sun nearby.

苏 颋

苏颋(670～727),字廷硕,京兆武功(今陕西武功)人。工文,当时朝廷重要文件多出其手。《全唐诗》存其诗两卷。

Su Ting(670～727), styled Tingshuo, was born in Wugong, Jingzhao (Wugong County, Shaanxi Province today). Su Ting was well versed in writing, for which many of the imperial documents were drafted by him. Of his poems two volumes are collected in *The Complete Collection of the Tang Poetry*.

汾上惊秋

北风吹白云,
万里渡河汾。
心绪逢摇落,
秋声不可闻。

Sigh over Autumn by Fen River

Float with the north wind white clouds in the sky,
Crossing the river from a remote place.
Gloomy I'm on seeing dead leaves fly,
Rustle in autumn frightens me always.

山鹧鸪词

玉关征戍久,
空闺人独愁。
寒露湿青苔,
别来蓬鬓秋。

Song of Mountain Francolin

You went to guard Yumen Pass long ago,
Sad in boudoir I'm a lonely shadow.
Green moss is wet through with cold heavy dew,
Since we parted on my head grey hairs grow.

张九龄

张九龄(678~740),字子寿,韶州曲江(今广东省韶关)人。唐玄宗时曾任宰相,其文为世人推崇,其诗淡雅清新。《全唐诗》存其诗三卷。

Zhang Jiuling(678~740), styled Zishou, was born in Qujiang, Shaozhou (Shaoguan City, Guangdong Province today). Zhang was the prime minister during the reign of Emperor Xuanzong(Li Longji), his articles were held in high esteem and his poems fresh and elegant in style, three volumes of which are collected in *The Complete Collection of the Tang Poetry*.

照镜见白发

宿昔青云志,
蹉跎白发年。
谁知明镜里,
形影自相怜。

Grey Hairs in the Mirror

My aspirations before were so high,
With grey hairs I dawdle time away.
Looking into the mirror with a sigh,
Oh, what a pity, gone is my heyday.

赋得自君之出矣

自君之出矣，
不复理残机。
思君如满月，
夜夜减清辉。

Since the Tearful Parting

Since you gave me a parting kiss that day,
No mood for weaving I put my loom away.
Yearning for you like the moon at its height,
On the wane I'm pining away day and night.

登荆州城望江

东望河悠悠，
西来昼夜流。
岁月既如此，
为心那不愁。

A View of the River from Jingzhou Gate Tower

Gazing east the river flowing away,
From the remote west it flows night and day.
Time flies like the river without stop,
Worries and sorrows turn my hair gray.

宋　惠崇　《沙汀烟树图》

崔国辅

崔国辅(678~755),吴郡(今江苏苏州)人。玄宗开元十四年进士,曾在朝为官。崔国辅擅长五言绝句,是盛唐的重要诗人之一。《全唐诗》存其诗一卷。

Cui Guofu(678~755) was born in Wu County(Suzhou City, Jiangsu Province today). Having succeeded in the highest imperial examination in 726, Cui was promoted to senior official in the court. Well versed in poems with five characters to each line, Cui was an important poet in the Tang Dynasty at its height. One volume of his poems is collected in *The Complete Collection of the Tang Poetry*.

魏宫词

朝日照红妆,
拟上铜雀台。
画眉犹未了,
魏帝使人催。

Song of the Wei Palace

In red attire was the imperial concubine,
She's going to Tongque Tower in the sunshine.
Well-dressed and painting eyebrows with great care,
Out of patience the king urged her to prepare.

吴声子夜歌

净扫黄金阶,
飞霜皓如雪。
下帘弹箜篌,
不忍见秋月。

A Midnight Song

I sweep the golden steps in the moon-lit night,
Brushing away the rime on the ground snow-white.
Back to my room I play konghou* behind the screen,
I can't bear to see the autumn moon so bright.

---

* Konghou is an ancient Chinese stringed instrument played by plucking.

采莲曲

玉溆花争发，
金塘水乱流。
相逢畏相失，
并著木兰舟。

Song of Gathering Lotus Seeds

Flowers are a riot of color by waterside,
Water from the golden pond flows far and wide.
Meeting by chance we're afraid of parting again,
Let's gather seeds together and row side by side.

丽人曲

红颜称绝代,
欲并真无侣。
独有镜中人,
由来自相许。

Song of a Beauty

She is a beauty matchless,
No one on a par with her grace.
Only the one in her mirror,
Is her mate worthy of a word praise.

中流曲

归时日尚早,
更欲向芳洲。
渡口水流急,
回船不自由。

Song of Midstream

It's still early to start the journey home,
On the fragrant shoal I desire to roam.
But the current is swift at the ferry,
To control the boat's beyond my carry.

怨词

楼头桃李疏,
池上芙蓉落。
织锦犹未成,
虫声入罗幕。

A Lady's Lament

Scattered peach and plum trees before the bower,
The pond is dotted with lotus without flower.
The pattern of brocade is far from well woven,
The chirping of crickets comes into my curtain.

今别离

送别未能旋,
相望连水口。
船行欲映洲,
几度急摇手。

Parting

Sending off my friend return is a sad plight,
Gazing after him by waterside I stand.
Slowly vanishing is the boat out of sight,
Time and again to my fried I wave my hand.

濮阳女

雁来书不至，
月照独眠房。
贱妾多愁思，
不堪秋夜长。

A Lady from Puyang

I catch sight of wild geese but no letters home,
Alone in the moon-lit room I want no comb.
Grief-stricken I am in a sorry plight,
Hardly can I bear such a long autumn night.

白纻词

洛阳梨花落如霰，
河阳桃叶生复齐。
坐惜玉楼春欲尽，
红绵粉絮裹妆啼。

Song of Beautiful Attire Dance

Like snowflakes pear petals are flying in Luoyang,
Peach twigs in Heyang are dressed with leaves young.
Afraid of spring from her boudoir fading away,
She is weeping well dressed in fragrant array.

王 翰

王翰(687~726),字子羽,并州晋阳(今山西太原)人。曾在朝为官,后遭贬。王翰恃才不羁,行为狂放,其诗在当时负盛名。《全唐诗》存其诗一卷。

Wang Han (687~726), styled Ziyu, was born in Jinyang, Bingzhou (Taiyuan City, Shanxi Province today). Wang was once a senior official, but was demoted later. Proud of his own talent and ability, Wang was arrogant and unrestrained, his poems had high reputation then and one volume is collected in *The Complete Collection of the Tang Poetry*.

春日思归

杨柳青青杏花发,
年光误客转思家。
不知湖上菱歌女,
几个春舟在若耶?

Yearning for Home in Spring

Green are willow and apricot blossoms blooming,
Lingering for spring I'm yearning for homecoming.
Girls picking water nut in autumn on Jinghu Lake were singing,
How many of them are still on Ruoye Stream boating?

宋　刘松年　《四景山水图·春》

凉州词

葡萄美酒夜光杯,
欲饮琵琶马上催。
醉卧沙场君莫笑,
古来征战几人回。

Song of Liangzhou

With fine wine in the luminous glasses shining bright,
Drinking with the *pipa* melody on horseback we're ready to fight.
Don't laugh at us if we lie drunk on the battleground,
Up to now few warriors could ever return sound.

王之涣

王之涣(688~742),字季凌,并州晋阳(今山西太原)人。性格豪放,诗风雄阔,深为时人所重。《全唐诗》仅存其诗六首。

Wang Zhihuan(688~742), styled Jiling, was born in Jinyang, Bingzhou (Taiyuan City, Shanxi Province toady). As a poet of uninhibited character, Wang's poems are vigorous and powerful in style, very much popular among the readers then. There are only six of his poems collected in *The Complete Collection of the Tang Poetry*.

送别

杨柳东风树,
青青夹御河。
近来攀折苦,
应为别离多。

Farewell to a Friend

Willow trees are dancing with vernal breeze,
Green is the imperial river on both sides.
So many twigs are snapped off from trees,
There must be lots of people waving goodbyes.

登鹳雀楼

白日依山尽,
黄河入海流。
欲穷千里目,
更上一层楼。

At the Top of the Stork Tower

Kissing the mountain ridge the sunshine fades away,
Towards the sea the Yellow River makes headway.
To gaze far and far away for a more splendid sight,
You have to go upstairs to a greater height.

九日送别

蓟庭萧瑟故人稀,
何处登高且送归。
今日暂同芳菊酒,
明朝应作断蓬飞。

Parting on Double Ninth Festival

I have few friends here it's a bleak and dismal day,
No height can I ascend and return in safe way.
Chrysanthemum wine is so sweet we drink today,
Like a fleabane tomorrow we've to go away.

凉州词

黄河远上白云间，
一片孤城万仞山。
羌笛何须怨杨柳，
春风不度玉门关。

Song of Liangzhou

Winding up to white clouds the Yellow River licks the sky,
Atop the soaring peaks lonely is the fort rising high.
The Qiang flute you need not bewail for weeping willows,
Beyond the Yumen Pass the vernal breeze never blows.

孟浩然

孟浩然(689～740),襄州襄阳(今湖北襄樊)人。长于五言诗,与王维齐名,是山水田园派的代表作家。《全唐诗》存其诗两卷。

Meng Haoran (689～740), styled Haoran, was born in Xiangyang, Xiangzhou (Xiangfan City, Hubei Province today). Well versed in poems with five characters to each line, Meng was on a par with Wang Wei and regarded as a famous representative of pastoral poetry. There are two volumes of his poems collected in *The Complete Collection of the Tang Poetry*.

扬子津望京口

北固临京口,
夷山近海滨。
江风白浪起,
愁杀渡头人。

The Yangtze Ferry Crossing

Close to Zhenjiang Beigu Mountain rises high,
Near the beach Yishan Mountain touches the sky.
Big waves rise and fall as the river wind blows,
Waiting at the ferry passengers' worry grows.

春晓

春眠不觉晓,
处处闻啼鸟。
夜来风雨声,
花落知多少。

Spring Dawn

Deep in spring slumber unaware of dawn light,
I'm awakened by birds singing all around.
It was raining and wind was blowing last night,
O, so many fallen petals on the ground.

赠王九

日暮田家远，
山中勿久淹。
归人须早去，
稚子望陶潜。

To Wang Jiu

Dusk falls but to my abode there's a long way,
Lingering in the mountains too much I stay.
It's time for homecoming, goodbye you'd better say,
Yearning for reunion your family are pining away.

寻菊花潭主人不遇

行至菊花潭，
村西日已斜。
主人登高去，
鸡犬空在家。

Waiting for the Owner of Chrysanthemum Pond

I got to Chrysanthemum Pond at the twilight,
To the west of the village the sun's setting.
Away from home the host went climbing a height,
Left at home fowls and dogs avail me nothing.

宿建德江

移舟泊烟渚，
日暮客愁新。
野旷天低树，
江清月近人。

A Night Berth on the River at Jiande

Berthed near the isle is my boat in the mist,
Dusk falls and a new worry is in the list.
In the wilds vast trees seem to kiss the sky,
Clear is the river and the moon is so nigh.

宋　马远　《寒江独钓图》

同储十二洛阳道中作

珠弹繁华子，
金羁游侠人。
酒酣白日暮，
走马入红尘。

On the Way to Luoyang

Pearls were used as shots they were too wealthy,
Hunting on horseback they led a life of luxury.
Until the sunset they did not drink to satiety,
And then riding high they vanished in night society.

送友人之京

君登青云去，
予望青山归。
云山从此别，
泪湿薜萝衣。

A Send-off to a Friend to the Capital

You'll have a meteoric rise to fame,
I hope to be a recluse worth the name.
Let's make our last farewell today,
Tears run down soaking my rattan array.

凉州词

浑成紫檀金屑文，
作得琵琶声入云。
胡地迢迢三万里，
那堪马上送明君。

Song of Liangzhou

Made of redwood *pipa* is carved with golden pattern,
Playing *pipa* the melody can be heard in heaven.
The native land from me is ten thousand miles away,
Parting her on horseback how can Zhaojun bear to play.

初秋

不觉初秋夜渐长,
清风习习重凄凉。
炎炎暑退茅斋静,
阶下丛莎有露光。

Early Autumn

In early autumn longer and longer is the night,
Cool breeze blows gently it is a great delight.
Gone are the scorching days, quiet is the cottage,
Beside the steps nut-grass is wet with dew bright.

送杜十四之江南

荆吴相接水为乡，
君去春江正淼茫。
日暮征帆何处泊，
天涯一望断人肠。

Sending Mr. Du to the South of the Yangtze River

Chu and Wu states are joined by lakes and rivers long,
Misty and vast is the spring river you sail along.
Where to berth your boat at dusk I really don't know,
Gazing far and wide, heart-broken now my worries grow.

刘方平

刘方平(生卒年不详)河南洛阳人。诗歌多悠远之思,超然物外,不落俗套。《全唐诗》存其诗26首。

Liu Fangping was born in Luoyang, Henan Province. Transcending worldly affairs, most of his poems are recollections of the remote past free from convention. Of his poems 26 are collected in *The Complete Collection of the Tang Poetry*.

采莲曲

落日清江里,
荆歌艳楚腰。
采莲从小惯,
十五即乘潮。

Gathering Lotus Seeds

Beautiful sunset glow on the clear river,
With slim waist the charming girl is a singer.
Good at picking lotus seeds since she's a child,
Who could play with waves in the weather wild.

春雪

飞雪带春风，
徘徊乱绕空。
君看似花处，
偏在洛阳东。

Spring Snow

With spring breeze snowflakes fly,
Lingering about under the open sky.
It seems to you they are flowers,
To the east of Luoyang at best hours.

夜月

更深月色半人家，
北斗阑干南斗斜。
今夜偏知春气暖，
虫声新透绿窗纱。

Moonlight at Night

The moonbeams peep into the chamber at the dead of night,
The slanting Plough and the South Dipper glitter with dim light.
Insects are aware of the warmth of the vernal breeze,
Through the green screen of the window come their songs of sheer bliss.

春怨

纱窗日落渐黄昏，
金屋无人见泪痕。
寂寞空庭春欲晚，
梨花满地不开门。

Grievance in Spring

The last glow of the sunset peeps into the window screen,
In the empty palace the maiden's tear stains can be seen.
No figure in the lonely courtyard spring's fading away,
Pear petals over the floor she keeps the door shut all day.

王昌龄

王昌龄(698～756),字少伯,京兆长安(今陕西西安)人。曾在朝为官,后遭贬遇害。其诗作以七言绝句最为杰出,边塞诗尤为出众。气势宏伟、语言圆熟、构思缜密、音节高亮是其作品的特色。《全唐诗》存其诗四卷。

Wang Changling (694～756), styled Shaobo, was born in Chang'an (Xi'an City, Shaanxi Province today). Wang once served as a senior official in the court, but was demoted and killed later. He was well versed in composing seven-syllable quatrains, the poems about the frontier zone in particular, which are characterized by tremendous momentum, skillful language, well-knit structure and sonorous rhythm. Four volumes of his poems are collected in *The Complete Collection of the Tang Poetry*.

送胡大

荆门不堪别,

况乃潇湘秋。

何处遥望君,

江边明月楼。

Farewell to Hu Da

I cannot bear the moment of parting pain,

The river is tinted with bleak autumn stain.

Where is the proper spot to gaze far and wide?

Atop the moon-lit tower by the riverside.

送张四

枫林已愁暮,
楚水复堪悲。
别后冷山月,
清猿无断时。

Farewell to Zhang Si

Dusk casts a deep gloom over maple trees,
Full of grief is the water in cold breeze.
Chilly is the moonlight since your parting,
Apes give wailing yelps without stopping.

从军行

大将军出战，
白日暗榆关。
三面黄金甲，
单于破胆还。

Service in the Army

The great general went into battle for fight,
Over Shanhai Pass dim and dull was the sunlight.
Troops in golden armor charged from three sides,
The Hun Chieftain ran away trembling with fright.

浣纱女

钱塘江畔是谁家？
江上女儿全胜花。
吴王在时不得出，
今日公然来浣纱。

Silk-washing Maidens

Whose abode is this on the bank of Qiantang River?
By flowers daughters of the family are so fair.
In the previous dynasty go out they could never,
Nowadays they dare to wash fibers in the open air.

长信秋词

奉帚平明金殿开，
且将团扇暂徘徊。
玉颜不及寒鸦色，
犹带昭阳日影来。

Grievance of a Deserted Empress in Autumn

She brings her broom to clean the golden palace at dawn,
A round fan in hand paving up and down she looks drawn.
Out of favor her rosy cheeks are gone forever,
Nowhere but Zhaoyang Palace can win the King's favor.

闺怨

闺中少妇不知愁，
春日凝妆上翠楼。
忽见陌头杨柳色，
悔教夫婿觅封侯。

Grievance of a Bride in her Chamber

The young lady in her chamber is free from sorrow,
Well-dressed on a spring day she mounts tower high.
Suddenly she catches sight of green leaves of a willow,
Regretting at her lord's seeking fame she gives a sigh.

芙蓉楼送辛渐

寒雨连江夜入吴,
平明送客楚山孤。
洛阳亲友如相问,
一片冰心在玉壶。

Farewell to Xin Jian at Lotus Tower

The cold rain lingers over the river at dead of night,
I see you off at dawn leaving the hill in sorrow plight.
If my relatives and friends in Luoyang ask about me,
Free from stains my heart is crystal clear and really bright.

重别李评事

莫道秋江离别难，
舟船明日是长安。
吴姬缓舞留君醉，
随意青枫白露寒。

Farewell to Judge Li Again

Don't say it's too hard to part by the autumn river,
Tomorrow your boat will berth in Chang'an however.
Graceful dance of the beauties will carry you away,
To the chilly dew drops green maples will give way.

送窦七

清江月色傍林秋,
波上荧荧望一舟。
鄂渚轻帆须早发,
江边明月为君留。

A Send-off to Dou Qi

The moonlight floods the river with the woods nearby,
Glimmering on the waves a small boat meets the eye.
From the small islet the light boat should start at dawn,
By the river you can see the bright moon on high.

别辛渐

别馆萧条风雨寒，
扁舟月色渡江看。
酒酣不识关西道，
却望春江云尚残。

Farewell to Xin Jian

Bleak is the villa and chilly are the wind and rain,
A small boat crossing the river in the moon light.
Tipsy with wine I have lost my way to Chang'an,
Gazing over the river I see broken clouds in flight.

采莲曲

荷叶罗裙一色裁,
芙蓉向脸两边开。
乱入池中看不见,
闻歌始觉有人来。

Song of Gathering Lotus Seeds

Lotus leaves and silk skirts are of the same color green,
Among the lotus flowers I see rosy cheeks with grin.
Mingled with flowers in the pond no cheeks are in sight,
Not until hearing the song do I know their hiding site.

明　陈洪绶　《荷花鸳鸯图》

西宫春怨

西宫夜静百花香,
欲卷珠帘春恨长。
斜抱云和深见月,
朦胧树色隐昭阳。

Spring Grievance of a Beauty Confined to West Palace

Scent of flowers wafts to the West Palace in still night,
About to roll up the bead screen she's in gloomy plight.
With a zither leaning her arms she gazes through moonlight,
Through dim tree shadows Zhaoyang Palace comes into sight.

西宫秋怨

芙蓉不及美人妆,
水殿风来珠翠香。
谁分含啼掩秋扇,
空悬明月待君王。

Autumn Grievance of a Beauty Confined to West Palace

Beside the well-made-up lady lotus flowers feel shy,
From the hall on water wafts of pearls and jade smoothly fly.
It's a pity she's to conceal her love with autumn fan,
Pining for the emperor at the moonlit night in vain.

从军行·其一

青海长云暗雪山，
孤城遥望玉门关。
黄沙百战穿金甲，
不破楼兰终不还。

Service in the Army（1）

Darkened by clouds are snowy mountains by Qinghai Lake,
Far away from the lonely fort Yumen Pass's out of sight.
Battle-seasoned our golden armor is worn out by sand,
Until we destroy our foe we can never cease our fight.

从军行·其二

大漠风尘日色昏，
红旗半卷出辕门。
前军夜战洮河北，
已报生擒吐谷浑。

Service in the Army（2）

The sand storm in the desert has dimmed the sunlight,
Red flags half unfurled, out of the barracks we're to fight.
After the battle in the north of the Taohe River,
It's said the enemy chieftain's captured alive at night.

青楼怨

香帏风动花入楼，
高调鸣筝缓夜愁。
肠断关山不解说，
依依残月下帘钩。

Grievance from the Boudoir

Sending petals into my room the wind kisses my curtain,
Turning the zither I try to allay my sorrow at night.
Heart-broken at the thought of my darling beyond the mountain,
Nobody knows my sorrow but the fading moon with dim light.

出塞

秦时明月汉时关,
万里长征人未还。
但是龙城飞将在,
不教胡马度阴山。

Beyond the Great Wall

The moon still shines on the former pass as before,
Soldiers sent to guard the border were now no more.
If General Li were sent to guard the borderland,
No steed of Huns would have invaded by the strong hand.

春怨

音书杜绝白狼西,
桃李无言黄鸟啼。
寒雁春深归去尽,
出门肠断草萋萋。

Grievance in Spring

No letters from the west of Bailang River,
Orioles are singing, flower petals floating.
Wild geese come back and spring is nearly over,
Heart-broken when she sees grass lushly growing.

王 维

王维(701~761),字摩诘,太原祁州(今山西祁县)人。开元九年进士,官至右丞,晚年过着亦官亦隐的优游生活。王维精通音乐,绘画,其山水田园诗诗中有画,而其画作则画中有诗,极见功力。《全唐诗》存其诗四卷。

Wang Wei(701~761), styled Mojie, was born in Qizhou, Taiyuan(Qi County, Shanxi Province today). Wang succeeded in the highest imperial examination during the reign of Li Longji and was promoted to a senior official, but demoted later and lived in seclusion in the sunset of his life. Wang was well versed in music, painting and poem writing as well. His landscape and idyllic poems are very much successful in integration of painting effect into poetry, and his painting vice versa. Four volumes of his poems are collected in *The Complete Collection of the Tang Poetry*.

鸟鸣涧

人闲桂花落,
夜静春山空。
月出惊山鸟,
时鸣春涧中。

Birds Chirping in the Dale

I'm at leisure when laurel blooms fall,
Deserted are spring hills still at night.
The moonrise startles birds with moonlight,
In the dale in spring birds sometimes call.

唐 王维 《辋川图》

萍池

春池深且广，
会待轻舟回。
靡靡绿萍合，
垂杨扫复开。

Duckweed in a Pond

Spring pond is deep and vast,
Homeward boat's swift and fast.
Duckweed split is gradually joined,
Swept by willows it comes apart.

孟城坳

新家孟城口，
古木余衰柳。
来者复为谁？
空悲昔人有。

The Gate of Mengcheng City

Near the city gate is my new abode,
Nothing left but a willow tree too old.
Who will be the future one after me?
No need to worry about who will be.

斤竹岭

檀栾映空曲，
青翠漾涟漪。
暗入商山路，
樵人不可知。

Bamboo Mountain Range

Winding along the range are bamboos of grace,
Undulating like green ripples in the breeze.
A path hidden in the grove leads to a good place,
Woodmen know nothing about the heaven of peace.

山中

荆溪白石出，
天寒红叶稀。
山路元无雨，
空翠湿人衣。

In the Mountains

In the blue brook white pebbles loom,
Red leaves like cold flowers that bloom.
There's no rain along the path serene,
But my dress is wet with the moist green.

文杏馆

文杏裁为梁,
香茅结为宇。
不知栋里云,
去作人间雨。

The Ginkgo Hut

Ginkgo is cut as the beam big and firm,
Made of fragrant thatch the room is warm.
Out of the thatched hut the clouds flow,
Turning into rain the owner does not know.

木兰柴

秋山敛余照，
飞鸟逐前侣。
彩翠时分明，
夕岚无处所。

The Magnolia Fence

The last ray of sunset glow fades away,
Chasing after each other flying birds play.
The evening glow sometimes shines bright,
The mountain mist finds no place to stay.

辛夷坞

木末芙蓉花，
山中发红萼。
涧户寂无人，
纷纷开且落。

The Magnolia Hollow

Flowers of magnolia blooming at tops of trees,
All over the mountains red pistils sweet in breeze.
Dead still in the valley with no figure in sight,
From bud to blossom they fade away all right.

山中寄诸弟妹

山中多法侣，
禅诵自为群。
城郭遥相望，
唯应见白云。

To Brothers and Sisters from the Mountain

I have friends studying sutra in the mountain,
Seeking truth we are lost in meditation.
From your city wall if you gaze far and wide,
Within your sight you will see the white clouds glide.

哭孟浩然

故人不可见，
汉水日东流。
借问襄阳老，
江山空蔡州。

Weeping for Meng Haoran

Oh, my bosom friend is brought to the ground,
The Han River still flows east day and night.
About him I ask the aged here and beyond,
The owner's gone; Caizhou Shoal* is in a sad plight.

---

* Caizhou Shoal is a famous scenic spot in Xianghang (a city in Hubei Province today) where Meng Haoran once took up his abode.

鹿柴

空山不见人，
但闻人语响。
返景入深林，
复照青苔上。

A Fenced Enclosure

Empty mountains, no figure in sight,
But sometimes come the echoes of sound.
Piercing the deep woods are rays of sunlight,
Gleams are scattered on the mossy ground.

临湖亭

轻舸迎上客，
悠悠湖上来。
当轩对尊酒，
四面芙蓉开。

The Lakeside Pavilion

Greeting distinguished guest on a light barge,
Floating leisurely on the lake ripples enlarge.
We drink to our heart's content by the boat window,
Lotus flowers around us frequently bow low.

欹湖

吹箫凌极浦,
日暮送夫君。
湖上一回首,
山青卷白云。

Qihu Lake

Melody of flute floats over the water vast,
Farewell to my friend I'm bathed in the twilight.
Turning round on the lake a charming view in sight,
Green mountains caped with white clouds floating fast.

栾家濑

飒飒秋雨中，
浅浅石溜泻。
跳波自相溅，
白鹭惊复下。

Luanjia Pebble Shoal

In the rustling of autumn wind it is raining,
Over the shallow pebble shoal rapids rushing.
Jumping waves splash onto stone break into foam,
Startled egrets away from the nest return home.

白石滩

清浅白石滩，
绿蒲向堪把。
家住水东西，
浣纱明月下。

White Pebble Shoal

White Pebble Shoal water is clear and shallow,
Bunches of green cattails in profusion grow.
We make our abodes to its east and the west,
Women washing in the moonlight look their best.

竹里馆

独坐幽篁里,
弹琴复长啸。
深林人不知,
明月来相照。

The Hut in Bamboo Forest

Sitting alone in the depth of bamboos,
I play flute and let out long and loud cries.
In the depth of the grove nobody knows,
Only the bright moon at me make sheep's eyes.

山中送别

山中相送罢，
日暮掩柴扉。
春草明年绿，
王孙归不归。

Farewell to a Friend in the Mountain

In the mountain the seed-off to my friend's given,
Dusk falls, I close the wicket gate of my garden.
Next year when spring comes grass will turn green for certain,
Oh, my friend, I wonder if you will come again.

班婕妤

玉窗萤影度,
金殿人声绝。
秋夜守罗帷,
孤灯耿不灭。

Ban Jieyu, a Palace Song

Through the jade window a firefly is passing,
From the imperial palace no voice's coming.
Too long to bear in the curtain is autumn night,
A lone figure faces the lone lamp that is bright.

红牡丹

绿艳闲且静,
红衣浅复深。
花心愁欲断,
春色岂知心。

Red Peony

Serene is the peony vividly green,
In red array shading into crimson.
The heart of flower sad and nearly broken,
But it makes no difference to spring season.

相思

红豆生南国，
春来发几枝。
愿君多采撷，
此物最相思。

Love Beans

In the southland red beans grow in profusion,
How many twigs do they branch in spring season?
I hope you gather more beans as you like,
The sweet memory of love they'll invite.

杂诗

君自故乡来，
应知故乡事。
来日绮窗前，
寒梅著花未？

A Poem Asking About the Native Land

Since you come from our native land,
You may have the news at first hand.
The time when you passed by my window,
Blooming or not the plums were you should know.

秋夜曲

桂魄初生秋露微，
轻罗已薄未更衣。
银筝夜久殷勤弄，
心怯空房不忍归。

Autumn Night Song

The new moon in the sky and autumn dew is light,
Thin is her dress but she's in no mood to groom.
Playing the silver lute in the dead of night,
She feels lonely, dare not enter the empty room.

少年行

新丰美酒斗十千,
咸阳游侠多少年。
相逢义气为君饮,
系马高楼垂柳边。

Song of Juvenile

Good wine brewed in Xinfeng is rare and fine,
Most knights errant in Xianyang are juveniles.
Like-minded at the first meeting they drink wine,
Around the windows by tall building are horses' ties.

送沈子福之江东

杨柳渡头行客稀，
罟师荡桨向临圻。
唯有相思似春色，
江南江北送君归。

Seeding a Friend Off to the East of the Yangtze River

At the willow-flanked ferry few people in sight,
The boatman rows his boat towards the other side.
Only my yearning for you like the charm of spring bright,
A send-off to you even if you go far and wide.

九月九日忆山东兄弟

独在异乡为异客,
每逢佳节倍思亲。
遥知兄弟登高处,
遍插茱萸少一人。

Pining for My Brothers on Double Ninth Festival

Alone, a lonely stranger I'm in a strange land,
Doubly pine for my kith and kin on holiday.
From afar I know my brothers at height today,
Best wishes to me they have cornel spray in hand.

送元二使安西

渭城朝雨浥轻尘,
客舍青青柳色新。
劝君更尽一杯酒,
西出阳关无故人。

Farewell to My Friend on His Mission to Anxi

After morning shower Xianyang is clear and clean,
Willows around the hotel look fresh and green.
Cheers then, please have one more glass of wine again,
Beyond the Yangguan Pass no more friends could be seen.

叹白发

宿昔朱颜成暮齿，
须臾白发变垂髫。
一生几许伤心事，
不向空门何处销。

Sigh over Grey Hairs

Gone are the rosy cheeks of the past,
Black hairs shade into grey before I know.
Heart-breaks in my life that forever last,
Nothing but Buddhism can get rid of sorrow.

伊州歌

清风明月苦相思，
荡子从戎十载馀。
征人去日殷勤嘱，
归雁来时数附书。

Song of Yizhou

Breeze is fresh, moon is bright, but I'm lovesick at night,
Ten years ago my darling joined the army to fight.
On the day of parting I told him time and again,
When swans fly southward more letters you must write.

田园乐·其一

采菱渡头风急，
策杖林西日斜。
杏树坛边渔父，
桃花源里人家。

An Idyll（1）

Picking water nuts at the ferry where wind blows,
Facing the village with a cane the setting sun glows.
Like a fisherman approaching the high altar,
I'm in Shangri-La, enjoying the bliss God knows.

明　仇英　《桃源仙境图》

田园乐·其二

萋萋芳草春绿，
落落长松夏寒。
牛羊自归村巷，
童稚未识衣冠。

An Idyll (2)

Spring grass fresh and green lushly grow,
It's cool enough under the pine trees high.
Herding homeward cattle sheep flocks low,
Naive are the children in the nude nigh.

田园乐·其三

山下孤烟远村，
天边独树高原。
一瓢颜回陋巷，
五柳先生对门。

An Idyll（3）

Rising from the mountain village is a curl of smoke,
Standing on the plateau is a tree touching the sky.
In a narrow and dark lane humble is my abode,
Opposite to Tao Qian's* home my gate is not so high.

---

* Tao Qian, Tao Yuanming, was an eminent poet of the East Jin Dynasty, who planted five willow trees before his abode, for that he styled himself "Mr. Five Willows".

田园乐·其四

桃红复含宿雨，
柳绿更带朝烟。
花落家童未扫，
鸟啼山客犹眠。

An Idyll (4)

Pink peach flowers are wet with sparkling rain drops,
Willows in the morning mist are a dim outline.
Page fails to sweep fallen petals from plant tops,
Birds are singing but in dream I'm drinking wine.

李 白

李白(701~762),字太白,号青莲居士,祖籍陇西成纪(今甘肃秦安),公元701年出生于碎叶城(今吉尔吉斯斯坦境内)。李白是伟大的浪漫主义诗人,被誉为"诗仙"。其诗风雄奇豪放,语言自然流畅,音韵和谐多变。《全唐诗》存其诗25卷。

Li Bai(701~762), styled Taibai, also known as Qinglian Buddhist, was born in Suiye(a city in Kyrgyzstan today), but his ancestral home was Chengji, Western Gansu(Qin'an County, Gansu Province today). Li is a great romanticist poet who is renowned for the poet-immortal in China. Characterized by harmonious and flexible rhyme and rhythm, his poems were composed with natural and smooth language in bold and unrestrained style, of which twenty-five volumes are collected in *The Complete Collection of the Tang Poetry*.

王昭君

昭君拂玉鞍,
上马啼红颊。
今日汉宫人,
明朝胡地妾。

To Wang Zhaojun

Zhaojun strokes lightly the saddle of jade,
On horseback in tears for her rosy cheeks fade.
In the Han Palace today she is the maiden,
But on the morrow the wife of a Hun chieftain.

玉阶怨

玉阶生白露,
夜久侵罗袜。
却下水精帘,
玲珑望秋月。

A Lady's Grievance by Steps

Jade steps are wet with dew drops white,
Soaked are silk socks in dead of night.
She comes in pulling down the crystal curtain,
Gazing at the autumn moon shining bright.

劳劳亭

天下伤心处，
劳劳送客亭。
春风知别苦，
不遣柳条青。

Pavilion Laolao

Here the very spot of heart break it is,
The pavilion sees many parting kisses.
The pain of parting only the spring wind knows,
It refuses to green the twigs of willows.

赠内

三百六十日，
日日醉如泥。
虽为李白妇，
何异太常妻。

To My Wife

In a year there are three hundred and sixty days,
I'm drinking every day and dead drunk always.
In fact you are playing a losing game,
Even though you are my wife in name.

静夜思

床前明月光,
疑是地上霜。
举头望明月,
低头思故乡。

Homesickness at Dead of Night

Afront the well a pool of the moonlight,
It seems to me that's the icy rime white.
Raising my head I see the moon so bright,
Bowing down I become homesick at night.

渌水曲

渌水明秋日，
南湖采白蘋。
荷花娇欲语，
愁杀荡舟人。

Song of Lushui River

The autumn sun on the river is so bright,
Picking clover fern in south lake with delight.
Delicate and charming are lotus flowers,
Ashamed of my looks I knit my brows.

重忆

欲向江东去,
定将谁举杯。
稽山无贺老,
却棹酒船回。

A Visit to He Zhizhang

I'm going to the east of the river,
With whom sharing my wine I'm a fever.
Mr. He is absent from Ji Mountain,
With wine on board I have to return.

秋浦歌·其一

秋浦千重岭，
水车岭最奇。
天倾欲堕石，
水拂寄生枝。

Song of Qiupu River (1)

By the River ridges upon ridges tower so high,
Grotesque most is Shuiche Peak striking the eye.
At the top huge rocks seem to fall from the sky,
And the water strokes parasitic plants nigh.

秋浦歌·其二

白发三千丈，
缘愁似个长。
不知明镜里，
何处得秋霜。

Song of Qiupu River（2）

Long, long is my hair in decay,
Endless worry lingers day and night.
I know not in the mirror bright,
Whence the rime dyes my hair grey.

秋浦歌·其三

炉火照天地，
红星乱紫烟。
赧郎明月夜，
歌曲动寒川。

Song of Qiupu River（3）

Blazing flames from the furnace are so bright,
Mingled with purple smoke sparks glow with light.
Red as beetroot the workers are busy,
Their songs echo on the river at night.

九日龙山饮

九日龙山饮，
黄花笑逐臣。
醉看风落帽，
舞爱月留人。

Drinking on Longshan Hill on Double Ninth Festival

Drinking on Longshan Hill on Double Ninth Festival,
Chrysanthemums laughed at me an exiled official.
The wind blew off my hat and I was pretty high,
Dancing with the bright moon under the open sky.

哭宣城善酿纪叟

纪叟黄泉里,
还应酿老春。
夜台无晓日,
沽酒与何人?

Elegy on Mr. Ji a Master Brewer in Xuancheng*

In the nether world you're still busy brewing
The time-honored wine of auspicious spring.
But in underworld the sun can never shine,
Who will be the connoisseur of thy choice wine?

---

* Xuancheng is a city in the south of Anhui Province today.

白鹭鸶

白鹭下秋水，
孤飞如坠霜。
心闲且未去，
独立沙洲傍。

Egrets

Over the autumn waters egrets fly,
As if frost falls from the open sky.
From my heart they never go afar,
As I stand alone by the sandbar.

独坐敬亭山

众鸟高飞尽,
孤云独去闲。
相看两不厌,
只有敬亭山。

Sitting in Face of Jingting Hill

All birds have soared out of sight,
A lonely cloud at leisure is in flight.
Face to face we gaze each other,
Both of us are greeted with delight.

清溪半夜闻笛

羌笛梅花引，
吴溪陇水情。
寒山秋浦月，
肠断玉关声。

Melody of Flute Heard at Midnight by Qingxi Stream

From the flute I hear the *Plum Prelude* at night,
Limpid as the water of the winding stream.
The cold hill and river share the same moonlight,
Heart-breaking is the melody of flute in dream.

夏日山中

懒摇白羽扇，
裸袒青林中。
脱巾挂石壁，
露顶洒松风。

Summer in Mountains

Languid I stop my feather-fan waving,
Stripped to waist in the woods I'm so fine.
Hanging from the rock is my head covering,
Bareheaded I cool myself in the woods of pine.

宋 刘松年 《四景山水图·夏》

怨情

美人卷朱帘,
深坐颦蛾眉。
但见泪痕湿,
不知心恨谁。

Grievance

The beautiful lady roll up the red curtain,
Sitting still alone she always knits her brows.
Tears spoil the rouge on her face like fountain,
Towards whom she bears the resentment like clouds.

夜下征虏亭

船下广陵去，
月明征虏亭。
山花如绣颊，
江火似流萤。

Passing by the Conquest Tower at Night

Towards Yangzhou my boat is in full sail at night,
The Conquest Tower is bathed in the moonlight.
Mountain flowers in bloom like rosy cheeks charming,
Lights on fishing boats like fireflies glowing bright.

越女词

镜湖水如月,
耶溪女如雪。
新妆荡新波,
光景两奇绝。

To the Maiden of the Yue State

Water of Mirror Lake ripples like moonbeam,
The maiden by waterside is fair as snow.
Her new dress ripples with soft waves in the stream,
Grace adds to the beauty both equally grow.

浣纱石上女

玉面耶溪女，
青蛾红粉妆。
一双金齿屐，
两足白如霜。

A Maiden on the Washing Stone

With good looks her face is so fair,
Dressed in pink her eyebrows are green rare.
A pair of clogs with golden racks,
Slim are her feet white as cream cakes.

黄鹤楼送孟浩然之广陵

故人西辞黄鹤楼，
烟花三月下扬州。
孤帆远影碧空尽，
唯见长江天际流。

Sending Meng Haoran Off to Guangling at Yellow Crane Tower

Farewell at Yellow Crane Tower my friend sails east,
Down to Yangzhou in mid-spring flowers are in mist.
Against the blue sky the sail's a speck on the horizon,
The Yangtze River stretches far beyond my vision.

春夜洛城闻笛

谁家玉笛暗飞声,
散入春风满洛城。
此夜曲中闻折柳,
何人不起故园情。

Melody of Flute Heard at Spring Night in Luoyang

From whose jade flute comes the melody at night?
Stealing into Luoyang with spring breeze so light.
On hearing *Breaking Willow Twigs* the sad tune,
Oh, who could free himself from nostalgic plight!

赠汪伦

李白乘舟将欲行,
忽闻岸上踏歌声。
桃花潭水深千尺,
不及汪伦送我情。

A Verse to Wang Lun

On board the ship I'm about to set sail,
Suddenly from the shore comes the song of farewell.
However deep the Pond of Peach Blossom may be,
But it can never equal Wang Lun's love for me.

峨眉山月歌

峨眉山月半轮秋，
影入平羌江水流。
夜发清溪向三峡，
思君不见下渝州。

Song of the Moon over E'mei Mountain

The half-moon in autumn over the E'mei Mountain,
On the River flowing southeast is your reflection.
From Qingxi Stream to Three Gorges we set sail at night,
On my way to Yuzhou I miss you out of my sight.

山中与幽人对酌

两人对酌山花开，
一杯一杯复一杯。
我醉欲眠卿且去，
明朝有意抱琴来。

Drinking Together with a Recluse in the Mountain

Drinking with a recluse and mountain flowers in bloom,
One glass after another we keep on free drinking.
Goodbye my friend pretty high I'm to sleep in my room,
If you like, please come with your lute tomorrow morning.

望庐山瀑布

日照香炉生紫烟,
遥看瀑布挂前川。
飞流直下三千尺,
疑是银河落九天。

Lushan Mountain Waterfall Viewed from Afar

The sun shines on the Censer Peak shrouded in purple mist,
Hanging from the cliff the waterfall's viewed from the east.
The torrent pours down from the crag three thousand feet high,
As if the Milky Way tumbles down from the blue sky.

早发白帝城

朝辞白帝彩云间，
千里江陵一日还。
两岸猿声啼不住，
轻舟已过万重山。

Departure from Baidi Town at Dawn

Morning farewell to Baidi Town in rosy clouds so high,
A thousand miles to Jiangling is but a one-day trip.
All the way along the river we can hear apes cry,
Thousands of ranges have been passed swiftly by my ship.

望庐山五老峰

庐山东南五老峰,
青天削出金芙蓉。
九江秀色可揽结,
吾将此地巢云松。

Wulao Peaks Viewed from Afar

In the southeast of Lushan Mountain five peaks rise high,
Like golden lotus buds piercing into the clear sky.
The charming views come into sight from Jiujiang River,
I'd like to take up my abode among pines near by.

宣城见杜鹃花

蜀国曾闻子规鸟,
宣城还见杜鹃花。
一叫一回肠一断,
三春三月忆三巴。

Enjoying Azaleas in Xuancheng

Once in Sichuan I heard the calls of cuckoo,
Now in Xuancheng I enjoy azaleas in bloom.
Heart-breaking are cuckoos that make me in sorrow,
Homesickness in late spring casts a deep gloom.

哭晁卿衡

日本晁卿辞帝都，
征帆一片绕蓬壶。
明月不归沉碧海，
白云愁色满苍梧。

Elegy on Chao Heng

Mr. Chao, a Japanese friend was leaving the capital,
Ploughing through waves past Penghu Mountain was his sail.
His ship in the storm like the bright moon sank to the bottom,
Clouds over Cangwu Mountain are gloomy and deadly pale.

望天门山

天门中断楚江开，
碧水东流至此回。
两岸青山相对出，
孤帆一片日边来。

A Distant View of Tianmen Mountain

Having slashed its way through Tianmen Mountain,
Flowing eastward but the river turns all of sudden.
Face to face on both sides are the mountains green,
On the horizon a lonely sail from east can be seen.

山中答俗人问

问余何意栖碧山，
笑而不答心自闲。
桃花流水窅然去，
别有天地非人间。

A Reply to a Friend

Dwelling in green mountains someone asks me why,
Smiling at leisure I give him no reply.
Peach petals fallen on water flowing far away,
Paradise on earth is better than that in the sky.

长门怨

天回北斗挂西楼,
金屋无人萤火流。
月光欲到长门殿,
别作深宫一段愁。

Grievance of a Deserted Empress

Over the west building the Plough's high in the sky,
Empty is the golden palace but fireflies fly.
The moon is going to shine on Changmen Palace,
Grief-stricken, it seems to her someone says goodbye.

清平调词·其一

云想衣裳花想容，
春风拂槛露华浓。
若非群玉山头见，
会向瑶台月下逢。

Song of Lady Yang to the Tune of Serenity（1）

Fair as a flower she's dressed in attire of rainbow,
Kissed by spring breeze charming is the peony with dew glow.
Nowhere but in the fairyland or Heavenly Palace,
Can you come across the belle with tremendous grace.

清平调词·其二

一枝秾艳露凝香，
云雨巫山枉断肠。
借问汉宫谁得似，
可怜飞燕倚新妆。

Song of Lady Yang to the Tune of Serenity (2)

More charming and sweet is the peony with dew,
The Goddess was no jealous of her the king knew.
Who is the match for her in the Han Palace?
Zhao Feiyan* if well-dressed can take belle's place.

---

* Zhao Feiyan, the empress of Emperor Cheng (Liu Ao), the tenth emperor of the Han Dynasty, was a beauty of beauties.

清平调词·其三

名花倾国两相欢，
长得君王带笑看。
解释春风无限恨，
沉香亭北倚阑干。

Song of Lady Yang to the Tune of Serenity（3）

Unmatched is the beauty and peony is charming,
To cherish her at his palm the emperor is dying.
Free from worries the emperor gives a happy smile,
Leaning on the pavilion rail they have an easy style.

戏赠杜甫

饭颗山头逢杜甫,
顶戴笠子日卓午。
借问别来太瘦生,
总为从前作诗苦。

Having a Joke with Du Fu

I came on Du Fu at the foot of Fanke Mountain,
Wearing a conical hat of bamboo at noontime.
Since we said farewell how could you be a skeleton?
Do you always rack your brain for rhythm and rhyme?

客中作

兰陵美酒郁金香,
玉碗盛来琥珀光。
但使主人能醉客,
不知何处是他乡。

A Poem Composed on the Journey

Brewed with tulip so sweet is Lanling Wine,
Contained in amber glass soft is the shine.
If I can get drunk with the wine of such brand,
Strange land is just the same with my homeland.

苏台览古

旧苑荒台杨柳新,
菱歌清唱不胜春。
只今惟有西江月,
曾照吴王宫里人。

Visiting the Ruins of Gusu Terrace

The garden's deserted, terrace bleak, but willows green,
Sweet melody from the boat adds charm to spring serene.
Nothing but the moon over the river from the west,
Witnessed the belle in the Wu Palace at its best.

越中览古

越王勾践破吴归，
义士还乡尽锦衣。
宫女如花满春殿，
只今惟有鹧鸪飞。

Visiting the Ruins of the Capital of the Yue State

At war with the Wu State the king of Yue was riding high,
Returned in glory warriors were dressed in silk attire.
Splendid was his palace full of beauties with strong desire,
We can see nothing today but partridges freely fly.

崔 颢

崔颢(704～754),汴州(今河南开封)人。唐开元十一年进士。早期诗作多写闺情,流于浮艳;后期作品风格雄浑奔放。《全唐诗》存其诗一卷。

Cui Hao(704～754), born in Bianzhou(Kaifeng City, Henan Province today), succeeded in the highest imperial examination in 723. His early poems mainly focused on maidens with florid language which was changed greatly in his late works composed in powerful and smooth style. There is only one volume of his poems collected in *The Complete Collection of the Tang Poetry*.

长干曲·其一

君家何处住?
妾住在横塘。
停船暂借问,
或恐是同乡。

The Antiphonal Songs on the River: A Lady's Song (1)

Where are you from, by the way?
Hengtang on the shore is my birth place.
Just a minute, I have something to say,
I wonder we are from the same place.

长干曲·其二

家临九江水，
来去九江侧。
同是长干人，
生小不相识。

The Antiphonal Songs on the River: A Young Man's Reply (2)

I take up my abode by the riverside,
Sailing with the ebb and flow of the tide.
Born in the same place on the same shore,
But we were strangers to each other before.

高　适

高适(704~765),字达夫,渤海蓨(今河北景县)人。少年家贫,潦倒失意,后被推荐为官。其诗多反映边塞风光和民众疾苦,是唐代边塞诗人的杰出代表。《全唐诗》存其诗四卷。

Gao Shi (704~765), styled Dafu, was born in Tiao, Bohai (Jingxian County, Hebei Province today). Gao led a dog's life and utterly frustrated when he was young, but he was later recommended for promotion as a secretary in the army. Gao was a prominent representative of frontier poets as most of his poems are vivid pictures of frontier landscape and weal and woe of common people. Four volumes of his poems are collected in *The Complete Collection of the Tang Poetry*.

田家春望

出门何所见,
春色满平芜。
可叹无知己,
高阳一酒徒。

Countryside View in Spring

Outside my cottage what comes into my sight?
All over the fields spring charm is so bright.
Alas, no alter ego now really knows me,
But a drunkard I'm lying idly on the lea.

闲居

柳色惊心事，
春风厌索居。
方知一杯酒，
犹胜百家书。

Living at Leisure

Terrified at the sight of green willows,
I'm in low spirits as soft breeze blows.
With a glass of wine I'm carried away,
Better than reading sage's works night and day.

逢谢偃

红颜怆为别,
白发始相逢。
唯馀昔时泪,
无复旧时容。

Meeting Xie Yan by Chance

Parting with you when we were in our prime,
Reunion happens when grey hairs grow long.
Attachment for each other as it were old time,
But rosy cheeks fade away, we're by no means young.

除夜作

旅馆寒灯独不眠,
客心何事转凄然。
故乡今夜思千里,
愁鬓明朝又一年。

A Poem Composed on New Year's Eve

Alone in the hotel I can't sleep by the cold light,
Sad and dreary why I'm heavy-hearted tonight?
Yearning for my return from home land far away,
New Year comes tomorrow and my hair turns gray.

塞上听吹笛

雪净胡天牧马还,
月明羌笛戍楼间。
借问梅花何处落,
风吹一夜满关山。

The Flute Melody Heard Outside the Great Wall

Herdsmen homeward from grazing land as snow melts away,
From the moon-lit watchtower comes the Qiang flute play.
The melody of *Plum-blossom*, where does it float tonight?
Flying with wind over the Guanshan Mountain overnight.

别董大

千里黄云白日曛,
北风吹雁雪纷纷。
莫愁前路无知己,
天下谁人不识君。

Farewell to Dong Tinglan

The sandstorm sweeping far and wide darkens the sky,
With north wind wild geese among the snowflakes fly.
No need to worry about alter egos on your way,
There is no connoisseur in the world but loves your play.

储光羲

储光羲(707~760),润州延陵(今江苏丹阳)人。官至监察御史,后遭贬死于岭南。储光羲长于五言诗,以山水田园诗居多,构思缜密,语言质朴自然。《全唐诗》存其诗四卷。

Chu Guangxi(707~760) was born in YanLin, Runzhou(Danyang City, Jiangsu Province today). Chu was once promoted to the imperial supervisor but later demoted and died in South China. Chu was well versed in poems of five characters to each line, many of which are idylls with well-knit structure and plain, natural language. Four volumes of his poems are collected in *The Complete Collection of the Tang Poetry*.

长安道

西行一千里,
暝色生寒树。
暗闻歌吹声,
知是长安路。

The Road to Chang'an

A thousand miles westward I travel on day and night,
The cold trees along the road are bathed in dusk light.
Faintly the songs and music come to my ears sometimes,
I know Chang'an, the capital will come into sight.

洛阳道

大道直如发,
春日佳气多。
五陵贵公子,
双双鸣玉珂。

The Road to Luoyang

Straight as an arrow is the road to Luoyang,
Wherever you go spring weather comes along.
Children of wealthy peers come out in pairs,
With jade bridles tinkling they put on airs.

清　恽寿平　《洛阳花》

江南曲

日暮长江里，
相邀归渡头。
落花如有意，
来去逐船流。

Song of the South of the Yangtze River

On the river glows the sunset glory,
We agreed to return to the ferry.
The fallen flowers if they pine for love,
Chase after our skiffs and give us a shove.

刘长卿

刘长卿(709~789),字文房,宣城(今安徽宣城)人。曾在朝为官,后遭贬谪。刘长卿自诩"五言长城",五言诗占其作品七成,其诗作气韵流畅,音调和谐。《全唐诗》存其诗五卷。

Liu Changqing (709~789), styled Wenfang, was born in Hejian (Hejian County, Hebei Province today). Liu once served as a government official of high rank, but he was demoted later. Famous for his poems with five characters per line, Liu praised himself as the "Great Wall of Five-character Poems". Poems of five-character per line amount 70% of all his poetry, which are smooth in style and beautiful in rhyme and rhythm. Five volumes of his poems are collected in *The Complete Collection of the Tang Poetry*.

逢雪宿芙蓉山主人

日暮苍山远,
天寒白屋贫。
柴门闻犬吠,
风雪夜归人。

Putting up for the Snowy Night in Lotus Mountain

The dim outline of mountains at dusk seems so far,
Cold enough are the thatched cottages in snow white.
From the wicker gate comes the dog's noisy barking,
I'm aware someone pleads to stay the snowy night.

湘妃

帝子不可见，
秋风来暮思。
婵娟湘江月，
千载空蛾眉。

The Goddesses of the River Xiang

Forever are the queens out of my sight,
As autumn wind blows I miss you at night.
The new moon over the River Xiang is so fair,
Like the beautiful eyebrows extremely rare.

斑竹

苍梧千载后，
斑竹对湘沅。
欲识湘妃怨，
枝枝满泪痕。

Mottled Bamboos

Having travelled to Cangwu* the King** passed away,
The bamboos by the River Xiang got mottled with dismay.
What marks the empress's sorrow for so many years?
The bamboos were speckled due to the drops of their tears.

---

* Cangwu is the place where King Shun passed away in twenty-first century BC and his two concubines committed suicide by drowning in the River Xiang (Hunan Province).
** The King here refers to King Shun.

春草宫怀古

君王不可见,
茅草旧宫春。
犹带罗裙色,
青青向楚人。

Meditations on the Former Palace of the Sui Dynasty

The former emperor is nowhere to be seen,
Near the old palace only the new grass in sight.
Verdant and tender in spring they are bright green,
Smiling at the new visitors with great delight.

正朝览镜作

憔悴逢新岁，
茅扉见旧春。
朝来明镜里，
不忍白头人。

Looking in the Mirror at Dawn

New year witnesses me pining away,
And the thatched hut sees the spring array.
Looking at myself in the mirror bright,
To my great surprise I find my hair white.

瓜洲道中送李端公南渡后，归扬州道中寄

片帆何处去，
匹马独归迟。
惆怅江南北，
青山欲暮时。

A Send-off to Imperial Envoy Li at Guazhou Sandbar

Where your boat is sailing for I think I know,
Homeward on horseback alone I'm in sorrow.
Parting pain comes from the river in between,
Green mountains at dusk can be dimly seen.

元　赵孟頫　《饮马图》

送灵澈上人

苍苍竹林寺,
杳杳钟声晚。
荷笠带夕阳,
青山独归远。

A Send-off to Ling Che, a Buddhist Monk

Hidden in green bamboos is an old temple high,
From which comes a peal of bells as dusk is nigh.
With a bamboo hat bathed in the evening glow,
In the green mountains he has a long way to go.

茱萸湾北答崔载华问

荒凉野店绝,
迢递人烟远。
苍苍古木中,
多是隋家苑。

The Cornel Bay

It's bleak and desolate there are no shops in sight,
Deserted long ago they were in the remote past.
Gardens hidden by the age-old trees of great height,
Most are the remains from the Sui Dynasty that last.

江中对月

空洲夕烟敛,
望月秋江里。
历历沙上人,
月下孤渡水。

Gazing at the Moon on the River

The mist on the sandbar slip away in dusk light,
The moon on the river looms at autumn night.
So clear is the figure moving on the sandbar,
Crossing the moonlit river alone from afar.

寄龙山道士许法棱

悠悠白云里，
独住青山客。
林下昼焚香，
桂花同寂寂。

To a Taoist Priest Xu in Longshan Mountain

Come and go through the floating clouds white,
All alone you're attached to mountains green.
In the woods you burn incense in daylight,
No companion but the laurel the flower queen.

赠崔九载华

怜君一见一悲歌，
岁岁无如老去何。
白屋渐看秋草没，
青云莫道故人多。

To Cui Jiu

Meeting you today I give my pity and a sad sigh,
Year after year senility for you is drawing nigh.
Your thatched cottage witnesses grass fading in autumn,
No need to envy your friends whose aspirations are high.

过郑山人所居

寂寂孤莺啼杏园,
寥寥一犬吠桃源。
落花芳草无寻处,
万壑千峰独闭门。

Passing by Mr. Zheng a Recluse's Residence

A lonely oriole sings in the apricot garden,
A solitary dog barks in the idyllic heaven.
Green grass and fallen flowers are nowhere in sight,
Through valleys and peaks I find his gate closed tight.

奉使鄂渚至乌江道中作

沧洲不复恋鱼竿，
白发那堪戴铁冠。
客路向南何处是，
芦花千里雪漫漫。

On a Mission to Ezhu

In no mood for angling by the riverside,
I'm too old to be on a mission far and wide.
Going southwards the right route I don't know,
All along my way reed catkins whirl like snow.

使回赴苏州道中作

春风何事远相催，
路尽天涯始却回。
万里无人空楚水，
孤帆送客到鱼台。

On the Way to Suzhou Back from My Mission

Spring wind urges to return I don't know why,
The end of the world my mission is drawing nigh.
All the way back no figure but water in sight,
A lonely boat sends me to Suzhou in sad plight.

重送裴郎中贬吉州

猿啼客散暮江头，
人自伤心水自流。
同作逐臣君更远，
青山万里一孤舟。

Sending Mr. Pei Off Again to Jizhou on His Demotion

Guests leaving, apes crying at dusk by the riverside,
Grief-stricken and my heart goes away with the tide.
Demoted as I was but you are sent further away,
No mate but a lonely boat and mountains all the way.

送李穆归淮南

扬州春草新年绿,
未去先愁去不归。
淮水问君来早晚,
老人偏畏过芳菲。

A Send-off to Li Mu on His Way to Huainan

After the New Year grass in Yangzhou turns green,
Before you start I'm worrying too long you'll stay.
The Huai River wants to know your date of return,
If you come back too late flowers will fade away.

杜 甫

杜甫(712～770),字子美,河南巩县(今河南巩义)人。自幼好学,知识渊博,诗风沉郁,语言精练,具有极高的表现力。杜甫是我国著名的现实主义诗人,国人称其为"诗圣"。其诗作现存1450余首。《全唐诗》存其诗十九卷。

Du Fu(712～770), Styled Zimei, was born in Gongxian, Henan(Gongyi City, Henan Province today). Du was fond of learning and erudite when he was a child. As a famous realistic poet Du Fu is praised a poet-sage in China. His poems, profound in meaning, terse in style, are much expressive. There are 1450 of his poems extant, of which 19 volumes are collected in *The Complete Collection of the Tang Poetry*.

武侯庙

遗庙丹青落,
空山草木长。
犹闻辞后主,
不复卧南阳。

Zhuge Liang Temple

Paintings on the temple wall are fading away,
Plants and trees in the vast mountains grow today.
As if making the farewell speech to the last king,
Return to the native land is lengthy delay.

八阵图

功盖三分国,
名成八阵图。
江流石不转,
遗恨失吞吴。

The Eight-Trigram Battle Array*

Three kingdoms were formed with his talents on display,
He became well-known due to the Eight-Trigram Array.
The river flows but the formation of stones stands fast,
Failure to recover the lost land is the regret to the last.

---

* The Eight-Trigram Battle Array was a famous military formation designed by Zhuge Liang during the period of Three Kingdoms Wei, Shu, Wu (220~280).

复愁

万国尚防寇,
故园今若何。
昔归相识少,
早已战场多。

Lingering Gloom

Flames of war spreading far and wide,
What about my hometown I don't know.
I ask the strangers by the roadside,
Many people went to war years ago.

绝句·其一

迟日江山丽,
春风花草香。
泥融飞燕子,
沙暖睡鸳鸯。

A Quatrain (1)

The sun is bright, river clear, and mountain green,
Flowers smiling, grass sweet, breeze soft and serene.
Nesting with mud so busy are swallows flying,
On the warm sands are the mandarin ducks lying.

绝句·其二

江碧鸟逾白，
山青花欲燃。
今春看又过，
何日是归年。

A Quatrain（2）

Against blue water birds seem bright white,
On green mountains flowers are to burn.
How time flies, spring is seen past its height,
Oh, I don't know the date of my return!

阙题

三月雪连夜,
未应伤物华。
只缘春欲尽,
留著伴梨花。

An Inscription on the Archway

It snows in late spring night and day,
But it does no harm to plants and flowers.
Because in March spring is fading away,
It adds much to pear blossoms for hours.

归雁

东来万里客,
乱定几年归。
肠断江城雁,
高高正北飞。

Homeward Swans

I'm roaming far away from my hometown,
Chaos is over for homecoming I yearn.
On seeing swans across the river in flight,
Heart-broken I dream to fly with birds at night.

绝句

江动月移石,
溪虚云傍花。
鸟栖知故道,
帆过宿谁家。

A Quatrain

The rocks move with the moon as the river flows,
Getting close to flowers a cloud on water floats.
Riverside is the place to perch on the birds know,
But to find a spot for the night we have to go.

赠李白

秋来相顾尚飘蓬，
未就丹砂愧葛洪。
痛饮狂歌空度日，
飞扬跋扈为谁雄。

To Li Bai

When autumn came you were drifting from place to place,
To find Taoist truth you had spent so many days.
Drinking and chanting wild with joy day and night,
For whom you're in an ecstasy of delight.

漫成一首

江月去人只数尺，
风灯照夜欲三更。
沙头宿鹭联拳静，
船尾跳鱼泼剌鸣。

A Quatrain at Random

The moon's only a few feet from the river in the sky,
Far advanced is the night and visible the lamplight.
Curling up on the sands the egrets soundly sleep at night,
From the boat stern comes the loud splash of fish jumping high.

漫兴·其一

眼见客愁愁不醒,
无赖春色到江亭。
即遣花开深造次,
便觉莺语太丁宁。

A Poem Composed at Random (1)

Deep in sorrow I'm in a trance behind the curtain,
Fascinating spring comes to the pavilion for certain.
Urging flowers into blooming spring comes with a quick dash,
Making orioles singing time and again you seem too rash.

漫兴 · 其二

熟知茅斋绝低小，
江上燕子故来频。
衔泥点污琴书内，
更接飞虫打着人。

A Poem Composed at Random (2)

Familiar with my cottage that is tiny and low,
But it's the haunt of swallows the reason I know.
They stain my books and strings while busy nesting,
Chasing insects without stop they fly to and fro.

漫兴·其三

二月已破三月来，
渐老逢春能几回。
莫思身外无穷事，
且尽生前有限杯。

A Poem Composed at Random（3）

February is over and March is ushered in,
To the aged how many times can we greet spring?
Think nothing about vanities in the world,
A glass of wine if possible enjoy your drinking.

漫兴·其四

肠断江春欲尽头,
杖藜徐步立芳洲。
颠狂柳絮随风舞,
轻薄桃花逐水流。

A Poem Composed at Random (4)

Heart-broken by the river as the spring fades away,
Paving on the sands with a cane I enjoy spring day.
Wild with joy willow catkins are dancing with breeze,
Frivolous peach blossoms float with stream in bliss.

漫兴·其五

糁径杨花铺白毡,
点溪荷叶叠青钱。
笋根雉子无人见,
沙上凫雏傍母眠。

A Poem Composed at Random (5)

Paved with catkins the path's like a long carpet white,
Dotting the stream lotus leaves are green coins bright.
Near the bamboo shoots are young pheasants lurking,
On the sands wild ducklings hug their mother sleeping.

漫兴·其六

隔户杨柳弱袅袅,
恰似十五女儿腰。
谁谓朝来不作意,
狂风挽断最长条。

A Poem Composed at Random(6)

Willows next door are so soft and graceful,
Like the slim waist of a teenage girl small.
A gust of wind blew in the morning at will,
Snapped the longest twig it cares not at all.

赠花卿

锦城丝管日纷纷，
半入江风半入云。
此曲只应天上有，
人间能得几回闻。

To Mr. Hua

The string and wind music in the town is so loud,
Wafting with wind over the river into cloud.
Only in the fairyland can such music be heard,
Scarcely can it be played in the human world.

少年行·其一

莫笑田家老瓦盆，
自从盛酒长儿孙。
倾银注瓦惊人眼，
共醉终同卧竹根。

Song of Juvenile（1）

Don't mock our pots which are humbly made of clay,
Containing wine the children are happy and gay.
Although your flagons are made of silver and gold,
When drunk lying by bamboos the same is our display.

少年行·其二

马上谁家薄媚郎，
临阶下马坐人床。
不通姓字粗豪甚，
指点银瓶索酒尝。

Song of Juvenile (2)

Who is the fair lad on horseback feeling so fine?
Dismounting near the steps he takes a seat to dine.
No greeting he is rough and arrogant enough,
He signals to the waiter for a flagon wine.

江畔独步寻花·其一

黄师塔前江水东,
春光懒困倚微风。
桃花一簇开无主,
可爱深红爱浅红。

Paving Alone along the River for Flowers(1)

Before the monk pagoda the river eastward flows,
I feel sleepy and tired in spring as the breeze blows.
Peach blossoms blooming without the owner today,
Crimson, or pink, they are all in splendid array.

江畔独步寻花·其二

黄四娘家花满蹊，
千朵万朵压枝低。
留连戏蝶时时舞，
自在娇莺恰恰啼。

Paving Alone along the River for Flowers（2）

Flanked with flowers is the path via Miss Huang's window,
Laden with clusters of flowers branches bow low.
Lingering around flowers butterflies are dancing,
I'm carried away with orioles singing in willow.

绝句

两个黄鹂鸣翠柳,
一行白鹭上青天。
窗含西岭千秋雪,
门泊东吴万里船。

A Quatrain

A couple of orioles in the green willow singing,
A flight of white egrets across the blue sky soaring.
From my window the snow-capped west peaks are seen white,
In front of my gate ships from the Wu Kingdom in sight.

解闷·其一

草阁紫扉星散居，
浪翻江黑雨飞初。
山禽引子哺红果，
溪友得钱留白鱼。

Free from Loneliness (1)

Thatched cottages here and there dot the green mountain,
Clouds over the waves form a huge rain curtain.
Leading the brood with red fruits the bird is feeding,
Satisfied is the fisherman on the stream fishing.

解闷·其二

一辞故国十经秋,
每见秋瓜忆故丘。
今日南湖采薇蕨,
何人为觅郑瓜州。

Free from Loneliness (2)

A sad farewell to the native land ten years ago,
Seeing autumn melon I think of home in sorrow.
Demoted I'm on the south lake where wild herbs grow,
Who is looking for the Melon Shoal I don't know.

戏为六绝句·其一

庾信文章老更成,
凌云健笔意纵横。
今人嗤点流传赋,
不觉前贤畏后生。

A Quatrain Composed for Fun(1)

More sound are the essays by Yu Xin in his old age,
At the acme of his works he wrote a glorious page.
Nitpicking of critics is far from fair and just,
I don't think they're any better than the ancient sage.

戏为六绝句·其二

王杨卢骆当时体,
轻薄为文哂未休。
尔曹身与名俱灭,
不废江河万古流。

A Quatrain Composed for Fun (2)

Wang, Yang, Lu and Luo* are poets with poems unique in style,
The critics make their shallow remarks with high profile.
Their bodies and names will certainly fade away,
While the poems of the eminent will go a long way.

---

* Wang, Yang, Lu and Luo refer to "Four Eminent Poets in the Early Tang Dynasty": Wang Bo, Yang Jiong, Lu Zhaolin and Luo Binwang, whose poems are considered unique in style.

江南逢李龟年

岐王宅里寻常见，
崔九堂前几度闻。
正是江南好风景，
落花时节又逢君。

A Chance Meeting with Li Guinian, a Famous Musician, South of the Yangtze River

Before long in Prince Qi's mansion we met all the time,
Even in Cui Jiu's chamber I heard you sing in your prime.
Now spring view south of the Yangtze is in its heyday,
Meeting you now again but flowers are fading away.

岑 参

岑参(715~770),荆州江陵(今湖北江陵)人。两次出征边塞,且久居塞外,对边塞风光景物有深刻体验,并真实地反映在其诗作中。与高适并享"边塞诗人"称号。《全唐诗》存其诗四卷。

Cen Shen(715~770) was born in Jiangling, Jingzhou(Jiangling County, Hubei Province today). Cen was sent to northwest frontier twice and stayed there for a long time, he was therefore very much familiar with the natural conditions and social customs which were vividly pictured in his poems. Together with Gao Shi, Cen Shen shared the title of "Frontier Poets". Four volumes of his poems are collected in *The Complete Collection of the Tang Poetry*.

西过渭州见渭水思秦川

渭水东流去,
何时到雍州。
凭添两行泪,
寄向故园流。

Longing for Qinchuan by Weishui River

Towards the east the Weishui River flows,
When it reaches Yongzhou nobody knows.
Thinking of this tears run down my cheeks,
Flowing to homeland are tears of sorrows.

题汾桥边柳

此地曾居住，
今来宛似归。
可怜汾上柳，
相见也依依。

To Willows by the Fenqiao Bridge

It was once my place of abode,
The visit is like homecoming today.
By the river so lovely are the willows,
Smiling at me with grace they sway.

秋思

那知芳岁晚，
坐见寒叶堕。
吾不如腐草，
翻飞作萤火。

Autumn Thoughts

Before I know gone is my heyday,
Sitting by tree I see fallen leaves fly.
Rotten grass is better than me fading away,
Like fireflies flitting up and down the sky.

逢入京使

故园东望路漫漫,
双袖龙钟泪不干。
马上相逢无纸笔,
凭君传语报平安。

Meeting a Messenger on His Way to the Capital

Gazing east an endless path to my homeland appears,
Never dry are the sleeves of my dress wet with tears.
Meeting you on horseback, no paper how can I write,
I ask you to pass the word to my wife,"I'm all right".

春梦

洞房昨夜春风起，
遥忆美人湘江水。
枕上片时春梦中，
行尽江南数千里。

Spring Dream

Last night spring breeze flowed to my chamber through window,
Came with zephyr my beauty from the Xiang River side.
Sweet was the dream but a fleeting moment on the pillow,
Over the south of the Yangtze I roamed far and wide.

隋　展子虔　《游春图》(局部)

草堂村寻罗生不遇

数株豁柳色依依，
深巷斜阳暮鸟飞。
门前雪满无行迹，
应是先生出未归。

A Vain Visit to a Recluse

A few willow trees appear faintly in sight,
Along the deep lane birds fly in setting sun light.
In front of his gate tracks disappear in snow,
Away from home perhaps he's still on the go.

碛中作

走马西来欲到天,
辞家见月两回圆。
今夜不知何处宿,
平沙万里绝人烟。

A Poem Composed in the Desert

Galloping westward I almost touch the sky,
Away from home twice the moon is full and high.
Dusk falls, but where to put up for the night,
Vast is the desert with no figure in sight.

山房春事

梁园日暮乱飞鸦,
极目萧条三两家。
庭树不知人去尽,
春来还发旧时花。

Spring in the Deserted Garden

Crows in the garden fly helter-skelter in twilight,
Two or three houses came into view, what a bleak sight!
Garden trees unaware that no figure can be seen,
Blooming still as they were last year when spring's ushered in.

金昌绪

金昌绪(生卒年不详),余杭(今浙江杭州)人。《全唐诗》存其诗一首。

Jin Changxu, was born in Yuhang (Hangzhou City, Zhejiang Province today). There is one of his poem collected in *The Complete Collection of the Tang Poetry*.

春怨

打起黄莺儿,
莫教枝上啼。
啼时惊妾梦,
不得到辽西。

Grievance in Spring

Shoo, shoo, I shouted orioles away,
To stop them from singing night and day.
Their singing awakes me from sweet dream,
Meeting my darling I can't find my way.

张　继

张继(715~779),字懿孙,襄州(今湖北襄樊)人。曾在朝为官。其诗风格清新,不事雕琢。《全唐诗》存其诗一卷。

Zhang Ji (715~779), styled Yisun, was born in Xiangzhou (Xiangfan City, Hubei Province today). He was once promoted to senior official and his poems were composed in pure and fresh style, of which one volume was collected in *The Complete Collection of the Tang Poetry*.

枫桥夜泊

月落乌啼霜满天,
江枫渔火对愁眠。
姑苏城外寒山寺,
夜半钟声到客船。

Nocturnal Berth at the Maple Bridge

The moon is setting, crows crying and rime fills the sky,
Dim lights through maples the fisherman's sad with a sigh.
Beyond Suzhou city wall, from the Hanshan Temple,
Midnight toll reaches the passenger boat on a ramble.

阊门即事

耕夫召募逐楼船，
春草青青万顷田。
试上吴门窥郡郭，
清明几处有新烟。

A Verse Composed at the West Gate of Suzhou

Recruited into the army few farmers did farming,
In the vast fields except spring weeds there is nothing.
Standing atop the city wall I gaze far and wide,
No cooking smoke curling up from the city outside.

裴 迪

裴迪(716～?)，关中(今属陕西)人。早年与王维友善，同居终南山，相互唱和，以田园诗著称。《全唐诗》存其诗29首。

Pei Di(716～?), born in Guanzhong(region of Shaanxi Province today), was on friendly terms with Wang Wei. They both lived in seclusion in Zhongnan Mountain, writing and replying in poems with each other. Pei was well known for his idylls, of which 29 poems are collected in *The Complete Collection of the Tang Poetry*.

欹湖

空阔湖水广，
青荧天色同。
舣舟一长啸，
四面来清风。

Qihu Lake

The expanse of lake water is vast and wide,
Blending into blue are the water and sky.
Sailing the boat into berth comes a loud cry,
Refreshing breeze blows from all sides with the tide.

柳浪

映池同一色,
逐吹散如丝。
结阴既得地,
何谢陶家时。

Sway of Willows

Same to water color you're reflected in the pond,
Swaying with breeze your twigs like hairs of nymph.
Casting your shadow your branches droop to ground,
Second to none your dance is graceful enough.

送崔九

归山深浅去,
须尽丘壑美。
莫学武陵人,
暂游桃源里。

A Send-off to Cui Xingzong

Along the winding path you return to the mountain,
Feast your eyes on the scenery living in seclusion.
Never follow the Wuling fishermen, the passers-by,
Visiting the Shangri-La for the time being with a sigh.

皇甫冉

皇甫冉(717～771)，字茂政，润州丹阳(今江苏丹阳)人。其诗多赠寄之作，语言工巧，格调清奇。《全唐诗》存其诗两卷。

Huangpu Ran(717～771), styled Maozheng, was born in Danyang, Runzhou (Danyang City, Jiangsu Province today). Most of his poems were composed as donation to his friends, of which some are exquisite in language and quaint in style. Two volumes of his poems are collected in *The Complete Collection of the Tang Poetry*.

远山

少室尽西峰，
鸣皋隐南面。
柴门纵复关，
终日窗中见。

Distant Views of Mountains

The west peak towers above the Shaoshi Mountain,
From the south Mountain Minggao is dimly in sight.
No matter the wicker gate is shut or open,
From the window I can glimpse them day and night.

同李三月夜作

霜风惊度雁，
月露皓疏林。
处处砧声发，
星河秋夜深。

A Verse Composed in the Moonlight with Li San

The passing swans are startled by wind and rime,
Dressed in frost sparse trees of the woods are bright.
Loud hammering can be heard from time to time,
Boundless is the Milky Way late at autumn night.

寄权器

露湿青芜时欲晚，
水流黄叶意无穷。
节近重阳念归否，
眼前篱菊带秋风。

To Quanqi

Wet with dew drops are green weeds in late autumn,
Away with water are yellow leaves floating.
On Double Ninth Day is your home in your bosom?
With autumn wind chrysanthemums are blooming.

元　赵孟頫　《鹊华秋色图》

贾 至

贾至(718～772),字幼邻,河南洛阳人。曾在朝为官,后遭贬。其诗语言朴实,风格俊逸。《全唐诗》存其诗一卷。

Jia Zhi(718～772), styled Youling was born in Luoyang(Luoyang City, Henan Province today). Jia Zhi once held a post in the government but was demoted later. His poems were plain in language and delicate in style, of which one volume was collected in *The Complete Collection of the Tang Poetry*.

西亭春望

日长风暖柳青青,
北雁归飞入窅冥。
岳阳城上闻吹笛,
能使春心满洞庭。

A Spring View of West Pavilion

Days are getting longer, breeze's warm and willows are green,
In the deep blue sky swans on the way home can be seen.
At Yueyang Gate Tower I hear the flute playing nigh,
Brimmed over with love for the lake I'm a bit high.

洞庭送李十二赴零陵

今日相逢落叶前,
洞庭秋水远连天。
共说金华旧游处,
回看北斗欲潸然。

Sending Li Bai off to Lingling on Dongting Lake

We meet by chance amid the fallen leaves today,
Dongting Lake in autumn kisses the sky far away.
Talking of the haunt in the capital in the past,
Turning round to the Plough my tears stream down the cheeks fast.

初至巴陵与李十二白裴九同泛洞庭湖

江上相逢皆旧游，
湘山永望不堪愁。
明月秋风洞庭水，
孤鸿落叶一扁舟。

Boating on Dongting Lake with Li Bai and Pei Yin

Old friends meet again on River Xiang, our haunt of the past,
Free from care we see the mountain on the lake standing fast.
Autumn wind strokes the water of the lake in the moonlight,
A lonely swan flies with fallen leaves and a boat in sight.

春思

草色青青柳色黄,
桃花历乱李花香。
东风不为吹愁去,
春日偏能惹恨长。

Gloom in Spring

Grasses are green and willows creamy yellow,
Plum blossoms are sweet and peach trees in full bloom.
Instead of blowing away my great sorrow,
The east wind brings me spring, but I'm deep in gloom.

钱 起

钱起(722～780),字仲文,吴兴(今浙江湖州)人。擅长五律、七绝,蕴藉含蓄,辞采清丽。《全唐诗》存其诗四卷。

Qian Qi(722～780), styled Zhongwen, was born in Wuxing(Huzhou City, Zhejiang Province today). Well versed in classic poems of eight lines with five characters per line, Qian's seven-syllable quatrains are implied with profound meanings. Four volumes of his poems are collected in *The Complete Collection of the Tang Poetry*.

戏鸥

乍依菱蔓聚,
尽向芦花灭。
更喜好风来,
数片翻晴雪。

Gulls at Play

About the water nuts now they gather and play,
Into the reed catkins they're fading away.
With nice wind they soar overhead with delight,
In the sky they are the beautiful snowflakes white.

江行

万木已清霜,
江边村事忙。
故溪黄稻熟,
一夜梦中香。

A Journey Along the River

All trees and plants are coated with the thin rime,
By the river for farmers it's the harvest time.
Ripe are crops in the paddies of my native land,
Sweet smell of rice is lingering in my dreamland.

宿洞口馆

野竹通溪冷，
秋泉入户鸣。
乱来人不到。
芳草上阶生。

An Overnight Stay at Dongkou Posthouse

Wild bamboos lead to a cold stream gurgling,
A spring in autumn around the house tinkling.
To and fro travelers seem hustling and bustling,
Along the steps fragrant grass keeps on creeping.

古藤

引蔓出云树,
垂纶覆巢鹤。
幽人对酒时,
苔上闲花落。

Age-old Vines

Vines hanging from a tree in the clouds are age-old,
Of the crane nest drooping canes keep a firm hold.
When hermits under the tree enjoy drinking wine,
Falling into the mossy ground are petals fine.

药圃

春畦生百药，
花叶香初霁。
好容似风光，
偏来入丛蕙。

A Garden of Herbs

Hundreds of herbs growing in the spring garden,
Flowers and leaves after rain fragrant and clean.
Vernal breeze comes up in the bright sunshine,
Stroking sweet herbs in thick clusters so fine.

石上苔

净与溪色连，
幽宜松雨滴。
谁知古石上，
不染世人迹。

Moss on Rocks

Clean and green as the small stream in peace,
Dew drops from pine trees make your necklace.
Nobody knows you grow on the ancient rocks,
Trodden by no one and stained with no trace.

潺湲声

乱石跳素波，
寒声闻几处。
飕飕暝风引，
散出空林去。

A Babbling Brook

Amid boulders and rocks waves spray,
Cold sound of babbling comes from the brook.
Gloomy and chilly wind comes on my way,
Through the empty woods it's a narrow crook.

窗里山

远岫见如近，
千重一窗里。
坐来石上云，
乍谓壶中起。

Views of Mountains from the Window

Views of caverns unfold before my eyes,
Ranges of mountains glide through my window.
Sitting in the clouds from the rock shadow,
As if in the fairyland it freely flies.

远山钟

风送出山钟,
云霞度水浅。
欲寻声尽处,
鸟灭寥天远。

Bells from the Distant Mountain

With the wind come the bells from the distant mountain,
Floating in the shallow water is the twilight.
Following the sound that fades on the horizon,
Up into the sky beyond birds fly out of sight.

长安落第

花繁柳暗九门深,
对饮悲歌泪满襟。
数日莺花皆落羽,
一回春至一伤心。

Failure in the Imperial Examination

Flowers blooming, willows dark and deep is the royal court,
Drinking in sad melody tears are wetting my garment.
Orioles are singing, flowers smiling, but now they are not,
Spring comes and goes once a year I'm sad at the moment.

夜泊鹦鹉洲

月照溪边一罩蓬,
夜间清唱有微风。
小楼深巷敲方响,
水国人家在处同。

Mooring to the Parrot Sandbar at Night

Over the awning by the stream the moon shines bright,
Light wind sends the sweet arias to my ears at night.
Percussion's heard from the tower in the deep lane,
Families by the waterside live with delight.

春郊

水绕冰渠渐有声,
气融烟坞晚来明。
东风好作阳和使,
逢草逢花报发生。

Spring in the Suburbs

The frozen ditch starts to thaw and water' gurgling,
It's warm in the hill hollows and setting sun bright.
The vernal breeze comes as a kind envoy of spring,
Speeding the growth of grass and flowers with delight.

过故洛城

故城门外春日斜，
故城门里无人家。
市朝欲认不知处，
漠漠野田空草花。

Passing Through the Former Luoyang City

Outside the gate of the former town the sun slants in spring,
Inside the former town you can find no human being.
Looking for the usual haunt but I know not the site,
Only grass and flowers in wilderness come into sight.

暮春归故山草堂

谷口春残黄鸟稀,
辛夷花尽杏花飞。
始怜幽竹山窗下,
不改清阴待我归。

Back to the Former Mountain Cottage in Late Spring

Few orioles sing at the valley mouth in late spring,
Magnolias are fading and apricot petals flying.
I love nothing but the bamboos by the window,
Waiting for my return they cast the green shadow.

归雁

潇湘何事等闲回,
水碧沙明两岸苔。
二十五弦弹夜月,
不胜清怨却飞来。

Wild Geese on Their Return

Why are you leaving here for the north flying so far?
With crystal water the River Xiang has the white sandbar.
The goddesses of the river* play lute at moonlit night,
The tune is so plaintive that we cannot bear the plight.

---

* The goddesses of the river here refer to the two-sister concubines(E Huang and Nv Ying who died in River Xiang, Hunan Province) of the sage King Shun in ancient China.

五代　董源　《潇湘图》

九日田舍

今日陶家野兴偏，
东篱黄菊映秋田。
浮云暝鸟飞将尽，
始达青山新月前。

Farmhouse on the Double Ninth Festival

In a good mood our family go outing today,
Along the east fence chrysanthemums a bright array.
Floating clouds and birds fly away in the after light,
Towards the new moon atop the green mountain bright.

韩翃

韩翃(生卒年不详),字君平,南阳(今河南省沁阳县)人。大历十才子之一,曾在朝为官。其绝句风格婉转雅致。《全唐诗》存其诗三卷。

Hang Hong, styled Junping, was born in Nanyang(Qinyang Country, Henan Province today). As a government official Han was ranked among the ten gifted talents in the period from 766 to 780. His quatrains are well-knit in syntax, beautiful in words and elegant in style. Three volumes of his poems are collected in *The Complete Collection of the Tang Poetry*.

汉宫曲

骏马绣障泥,
红尘扑四蹄。
归时何太晚,
日照杏花西。

Song of the Han Palace

Nicely embroidered are pads on the horse belly,
Four horse hooves are stained with dust thickly.
Late enough for homecoming as I travel around,
Sun in the west kisses apricot trees on the ground.

唐　韩干　《圉人呈马图》

宿石邑山中

浮云不共此山齐,
山霭苍苍望转迷。
晓月暂飞高树里,
秋河隔在数峰西。

An Overnight Stay in Shiyi Mountain

Floating clouds can hardly touch the top of the mountain,
Shimmering round the peaks is the haze faintly golden.
Behind the thicket the moon at dawn is now hidden,
Beyond the peaks the river in autumn can be seen.

寒食即事

春城无处不飞花，
寒食东风御柳斜。
日暮汉宫传蜡烛，
轻烟散入五侯家。

The Cold Food Festival

Capital in spring witnesses flowers fading away,
Willow trees sway in the vernal breeze on the Cold Food Day.
From palace to palace at dusk bright is the candle light,
Nowhere but in the court smoke and fire can be seen at night.

顾 况

顾况(725～806),字逋翁,苏州海盐(今浙江海盐)人。曾在朝为官,后遭贬,归隐茅山。其诗重气骨,绝句清隽自然。《全唐诗》存其诗四卷。

Gu Kuang (725～806), styled Buweng, was born in Haiyan (Haiyan County, Zhejiang Province today). Gu Kuang served as a high-rank official in the imperial government but was demoted later and led a secluded life in Maoshan Mountain. His poems are full of spirit and lucid in style, of which four volumes are collected in *The Complete Collection of the Tang Poetry*.

梦后吟

醉中还有梦,
身外已无心。
明镜唯知老,
青山何处深。

A Poem Composed After Dreaming

In state of being drunk I'm still dreaming,
About fame and fortune I care nothing.
Before the mirror I know I am old,
In mountains I'm relieved of heavy load.

青弋江

凄清回泊夜,
沧波激石响。
村边草市桥,
月下罟师网。

Qingyi River

Slightly cold in the boat berthed at night,
Beating the rocks small waves skip with delight.
Near the village bridge there's a country fair,
In the moonlight looms the fisherman's snare.

洛阳陌

莺声满御堤,
堤柳拂丝齐。
风送名花落,
香红衬马蹄。

The Path to Luoyang

Along the dykes orioles are singing,
Willows on dykes are neatly swaying.
Dancing with wind are flower petals,
Sticking to horse hooves are sweet ravels.

山中夜宿

凉月挂层峰,
萝林落叶重。
掩关深畏虎,
风起撼长松。

An Overnight Stay in Mountains

Atop the mountain peak is the moon bright,
Leaves of trailing plants thickly cover the ground.
Afraid of tiger we close the door at night,
Through the pine trees the sough of the wind comes round.

溪上

采莲溪上女,
舟小怯摇风。
惊起鸳鸯宿,
水云撩乱红。

On the Stream

Picking lotus is a girl on the stream,
Afraid of wind that shakes her tiny boat.
Startled are the lovebirds in the sweet dream,
On the misty water pink petals float.

山径柳

宛转若游丝，
浅深栽绿崦。
年年立春后，
即被啼莺占。

Willows Along the Mountain Path

Soft enough are the willow twigs slim,
Through the mountain path shines the willow gleam.
Year after year when spring comes around,
Orioles are singing here as the firm ground.

石上藤

空山无鸟迹,
何物如人意。
委曲结绳文,
离披草书字。

Vines Twining around the Rocks

Deep in the mountains no bird is in sight,
What on earth caters to human delight?
Around the rocks are vines like tying knots,
Which seem to calligraphy strokes and dots.

芙蓉榭

风摆莲衣干,
月背鸟巢寒。
文鱼翻乱叶,
翠羽上危栏。

A Waterside Pavilion

Swaying with wind lotus leaves are soon dry,
It's chilly in the nest with no moon in the sky.
Colorful fishes turn upside down among leaves,
A kingfisher flies onto the railings nigh.

题山顶寺

遥闻林下语，
知是经行所。
日暮香风时，
诸天散花雨。

To the Temple atop the Mountain

Afar in the woods I hear someone chatting,
I know around the haunt Buddhists are paving.
When fragrance comes with wind at sun setting,
Flower petals all over the sky are dancing.

过山农家

板桥人渡泉声,
茅檐日午鸡鸣。
莫嗔焙茶烟暗,
却喜晒谷天晴。

A Farmyard in the Mountain

Across the wooden bridge a stream is murmuring,
Atop the eaves cock crows and the noon sun glaring.
Baking tea the cottage's filled with smoke, don't blame,
To dry grain they like the fine day and the sun's flame.

湖中

青草湖边日色低，
黄茅嶂里鹧鸪啼。
丈夫飘荡今如此，
一曲长歌楚水西。

On the Lake

The sun is setting beyond the Qingcao Lake side,
Partridges in the mountains are crying far and wide.
All over the world my husband's still wandering,
A song of heartstrings in his ears is lingering.

小孤山

古庙枫林江水边,
寒鸦接饭雁横天。
大孤山远小孤出,
月照洞庭归客船。

An Isolated Peak Towering in the River

Amid the maples an old temple stands by the river,
Crows cry for food and a flight of swans fly across the sky.
The big mountain's dim as the small one comes into sight,
On the moon-lit Dongting Lake the passenger boat draws nigh.

元　王蒙　《青卞隐居图》

忆故园

惆怅山多人复稀,
杜鹃啼处泪沾衣。
故园此去千馀里,
春梦犹能夜夜归。

The Native Land in My Memory

Sad for so many mountains with few figures in sight,
When cuckoos cry my tears wet my dress in dismay.
My native land is now a thousand miles away,
Homecoming comes true only in dream every night.

听子规

栖霞山中子规鸟,
口边血出啼不了。
山僧后夜初出定,
闻似不闻山月晓。

Calls of Cuckoos

In the depth of the Mountain cuckoos call and call,
Never stop crying until bleeding from beaks at all.
The monk sits in meditation in the dead of night,
Pretending to be a deaf to them in the moonlight.

桃花曲

魏帝宫人舞凤楼，
隋家天子泛龙舟。
君王夜醉春眠晏，
不觉桃花逐水流。

Song of Peach Blossoms

To cater to Cao Cao* the palace maids were dancing,
For the sake of Yang Guang** a canal was dug for boating.
Drunk at night in spring the king used to sleep by day,
He knew nothing about peach petals floating away.

---

*   Cao Cao(155~220), the king of the Wei State, was awarded posthumously the title of Emperor Wu of the Wei Kingdom.
** Yang Guang(569~618), became the second emperor of the Sui Dynasty by killing his father Yang Jian, the first emperor. Yang Guang was crazy about sightseeing by dragon boat along the canal, and dug for the convenience of his sightseeing.

送郭秀才

故人曾任丹徒令,
买得青山拟独耕。
不作草堂招远客,
却将垂柳借啼莺。

A Verse to Mr. Guo

My old friend, you were once a county magistrate,
Now you have bought a green mountain to cultivate.
Putting up a thatched cottage for seclusion,
Planting willows for orioles to sing in season.

宫词

玉楼天半起笙歌,
风送宫嫔笑语和。
月殿影开闻夜漏,
水晶帘卷近秋河。

Song of Palace

From the jade tower music floats halfway up the sky,
Wafts from the palace the laughing of maids on a high.
Water clock drips, the moon-lit palace casts its shadow,
Up rolled is the screen and the Milky Way drawing nigh.

戴叔伦

戴叔伦(732～789)，字幼公，润州金坛(今江苏金坛)人。其七绝语言含蓄婉转。《全唐诗》存其诗两卷。

Dai Shulun(732～789), styled Yougong, was born in Jintan, Yunzhou (Jintan County, Jiangsu Province today). His quatrains were elegantly composed with profound implications. Two volumes of his poems are collected in *The Complete Collection of the Tang Poetry*.

过三闾庙

沅湘流不尽，
屈子怨何深。
日暮秋风起，
萧萧枫树林。

Homage Paid to Qu Yuan Temple

Like the Yuan and Xiang rivers that flow forever,
You want to vent your resentment but can never.
As dusk falls the autumn wind wails and cries,
Through the maple woods the wind soughs and sighs.

清　王翚　《虞山枫林图》

泊湘口

湘山千岭树，
桂水九秋波。
露重猿声绝，
风清月色多。

Mooring at the Mouth of the River Xiang

Cloaked in woods are peaks of Mountain Xiang high,
River Gui in autumn is rippling with waves white.
Heavy is dew and you can hear no apes cry,
Cool is the breeze and the bright moon shines at night.

新别离

手把杏花枝,
未曾经别离。
黄昏掩闺后,
寂寞心自知。

Fresh Pain of Parting

I hold a twig of apricot blossoms in hand,
Never before had I sent him for a strange land.
As dusk falls I shut the door and close the window,
Nobody but myself feels lonely with my shadow.

松鹤

雨湿松阴凉,
风落松花细。
独鹤爱清幽,
飞来不飞去。

Pine and Crane

Wet with rain it's cool in the shade of pine,
Fallen with wind are pine flowers so fine.
Solitary is the crane who favors peace,
Attached to the new place he really is.

关山月

月出照关山,
秋风人未还。
清光无远近,
乡泪半书间。

The Moon atop Guanshan Mountain

Atop Guanshan Mountain is the moon bright,
Bleak wind blows and I wait for him at night.
Bathed in the moonlight is the world vast,
Tears of homesickness wet my letter fast.

遣兴

明月临沧海,
闲云恋故山。
诗名满天下,
终日掩柴关。

Giving Vent to My Feelings

The bright moon shines over the blue sea vast,
The clouds drift around the peaks of the past.
Well-known in the world are my poems at their height,
With door closed I enjoy peace day and night.

山居

麋鹿自成群,
何人到白云。
山中无外事,
终日醉醺醺。

Dwelling in the Mountain

Elk and deer flock into herds of their own,
I take up my abode in the clouds white.
Free from affairs of the vanity world,
Wine glass in hand I'm tipsy day and night.

题天柱山图

拔翠五云中,
擎天不计功。
谁能凌绝顶,
看取日升东。

A Verse on the Drawing of Tianzhu Mountain

Looming over the clouds is the peak so high,
But you never show off you hold up the sky.
Who can climb the mountain and reach the summit,
To enjoy the sunrise from the east so nigh?

堤上柳

垂柳万条丝，
春来织别离。
行人攀折处，
闺妾断肠时。

Willows Along the Dyke

Thousands of weeping willow twigs droop long,
The advent of spring marks the parting song.
When pedestrians break twigs off from branches,
The lovesick know their pining is so strong.

对酒示申屠学士

三重江水万重山，
山里春风度日闲。
且向白云求一醉，
莫教愁梦到乡关。

Drinking with the Scholar Shentu

Waves lash thousands of crags of great height,
Mild's spring breeze I'm at leisure in mountain.
Cup to cup I'm drinking with the clouds white,
Tipsy I'm carefree at night in my curtain.

闺怨

看花无语泪如倾，
多少春风怨别情。
不识玉门关外路，
梦中昨夜到边城。

Grievances in the Boudoir

Silent before flowers she's in torrential tears,
Spring wind witnessed parting pain of many peers.
The road beyond Yumen Pass was strange to her,
Last night in dream she got to a town of frontiers.

过柳溪道院

溪上谁家掩竹扉，
鸟啼浑似惜春晖。
日斜深巷无人迹，
时见梨花片片飞。

Passing by a Taoist Temple by Willow Stream

Whose bamboo gate shut by the stream I don't know,
Singing are the birds as if they love spring sunshine.
Deep is the lane but no figure in the sunset glow,
From time to time dancing are pear petals so fine.

苏溪亭

苏溪亭上草漫漫,
谁倚东风十二阑。
燕子不归春事晚,
一汀晚雨杏花寒。

Suxi Pavilion

From the pavilion a vast view of grass comes into sight,
Who is the one leaning on the rail in the east wind light?
Reluctant to return are swallows and spring farming's late,
On the shoal apricots feel chilly with rain in the twilight.

兰溪棹歌

凉月如眉挂柳湾,
越中山色镜中看。
兰溪三日桃花雨,
半夜鲤鱼来上滩。

Boatmen's Song on Lanxi River

Atop the willows the crescent moon is cool and bright,
Reflected on the river are the mountains in sight.
Three days of raining result in peach blossoms blooming,
You can hear carps jumping out of water at midnight.

韦应物

韦应物(737~792),京兆长安(今陕西西安)人。唐玄宗时,韦应物在朝为官。其诗以写田园风物著名,诗风恬淡清幽,语言洗练。《全唐诗》存其诗十卷。

Wei Yingwu (737~792) was born in Chang'an (Xi'an City, Shaanxi Province today). During the reign of Emperor Xuanzong (the tenth emperor of the Tang Dynasty). Wei was a senior government official. Most of his poems are pictures of pastoral scene with succinct language in elegant style, of which ten volumes are collected in *The Complete Collection of the Tang Poetry*.

九日

一为吴郡守,
不觉菊花开。
始有故园思,
且喜众宾来。

On the Double Ninth Festival

As a prefect I focus on the work day and night,
Chrysanthemums are now blooming before I know.
I think of my homeland at the glimpse of the sight,
But I'm delighted to see many guests come and go.

寄卢陟

柳叶遍寒塘，
晓霜凝高阁。
累日此流连，
别来成寂寞。

To Lu Zhi My Friend

Willow leaves flow all over the cold pond.
The tall tower is cloaked in the thick rime.
For a few days we've been lingering around,
But loneliness looms up at the parting time.

登楼

兹楼日登眺,
流岁暗蹉跎。
坐厌淮南守,
秋山红树多。

Going Upstairs

Going upstairs I look far and wide,
Years elapse but I just let things slide.
Satisfied with the post a prefect,
Bathed in the gold autumn tints perfect.

咏露珠

秋荷一滴露，
清夜坠玄天。
将来玉盘上，
不定始知圆。

Ode to Dewdrops

Dewdrops on the lotus leaves in autumn,
Fall from the north sky in the still of night.
Collecting them on the jade plate into column,
But they roll around like pearls shining bright.

咏珊瑚

绛树无花叶，
非石亦非琼。
世人何处得，
蓬莱石上生。

Ode to Coral

It is a crimson tree with no flower,
Neither stone nor jade it has no leaves.
To get it is beyond common people's power,
On the fairy island no one achieves.

咏晓

军中始吹角，
城上河初落。
深沉犹隐帷，
晃朗先分阁。

Ode to Dawn

The bugle is sounded in the army camp,
Dim is the Milky Way at dawn and the lamp.
The night curtain is still in the gloom,
And the outlines of buildings dimly loom.

秋斋独宿

山月皎如烛，
风霜时动竹。
夜半鸟惊栖，
窗间人独宿。

A Lonely Overnight Stay in Autumn

Atop the mountain the moonbeams are bright,
In the frosted bamboos the wind is rustling.
Startled are the birds in the still of night,
Behind the window screen alone I'm sleeping.

咏春雪

裴回轻雪意，
似惜艳阳时。
不悟风花冷，
翻令梅柳迟。

Ode to Spring Snow

Dancing with grace so light is your sway,
You seem to cherish the bright spring day.
Unaware of snowflakes that are cold enough,
To flowering plants it's only a delay.

夜闻独鸟啼

失侣度山觅，
投林舍北啼。
今将独夜意，
偏知对影栖。

A Lonely Bird Crying at Night

All over the valleys and hills she looks for her mate,
She perches to the north of my room and cries till late.
Having no mate she feels lonely throughout the night,
With my shadow she stays in a sorry plight.

玩萤火

时节变衰草，
物色近新秋。
度月影才敛，
绕竹光复流。

Fireflies

Wilting are weeds with the change of seasons,
Early autumn tints plants with various patterns.
Weak and dim when thou fly in the moonlight,
But in the bamboo grove thy light turns bright.

秋夜寄邱二十二员外

怀君属秋夜，
散步咏凉天。
山空松子落。
幽人应无眠。

To Mr. Qiu Dan a Hermit on an Autumn Night

Thinking of thee at the dead of autumn night,
Chanting the cool in the air my pace is light.
Pine corns fall from trees in the quiet mountain,
Mr. Hermit, thou must be awake behind curtain.

闻雁

故园渺何处，
归思方悠哉。
淮南秋雨夜，
高斋闻雁来。

Honks of Wild Geese Heard at Night

For my native place I'm looking far and wide,
Homesickness lingers I'm suffering inside.
It drizzles in the strange land at autumn night,
From the sky come the honks of wild geese in flight.

闲居寄诸弟

秋草生庭白露时，
故园诸弟益相思。
尽日高斋无一事，
芭蕉叶上独题诗。

To My Brothers in My Idle

Around the courtyard autumn weeds are wet with dew bright,
I yearn for reunion with my brothers in my hometown.
In my study I've nothing to do all day and night,
On plantain leaves I have some verses written down.

同越琅玡山

石门有雪无行迹，
松壑凝烟满众香。
馀食施庭寒鸟下，
破衣挂树老僧亡。

Langya Mountain

Near the stone gate no trace on the snow-covered way,
From the gully of pine trees sweet smell wafts away.
Leftovers on the yard ground are inviting to birds,
Hanging from the tree top is the dead monk's array.

清　王鉴　《长松仙馆图》

滁州西涧

独怜幽草涧边生,
上有黄丽深树鸣。
春潮带雨晚来急,
野渡无人舟自横。

The West Stream at Chuzhou

Alone by the streamside I love the grass green,
Deep in the grove the orioles call with delight.
At dusk spring tide comes with the sudden rain screen,
No one at the ferry but a boat in sight.

子规啼

高林滴露夏夜清,
南山子规啼一声。
邻家孀妇抱儿泣,
我独展转何时明。

The Call of a Cuckoo

Dew drips from big trees and quiet is the summer night,
From the south mountain a cuckoo calls in sad plight.
A baby in arms the next-door widow's crying,
Tossing and turning alone sleepless I'm lying.

司空曙

司空曙(720~790)，字文明，广平(今河北永年)人。为大历十才子之一。其诗多描摹自然景色和乡情旅思，长于抒情，风格清婉。《全唐诗》存其诗两卷。有《司空曙文集》存世。

Sikong Shu(720~790), styled Wenming, was born in Guangping(Yongnian County, Hebei Province today). He was ranked among the ten gifted talents in the period from 766 to 780. His poems give a vivid description of natural scenery and nostalgia with emotion in delicate style, of which one volume was collected in *The Complete Collection of the Tang Poetry*. There is *Sikong Shu's Anthology of Poems* extant.

竹里径

幽径行迹稀，
清阴苔色古。
萧萧风欲来，
乍似蓬山雨。

A Path Through the Bamboo Grove

Along the secluded path few tracks can be seen,
In the quiet shade the color of moss is dark green.
The wind rustles the bamboo as it sighs and soughs,
As if in the fairyland it suddenly showers.

松下雪

不随晴野尽,
独向深松积。
落照入寒光,
偏能伴幽寂。

Snow Under Pine Trees

In the vast sunny country snow always in sight,
But deep in pine woods it piles up to a great height.
The setting sun casts a cold glow gleaming at dusk,
Quiet and secluded it's the companion of night.

金陵怀古

辇路江枫暗,
宫庭野草春。
伤心庾开府,
老作北朝臣。

Meditations on the Past at Jinling

Along the royal street maple shade is sullen,
Around the court spring weeds grow in profusion.
Heart-broken was Yuxin detained on a mission,
Serving the north dynasty he'd never return.

晚思

蛩馀窗下月,
草湿阶前露。
晚景凄我衣,
秋风入庭树。

Thoughts on the Autumn Night

By the window crickets chirp in the moonlight,
Before the steps weeds are wet with dew drops.
I feel chilly at the desolate sight,
The autumn wind rustles through the tree tops.

江村即事

钓罢归来不系船,
江村月落正堪眠。
纵然一夜风吹去,
只在芦花浅水边。

An Extempore Verse Composed in Riverside Village

My boat's not tied on my return from fishing,
The moon sets near the village it's time for sleeping.
Even if the wind at night blows my boat away,
Amid the reeds in the shallows it must stay.

唐人绝句精粹

中英文版

A Translation of the Choice Tang Quatrains

中卷

Volume Two

献给共和国七十华诞

周方珠 编译

By Zhou Fangzhu

北京师范大学出版集团
BEIJING NORMAL UNIVERSITY PUBLISHING GROUP
安徽大学出版社

卢　纶	1	王　建	131
李　益	10	韩　愈	172
孟　郊	22	薛　涛	190
杨巨源	32	张仲素	196
武元衡	39	李　绅	208
权德舆	50	白居易	214
令狐楚	67	刘禹锡	271
朱庆馀	79	柳宗元	304
杨　凌	86	姚　合	309
杨　凝	92	元　稹	323
雍裕之	97	贾　岛	344
张　籍	110		

卢 纶

卢纶(748~800),字允言,河中蒲州(今山西永济)人。为"大历十才子"之一。其诗多为送别酬答之作,较有名的为反映军旅生活的《塞下曲》。《全唐诗》存其诗五卷。

Lu Lun (739~799), styled Yunyan, was born in Puzhou (Yongji County, Shanxi Province today). Lu was ranked among the ten gifted talents in the period from 766 to 780. Most of his poems were composed in response to the works of his friends, of which the most famous are "Songs of the Frontier Fortress" that reflect the military life. Five volumes of his poems are collected in *The Complete Collection of the Tang Poetry*.

塞下曲·其一

林暗草惊风,
将军夜引弓。
平明寻白羽,
没在石棱中。

Song of the Frontier Fortress (1)

Against the wind grass in woods shivers with fright,
Drawing his bow the general aimed at night.
At dawn he looked for along the path narrow,
Only to find the rock pierced by his arrow.

塞下曲·其二

月黑雁飞高,
单于夜遁逃。
欲将轻骑逐,
大雪满弓刀。

Song of Frontier Fortress (2)

Across the sky are wild geese at night,
The Hun Chieftain through the dark takes flight.
To chase him with the bow and arrow,
But our swords are deeply buried in snow.

天长地久词

玉砌红花树,
香风不敢吹。
春光解人意,
偏发殿南枝。

Song of Everlasting Love

Marble stairs are flanked by red flowers blooming,
Waft of flowers is lingering with no wind blowing.
Spring scenery can well read the owner's mind,
First comes to branches on the south side of its kind.

赠别司空曙

有月曾同赏,
无秋不共悲。
如何与君别,
又是菊花时。

A Parting Poem to Sikong Shu

Once we shared the beautiful moonlight,
Autumn came when we were in sorry plight.
The moment of parting filled us with gloom,
It happened when chrysanthemums would bloom.

同李益伤秋

岁去人头白,
秋来树叶黄。
搔头向黄叶,
与尔共悲伤。

Sharing Grief in Autumn with Li Yi

As time passes by my hair turns grey,
When autumn comes trees wear yellow array.
Deeply vexed I turn to leaves fallen,
Sharing your grief I'm now crestfallen.

山中一绝

饥食松花渴饮泉,
偶从山后到山前。
阳陂软草厚如织,
因与鹿麛相伴眠。

Dwelling in Mountains

Eating pine nuts, drinking from spring in time of hunger,
Traveling from slope to slope I'm a happy roamer.
Grass in the southern slope is like soft and thick fiber,
As if a cozy blanket on which I sleep with deer.

清　髡残　《层岩叠嶂图》

逢病军人

行多有病住无粮,
万里还乡未到乡。
蓬鬓哀吟古城下,
不堪秋气入金疮。

Meeting a Sick Soldier on His Way Home

Sick, tired and hungry he is plodding along,
On the way home but he finds the way too long.
Disheveled at the city wall he's moaning,
Badly injured in autumn on the wall he's leaning.

春日登楼有怀

花正浓时人正愁，
逢花却欲替花羞。
年来笑伴皆归去，
今日晴明独上楼。

Sentimental Feeling in Spring atop the Tower

Flowers smiling at me but I'm in sorry plight,
Together with flowers instead of them I'm shy.
In recent years all my mates return I've to sigh,
Upstairs alone today it is a nice day bright.

李 益

李益(748～827),字君虞,陇西姑臧(今甘肃武威县)人。李益有十多年军旅生活,其间横槊赋诗,其诗多悲凉慷慨之作。《全唐诗》存其诗两卷。

Li Yi(748～827), styled Junyu, was born in Guzang, Longxi(Wuwei County, Gansu Province today). Li once served in the army as a senior-rank officer for over ten years and had many poems composed about military life with solemn fervor. Two volumes of his poems are collected in *The Complete Collection of the Tang Poetry*.

江南曲

嫁得瞿塘贾,
朝朝误妾期。
早知潮有信,
嫁与弄潮儿。

Song of the South of the River

Since I became a trader's wife,
I have lived a grass widow's life.
If I knew a wise man caught the tide on time,
I'd have married him in my prime.

照镜

衰鬓临朝镜，
将看却自疑。
惭君明似月，
照我白如丝。

Looking in the Mirror

In the mirror I look at myself in the morning,
I can hardly believe my hair is withering.
Ashamed of myself before the mirror so bright,
In the mirror I see my hair like silk snow-white.

上洛桥

金谷园中柳,
春来似舞腰。
何堪好风景,
独上洛阳桥。

On Luoyang Bridge

Willows in the deserted Jingu Garden,
Tall and slim in spring gracefully sway.
Beautiful enough is the scenery today,
But alone on Luoyang Bridge I'm crestfallen.

扬州早雁

江上三千雁，
年年过故宫。
可怜江上月，
偏照断根蓬。

Wild Geese via Yangzhou

Across the river thousands of wild geese flying,
Year after year through the site of palace crying.
So lively is the moon over the river bright,
Shining me alone like weeds uprooted at night.

蜀川闻莺

蜀道山川心易惊,
绿窗残梦晓闻莺。
分明似雪文君恨,
万怨千愁弦上声。

Orioles Singing Heard in the Mountain of Sichuan

Along the mountain path to Sichuan I'm fear-ridden,
Orioles singing near the window makes my dream's broken.
Grief-stricken is Wenjun and her hair is white as snow,
She's playing zither pouring out her endless sorrow.

唐　李昭道　《明皇幸蜀图》

行舟

柳花飞入正行舟,
卧引菱花信碧流。
闻道风光满扬子,
天晴共上望乡楼。

Sailing a Boat

Flying into the sailing boat are catkins white,
Lying on board I drift freely with the tide.
It's said the Yangtze River is of splendid sight,
But atop the tower I gaze homeward far and wide.

宫怨

露湿晴花春殿香，
月明歌吹在昭阳。
似将海水添宫漏，
共滴长门一夜长。

Grief of a Palace Maid

Fragrant with flowers Zhaoyang Palace's wet with dew,
From the moon-lit palace comes the music anew.
The water-clock seems filled up with sea water vast,
Pit-a-pat the steady drip at night never goes fast.

隋宫燕

燕语如伤旧国春,
宫花一落已成尘。
自从一闭风光后,
几度飞来不见人。

Swallows in the Imperial Palace of Sui Dynasty

Twittering swallows as if sigh over the spring past,
Fallen petals in the court are reduced to dust fast.
Gone are the days when the splendor did last,
Time and again swallows could see no shadow cast.

夜上受降城闻笛

回乐峰前沙似雪,
受降城外月如霜。
不知何处吹芦管,
一夜征人尽望乡。

A Flute Tune Heard at Night atop the Surrender-taking Wall

Below the beacon tower the sand dunes are snow white,
Beyond the city wall the moonbeams are like rime bright.
Nobody knows from where the tune of reed flute comes,
Wide awake are all soldiers homesick throughout the night.

写情

水纹珍簟思悠悠，
千里佳期一夕休。
从此无心爱良夜，
任他明月下西楼。

Pouring Out My Heavy Heart

Lying on the gorgeous bamboo mat I'm upset and sigh,
Fizzling out all of sudden is the wedding drawing nigh.
From now on I'm in no mood for the charming night,
Let the moon rise set I've no interest in moonlight.

汴河曲

汴水东流无限春,
隋家宫阙已成尘。
行人莫上长堤望,
风起杨花愁杀人。

Meditation on the Past of Bianhe Canal

Bianhe Canal flows eastward with spring on rising tide,
The palaces of Sui Dynasty are reduced to dust.
Never walk along the long dam and gaze far and wide,
Like gloomy clouds catkins follow you with a great gust.

孟 郊

孟郊(751～814),字东野,湖州武康(今浙江德清)人。孟郊生性耿介,四十六岁时中进士,曾任溧阳县令。其诗尚古风,重比兴,被誉为"苦吟诗人"。《全唐诗》存其诗十卷。

Meng Jiao (751～814), styled Dongye, was born in Wukang, Huzhou (Deqing County, Zhejiang Province today). Meng was upright by nature and appointed the magistrate of Liyang County after he passed successfully the imperial examination at the age of 46. He was well versed in poetry in ancient style composed with analogy and metaphor and thus regarded a famous assiduous poet. There are ten volumes of his poems collected in *The Complete Collection of the Tang Poetry*.

叹疆场

闻道行人至,
妆梳对镜台。
泪痕犹尚在,
笑靥自然开。

A Sigh of Relief for Her Husband from the Battlefield

Informed of good news about her darling,
To make up she sits before the dressing table.
Tear stains still visible but she's now smiling,
On either side of her cheeks appears a dimple.

闺怨

妾恨比斑竹，
下盘烦冤根。
有笋未出土，
中已含泪痕。

A Grief-stricken Lady

Like mottled bamboo with stains my grief's profound,
It's deeply rooted in the soil of grievance.
Before the bamboo shoots grow out of the ground,
They're already stained with tears in appearance.

古意

河边织女星,
河畔牵牛郎。
未得渡清浅,
相对遥相望。

A Poem in Classic Style

The Weaver Maid stands on one side of the Milky Way,
On the other the Cowherd's waiting day after day.
No chance for the couple to cross the river so wide,
They have to gaze across the river on either side.

古别离

欲别牵郎衣,
郎今到何处?
不恨归来迟,
莫向临邛去。

A Tearful Parting

Grasping your robe lest you should go away,
Tell me, darling, where are you going today?
Your late return won't bring me great sorrow,
But if you stay in Linqiong* you'd be led astray.

---

* Linqiong was a county town in ancient China (Qionglai City, Sichuan Province today), in which Sima Xiangru lured Zhuo Wenjun into eloping with him according to an old tale. Since then people use the metaphor of Linqiong as a snare for those who will be led astray.

喜雨

朝见一片云，
暮成千里雨。
凄清湿高枝，
散漫沾荒土。

The Timely Rain

A layer of morning cloud floating in the sky,
In the evening it is raining far and wide.
Wet with rain drops are the tree branches high,
The wild country is moistened on every side.

春后雨

昨夜一霎雨，
天意苏群物。
何物最先知，
虚庭草争出。

A Shower in Spring Time

It happened to shower timely last night,
A gift from heaven brings all things back to life.
What creature is the first to be aware?
The new sprout of grass like the point of a knife.

征妇怨

良人昨日去，
明月又不圆。
别时各有泪，
零落青楼前。

Grief of a Soldier's Wife

My darling parted from me yesterday,
The moon happened to be on the wane.
We had a tearful parting with dismay,
Before the boudoir tears poured like rain.

登科后

昔日龌龊不足夸,
今朝放荡思无涯。
春风得意马蹄疾,
一日看尽长安花。

On the Crest of Honor

Gone are the gloomy days greeted with dismay,
Free from care I am unrestrained today.
On the crest of honor I'm riding high in spring,
I've seen all flowers in Chang'an within a day.

济源寒食

长安落花飞上天，
南风引至三殿前。
可怜春物亦朝谒，
唯我孤吟渭水边。

The Cold Food Festival in Jiyuan

Petals in the capital are flying across the sky,
Blown to the royal palace by the south gale draws nigh.
Pity is that flowers pay homage to His Majesty,
It's me alone by the riverside chanting with deep sigh.

洛桥晚望

天津桥下冰初结，
洛阳陌上行人绝。
榆柳萧疏楼阁闲，
月明直见嵩山雪。

An Evening View from Tianjin Bridge

Under Tianjin Bridge water freezes for the first time,
Along the road to Luoyang no figure is in sight.
Around the tower trees are bare of leaves with rime,
Snow-capped Mount Song is visible in the moonlight.

杨巨源

杨巨源(755～?),字景山,河中(今山西永济)人。其诗语言质朴,风格清新自然。《全唐诗》存其诗一卷。

Yang Juyuan (755～?), styled Jingshan, was born in Hezhong (Yongji City, Shanxi Province today). His poems were written with plain language in simple style, of which one volume is collected in *The Complete Collection of the Tang Poetry*.

衔鱼翠鸟

有意莲叶间,
瞥然下高树。
擘波得全鱼,
一点翠光去。

A Kingfisher

Aiming at the fish amid the lotus leaves,
Like an arrow shot from the top of a tree high.
Splitting ripples you catch the fish underwater,
Rapid as a green spark you dart into the sky.

寄薛侍御

世上无穷事，
生涯莫废诗。
何曾好风月，
不是忆君时。

To Mr. Xue My Friend

Worldly matters however complex they are,
Throughout my life I make my poem up to par.
Whenever a charming view comes into sight,
A poem on our parting will be my delight.

山中主人

十里青山有一家,
翠屏深处更添霞。
若为说得溪中事,
锦石和烟四面花。

The Host of the Mountain

There is a cottage in the green mountain deep and high,
In the depth of the mountain rosy clouds freely fly.
How to start the topic of the stories in the stream,
Flowers around the golden rocks in the mist like cream.

和练秀才杨柳

水边杨柳麹尘丝,
立马烦君折一枝。
惟有春风最相惜,
殷勤更向手中吹。

Ode to Willows in Reply to Mr. Lian

Slim and soft are the willow twigs by the waterside,
Halting my steed I ask my friend to snap a twig for me.
Kind enough is the spring breeze to be close to my side,
And keep stroking the twig in my hand on bended knee.

城东早春

诗家清景在新春,
绿柳才黄半未匀。
若待上林花似锦,
出门俱是看花人。

Early Spring in the East of the Capital

Early spring triggers my poetic inspiration,
Willow buds turn half yellow and half green.
If all flowers bloom in the imperial garden,
People will seize the time of flowering season.

宋　李嵩　《花篮图》

临水看花

一树红花映绿波，
晴明骑马好经过。
今朝几许风吹落，
闻道箫郎最惜多。

Feasting My Eyes on Flowers by Waterside

Red flowers are mirrored on the light ripples green,
Crossing the river I'm on horseback on a fine day.
By wind some flowers at present are blown away,
My sweetheart will regret many petals clean.

武元衡

武元衡(758~815),字伯苍,河南缑氏(今河南偃师)人。早年曾在朝为官,后遭刺客暗害。《全唐诗》存其诗两卷。

Wu Yuanheng (758~815), styled Bocang, was born in Goushi, Henan (Yanshi City, Henan Province today). In his early years, Wu was a high-rank official but later he was assassinated. Two volumes of his poems are collected in *The Complete Collection of the Tang Poetry*.

左掖梨花

巧笑解迎人,
晴雪香堪惜。
随风蝶影翻,
误点朝衣赤。

Pear Blossoms by the Postern Gate

At the gate you greet the guests with a sweet smile,
White as snowflakes in fine days you lovely fly.
Dancing with the wind like butterflies in the sky,
Dotting my red dress with white petals with style.

春兴

杨柳阴阴细雨晴,
残花落尽见流莺。
春风一夜吹香梦,
梦逐春风到洛城。

Inspiration in Spring

After rain willows are lush in spring sunshine,
Flowers have faded and orioles sing so fine.
Vernal breeze sends me into sweet dream at night,
With spring wind my dream goes to Luoyang in flight.

宿青阳驿

空山摇落三秋暮,
萤过疏帘月露团。
寂寞银灯愁不寐,
萧萧风竹夜窗寒。

An Overnight Stay at Qingyang Posthouse

Bare are the trees in the mountains in late autumn,
Through the curtain a firefly glows at the moonrise.
Facing the bleak lamp alone I'm gloomy in bosom,
By the window at night the cold wind in bamboos sighs.

题嘉陵驿

悠悠风斾绕山川,
山驿空濛雨似烟。
路半嘉陵头已白,
蜀门西上更青天。

A Verse on Jialing Posthouse

Around the mountains and rivers flags and banners sway,
Shrouded in mist is the posthouse faintly looming nigh.
Halfway on the journey to Jialing my hair turns grey,
Heading westward is a hard work like climbing the sky.

赠道者

麻衣如雪一枝梅，
笑掩微妆入梦来。
若到越溪逢越女，
红莲池里白莲开。

To a Female Taoist

Like a plum blossom her Taoist dress is snow-white,
Bashful smile on her face she appears in my dream.
Among the fair belles washing fiber by the stream,
As if a white flower blooming among nymphs bright.

听歌

月上重楼丝管秋，
佳人夜唱古梁州。
满堂谁是知音者，
不惜千金与莫愁。

Listening to the Music

Music of strings comes from the tower in the moonlight,
The pretty girl is singing the classical song at night.
Who is the alter ego among the present attenders?
Spending money like dirt he's number one of spenders.

陌上暮春

青青南陌柳如丝,
柳色莺声晚日迟。
何处最伤游客思,
春风三月落花时。

The Scenery in Late Spring by Roadside

Along the south road willow twigs are soft and green,
In the green willows orioles are singing happy and gay.
The possible trigger for visitor's grief is the late spring,
In which breeze blows and flowers are fading away.

缑山道中口号

秋山寂寂秋水清，
寒郊木叶飞无声。
王子白云仙去久，
洛滨行客夜吹笙。

On the Path Along Goushan Mountain

Deserted is the mountain and autumn water green,
Cold in the suburbs and withered leaves have fallen.
Seeking the fairyland the prince rode the clouds white,
Along the Luoshui River he played *sheng** at night.

---

* *Sheng* is a traditional bamboo pipe wind instrument in China.

清　赵之谦　《枝头秋色图》

寓兴呈崔员外诸公

三月杨花飞满空,
飘飘十里雪如风。
不知何处香醪熟,
愿醉佳园芳树中。

A Verse Composed in High Spirits

Over the sky are the catkins in late spring all day,
Like snowflakes they float with wind ten miles away.
From where comes the sweet smell of mellow wine?
To be drunk in a fragrant garden is so fine.

春晓闻莺

寥寥兰台晓梦惊,
绿林残月思孤莺。
犹疑蜀魄千年恨,
化作冤禽万啭声。

An Oriole Singing in Spring

From a dream I wake up with a start in the still court,
In the woods a lone bird cries in the waning moon light.
Grief-stricken is the soul of the king* weeping a lot,
Deeply wronged he is a bird crying day and night.

---

* The king here refers to the king of the Shu State who was wrongly treated, and his soul turned into a bird after his death that cried day and night according to a Chinese tale.

权德舆

权德舆(759～818),字载之,天水略阳(今甘肃秦安)人。权德舆曾官拜礼部尚书。其诗风格古雅,文字洗练。《全唐诗》存其诗十卷。

Quan Deyu (759～818), styled Zaizhi, was born in Luoyang, Tianshui (Qin'an County, Gansu Province today). Quan once served the government as the Minister of Rites. Terse language in a graceful classical style is characteristic of his poems, of which ten volumes are collected in *The Complete Collection of the Tang Poetry*.

岭上逢久别者又别

十年曾一别,
征路此相逢。
马首向何处,
夕阳千万峰。

Meeting a Friend After a Long Parting and Parting from Him Again

We parted from each other ten years ago,
Now we meet on our journey before we know.
Riding on horseback where are you to go?
Towards the peaks bathed in the sunset glow.

晓

晓风摇五两,
残月映石壁。
稍稍曙光开,
片帆在空碧。

Dawn

Swaying is the weathercock with dawn breeze,
The waning moon shines on the precipice.
Dawn breaks and twilight appears on high,
Sails in sight are floating in the blue sky.

昼

孤舟漾暖景,
独鹤下秋空。
安流正日昼,
净绿天无风。

Daytime

Ripples around the boat adds much to the mild sight,
A solitary crane dives from the autumn sky.
Gently flowing is the river and the sun's bright,
Smooth are the green currents and no wind from on high.

晚

古树夕阳尽,
空江暮霭收。
寂寞扣船坐,
独生千里愁。

Evening

An old tree is bathed in the sunset glow,
Over the vast river thin mist and haze flow.
Sitting alone in the boat I knock the side,
My sorrow grows and my mind roams far and wide.

夜

猿声到枕上，
愁梦纷难理。
寂寞深夜寒，
青霜落秋水。

Night

From afar yelps of apes come to my pillow,
In a complete haze in dream I'm in sorrow.
Sleeping alone I feel chilly in a sad plight,
Dew drops drip into water in autumn night.

相思树

家寄江东远,
身对江西春。
空见相思树,
不见相思人。

Tree of Romance

My home is in the east of the river,
Spring view in the west I look over.
I catch sight of the tree of romance,
But nowhere can I find my lover.

酬九日

重九共游娱，
秋光景气殊。
他日头似雪，
还对插茱萸。

Celebrating the Double Ninth Festival

Double Ninth Festival is a delight day,
But scene in autumn puts on different array.
In the coming year when our hairs turn grey,
A brunch of cornels for each we piously pray.

玉台体·其一

君去期花时，
花时君不至。
檐前双燕飞，
落妾相思泪。

A Poem in Imperial Style（1）

You promised to return at the flowering season,
Flowers are blooming but you're nowhere to be seen.
Nesting under the eaves two swallows fly to and fro,
Lovesick I'm in tears and my dress is soaked through.

玉台体·其二

婵娟二八正娇羞,
日暮相逢南陌头。
试问佳期不肯道,
落花深处指青楼。

A Poem in Imperial Style(2)

Graceful is the belle in her teens timid and shy,
We meet by the roadside as the sunset tinges the sky.
I plead for the wedding date but she refuses to say,
Pointing to the mansion in flowers instead of the way.

宫人斜绝句

一路斜分古驿前，
阴风切切晦秋烟。
铅华新旧共冥寞，
日暮愁鸱飞野田。

Tombs of the Palace Maids

A slant fork branches off before the old posthouse,
Gloomy is the autumn mist and the cold wind soughs.
Quiet are all the maids in the neither world lonely,
Over the wilds are the sad crows at dusk chilly.

舟行夜泊

萧萧落叶送残秋,
寂寞寒波急暝流。
今夜不知何处泊,
断猿睛月引孤舟。

Mooring at Night

Rustling leaves witness the autumn waning,
Lonesome waves surge forward in the evening.
I wonder where I can moor my boat tonight,
Heart-rending yelps lead the boat to the moon bright.

杂言和常州李员外副使春日戏题

檐前晓色惊双燕，
户外春风舞百花。
粉署可怜闲对此，
唯令碧玉泛流霞。

A Poem in Jest in Spring

Awakened by twilight are two swallows before screen,
Outdoors flowers dancing with vernal breeze can be seen.
Lovely are the beauties in the painting on the wall,
Singing girls are to dance in the rosy clouds on call.

舟行见月

月入孤舟夜半晴,
寥寥霜雁两三声。
洞房烛影在何处,
欲寄相思梦不成。

Sailing in the Moonlight

Moonlight peeps into the solitary boat at midnight,
Lonely is the autumn wild geese screaming in flight.
At the thought of nuptial bliss in the bridal chamber,
Pining for you but I can't go into dreamland at night.

题崔山人草堂

竹径茆堂接洞天,
闲时麈尾漱春泉。
世人车马不知处,
时有归云到枕前。

To the Cottage of Hermit Cui

From the cottage a bamboo path leads to the fairyland,
At leisure in spring he washes the horsetail whisk in hand.
Free from hustle and bustle his abode nobody knows,
But the clouds on the way home often haunt his pillows.

斗子滩

斗子滩头夜已深,
月华偏照此时心。
春江风水连天阔,
归梦悠扬何处寻。

Douzi Sandbar

Night is far-advanced over Douzi Sandbar,
The moon light tries to peep into my mind so far.
With wind the spring river stretches vast to the sky,
My dream to go home is still wandering on high.

杂兴

乳燕双飞莺乱啼，
百花如绣照深闺。
新妆对镜知无比，
微笑时时出瓠犀。

An Extempore

Baby swallows fly in pairs and orioles sing at random,
Around the boudoir various kinds of flowers in blossom.
Peerless is the maiden in the new dress in the mirror bright,
Smiling from time to time like pearls her teeth gleam white.

七夕

今日云軿渡鹊桥，
应非脉脉与迢迢。
家人竞喜开妆镜，
月下穿针拜九霄。

Double Seventh Festival*

By the curtained carriage they cross the Magpie Bridge today,
What a bliss! Reunion comes true across the Milky Way.
Wild with joy the family are decked out at midnight,
The female pray Heaven for needlecraft in the moonlight.

---

* Double Seventh Festival refers to the seventh evening of the seventh month in Chinese lunar calendar when the Herd-boy and Weaving-maid are supposed to meet, which is also colloquially called Valentine's Day in China.

令狐楚

令狐楚(766~837),字壳士,宜州华原(今陕西铜川)人。令狐楚曾在朝为官,其绝句内容含蓄,语言精炼,多写闺情及边塞军旅生活。《全唐诗》存其诗一卷。

Linghu Chu (766~837), styled Keshi, was born in Huayuan, Yizhou (Tongchuan City, Shaanxi Province today). Linghu served as an official in the court after his success in the imperial examination. His quatrains are profound in meaning and terse in words, most of which are the picture of life in boudoir and army. There is one volume of his poems collected in *The Complete Collection of the Tang Poetry*.

宫中乐

柳色烟相似,
梨花雪不如。
春风真有意,
一一丽皇居。

Joy of Life in the Palace

Tinged with mist is the tint of willow,
Blossoms of pear trees are whiter than snow.
It's kind of spring breeze to add so much
To the imperial palace, a nice view.

春游曲

晓游临碧殿，
日上望春亭。
芳树罗仙仗，
晴山展翠屏。

Song of Spring Outing

Visiting Linbi Palace in the twilight,
From Wangchun Pavilion rises the sun so bright.
The imperial flags are hidden by trees green,
Before my eyes mountains are a long fresh screen.

元 黄公望 《丹崖玉树图》

远别离

杨柳黄金穗,
梧桐碧玉枝。
春来消息断,
早晚是归期。

A Long Separation

Willow flowers shade into green yellow light,
Branches of phoenix trees grow verdant bright.
Since the advent of spring I've no news from him,
The date of his return is still a day dream.

长相思

君行登陇上，
妾梦在闺中。
玉箸千行落，
银床一半空。

Pining for Love

You travel along the mountain path northwest,
Dreaming in my boudoir is a bitter test.
In floods of tears my pillow is wet at night,
To be a grass widow on me is a blight.

从军行

孤心眠夜雪,
满眼是秋沙。
万里犹防塞,
三年不见家。

Service in the Army

Sleepless on a snowy night I feel lonely,
The sight that greets me is the vast land sandy.
Garrisoning the endless frontiers far away,
For three years home's on my mind night and day.

王昭君

锦车天外去,
毳幕雪中开。
魏阙苍龙远,
萧关赤雁哀。

Wang Zhaojun

A brocade carriage is plodding on northwest,
The felt tent is put up in the snow for rest.
Far away from the imperial court she's moving,
Beyond the Great Wall red swans are sadly wailing.

赴东都别牡丹

十年不见小庭花，
紫萼临开又别家。
上马出门回首望，
何时更得到京华。

Farewell to Peony

I haven't seen peony in my courtyard for ten years,
But I've to leave my home as peony's ready to bloom.
Mounting my steed I turn round at the gate in tears,
The date to back to the capital casts a deep gloom.

少年行·其一

少小边州惯放狂，
骣骑蕃马射黄羊。
如今年老无筋力，
独倚营门数雁行。

Song of a Man in His Prime (1)

Unrestrained on the frontiers when I was in my prime,
Riding on horseback I shot gazelles from time to time.
But worn-out with age I am feeble enough today,
Leaning on the door alone I count swans flying away.

少年行·其二

弓背霞明剑照霜，
秋风走马出咸阳。
未收天子河湟地，
不拟回头望故乡。

Song of a Man in His Prime (2)

Glittering is the back of my bow and my sword shines,
Galloping out of the capital as autumn wind sighs.
Before recovering the lost land for the empire,
To have a glance at my hometown I never desire.

塞下曲

边草萧条塞雁飞，
征人南望泪沾衣。
黄尘满面长须战，
白发生头未得归。

Song of the Frontier Fortress

Bleak is the frontier grassland with wild geese a long flight,
Gazing southward soldiers on an expedition shed tears.
Covered with dust many long-bearded soldiers still fight,
Hoary-headed they've been in the army for many years.

游春词

高楼晓见一花开,
便觉春光四面来。
暖日晴云知次第,
东风不用更相催。

Song of Spring Outing

Atop the tall building I see a flower blooming,
It seems to me from all sides spring is coming.
Clouds float one after another on a fine day,
There's no need for the east wind to drive them away.

朱庆馀

朱庆馀(生卒年不详),字可久,越州(今浙江绍兴)人。宝历二年进士,授校书郎。其诗风格清新,工于言情。《全唐诗》存其诗两卷。

Zhu Qingyu, styled Kejiu, was born in Yuezhou (Shaoxing City, Zhejiang Province today). Zhu successfully passed the imperial examination in 826 and was promoted to secretary of collation. His poems are refreshing in style with the focus on sentiment, of which two volumes are collected in *The Complete Collection of the Tang Poetry*.

杭州送萧宝校书

马识青山路,
人随白浪船。
别君犹有泪,
学道谩经年。

A Send-off to Mr. Xiao Bao My Colleague

The horse knows the route along the hill green and bright,
My colleague on board the ship braving the waves white.
Parting from my friend my coat is wet with tears,
To master Taoist doctrine it takes many years.

同友人看花

寻花不问春深浅,
纵是残红也入诗。
每个树边行一匝,
谁家园里最多时。

Enjoying Flowers with Friends

Spring, early or late, is the best time to enjoy flowers,
Even the withered flowers are truly poetic indeed.
We circle a tree once every time in the spring hours,
In whose garden I wonder the longest time we need.

闺意献张水部

洞房昨夜停红烛，
待晓堂前拜舅姑。
妆罢低声问夫婿，
画眉深浅入时无？

A Poem Presented to Minister Zhang Ji

Wedding candles were bright in the bridal chamber last night,
I'm to pay a call on my parents-in-law at twilight.
Having made up I invite my darling to pass comment,
What about my eyebrows: Is the color strong or light?

采莲

隔烟花草远濛濛,
恨个来时路不同。
正是停桡相遇处,
鸳鸯飞去急流中。

Gathering Lotus Seeds

Misty are the grass and flowers beyond the water,
Pity is that we'll return along another way.
We are to meet just at the spot where we're to anchor,
From the rapid stream some mandarin ducks fly away.

西亭晚宴

虫声已尽菊花干,
共立松阴向晚寒。
对酒看山俱惜去,
不知斜月下栏干。

An Evening Dinner at West Pavilion

No insects chirp and chrysanthemums are fading away,
Standing in the shades of pines we feel chilly in cold glow.
Gazing at mountains while drinking we're in blank dismay,
The moon is hidden below rails before we know.

宫词

寂寂花时闭院门,
美人相并立琼轩。
含情欲说宫中事,
鹦鹉前头不敢言。

Song of the Palace

Oddly lonely at the flower season they close the door,
Side by side the palace maids stand along the corridor.
Sentimental about the palace affairs they're to say,
But in front of the parrots only on words they dare play.

登玄都阁

野色晴宜上阁看,
树阴遥映御沟寒。
豪家旧宅无人住,
空见朱门锁牡丹。

At the Top of Xuandu Pagoda

At the top of tower a bird's-eye view is charming,
Tree shades mirrored in the chilly moat are gleaming.
Splendid are the mansions of peers but no candle light,
Behind the crimson gates nothing but peony in sight.

杨 凌

杨凌(生卒年不详),字恭履,虢州弘农(今河南灵宝)人。曾在朝为官。其诗语言平实,风格清新自然。《全唐诗》存其诗一卷。

Yang Ling, styled Gonglv, was born in Hongnong, Guozhou (Lingbao, Henan today). Yang once served the imperial court as a high-rank official. His poems were composed with plain language in refreshing style. There is one volume of his poems collected in *The Complete Collection of the Tang Poetry*.

送客往睦州

水阔尽南天,
孤舟去渺然。
惊秋路傍客,
日暮数声蝉。

Seeing a Friend Off to Muzhou

Vast is the water stretching southward to the horizon,
A solitary boat fades from my field of vision.
Very much surprised I am standing by the roadside,
To hear cicadas buzzing at autumn dusk far and wide.

剡溪看花

落花千回舞,
莺声百啭歌。
还同异方乐,
不奈客愁多。

Enjoying Flowers Along Shanxi River

Falling petals dance time after time,
Orioles sing without stop in their prime.
Sharing their joy far away from home,
I am in sorrow and deep in gloom.

早春雪中

新年雨雪少晴时,
屡失寻梅看柳期。
乡信忆随回雁早,
江春寒带故阴迟。

Snow in Early Spring

Too much snow in the New Year I am yearning for fine day,
To look for plum flowers and willows but snow blocks the way.
News from my home should come early with wild geese on return flight,
But it's cold along the river that makes the spring delay.

宋　郭熙　《早春图》

秋原野望

客雁秋来次第逢,
家书频寄两三封。
夕阳天外云归尽,
乱见青山无数峰。

An Evening View of the Open Country in Autumn

Wild geese in autumn fly southward one after another,
Some letters from my family come to me together.
The sun is setting in the west beyond the cloudless sky,
From time to time green peaks come into sight so high.

明妃怨

汉国明妃去不还,
马驮弦管向阴山。
匣中纵有菱花镜,
羞对单于照旧颜。

Grievance of Wang Zhaojun

Having left the Han Dynasty she could never return,
With the strings on horseback she headed for Yinshan Mountain.
In her casket there's a mirror bright but she looked stern,
She's ashamed of looking herself before the Hun Chieftain.

杨　凝

杨凝(?～803)，字懋功，虢州弘农(今河南灵宝)人。曾在朝为官，终任兵部郎中。其诗语言朴实，风格明快。《全唐诗》存其诗一卷。

Yang Ning (?～803), styled Maogong, was born in Hongnong, Guozhou (Lingbao County, Henan Province today). Yang was finally promoted to a Deputy Minister in Ministry of War. His poems were composed with simple and plain language in lucid style, of which one volume is collected in *The Complete Collection of the Tang Poetry*.

柳絮

河畔多杨柳，
追游尽狭斜。
春风一回送，
乱入莫愁家。

Willow Catkins

Along the river banks many willows grow,
Street walkers' haunt is the small lane narrow.
Whenever spring breeze brings warmth in the air,
Young women's desire will be stirred in sorrow.

花枕

席上沉香枕，
楼中荡子妻。
那堪一夜里，
长湿两行啼。

A Pair of Embroidered Pillows

On the mat lies idle an eaglewood pillow,
Upstairs a wanderer's wife alone in sorrow.
The night is so long that she can hardly bear,
Always in tears sleeping for her is a nightmare.

春怨

花满帘栊欲度春，
此时夫婿在咸秦。
绿窗孤寝难成寐，
紫燕双飞似弄人。

Loneliness in Late Spring

Flowers bloom in late spring outside the painted window,
At the moment my husband is absent in Chang'an.
Beside the window I feel lonely on the pillow,
Flying in pairs swallows seem to tease me like a fan.

送别

春愁不尽别愁来,
旧泪犹长新泪催。
相思倘寄相思字,
君到扬州扬子回。

A Tearful Farewell

The parting pain comes after the sorrow in spring,
The new teardrops pile on the old ones glistening.
Send me red beans the token of love if you pine,
As you get to Yangzhou let me know you are fine.

残花

五马踟蹰在路岐,
南来只为看花枝。
莺衔蝶弄红芳尽,
次日深闺那得知。

Faded Flowers

At the crossroads the prefect hesitates to move forward,
Only for enjoying flowers he's traveling southward.
Orioles are nesting, butterflies dancing and petals flying,
But nobody knows kept deep in the boudoir I'm fading.

雍裕之

雍裕之（生卒年不详），蜀地（今四川省）人。其诗语言洗练，情景交融。《全唐诗》存其诗一卷，皆为绝句。

Yong Yuzhi was born in the Shu State (Sichuan Province today). Blending his sentiment with the natural setting his poems were composed with succinct language in lucid style. There is one volume of his quatrains collected in *The Complete Collection of the Tang Poetry*.

自君出之矣

自君出之矣，
宝镜为谁明。
思君如陇水，
长闻呜咽声。

The Pain of Parting

Ever since my darling from me parted,
Left idle my mirror's by no means bright.
Pining away for you I'm broken hearted,
And the river wails in my ears at night.

三月晦日郊外送客

野酌乱无巡，
送君兼送春。
明年春色至，
莫作未归人。

Farewell to My Friend in Late Spring

Drinking in the outskirts how happy I can't tell,
A farewell drink to you and to spring as well.
In the coming year spring itself is sure to present,
You must return in time and nothing can prevent.

四气

春禽犹竞啭，
夏木忽交阴。
稍觉秋山远，
俄惊冬霰深。

Alternations of the Four Seasons

Spring birds are still competing in singing,
Summer plants provide shade all of sudden.
Autumn mountains beyond are dimly looming,
Suddenly covered by snow I'm panic-stricken.

山中桂

八树拂丹霄，
四时青不凋。
秋风何处起，
先袅最长条。

To Laurels in the Mountains

Laurels in the mountains grow high and tall,
Green all the year round do not wilt at all.
Whenever the bleak wind blows from the west,
It is the longest branch that takes the test.

芦花

夹岸复连沙,
枝枝摇浪花。
月明浑似雪,
无处认渔家。

To Reed Catkins

Lining both banks stretching out to the sandbar,
Dancing with wind like foamy waves surging far.
When the moonlight over the world is snow-white,
Fishing boats are nowhere to be found at night.

江边柳

裊裊古堤边,
青青一树烟。
若为丝不断,
留取系郎船。

To Willows by the Riverside

Slim are your long twigs swaying by riverside,
Tender is your foliage like smoke wreaths that float.
"If supple and tough enough you are," she sighed,
"I'd let you tie up my darling's parting boat."

江上山

绮霞明赤岸,
锦缆绕丹枝。
楚客正愁绝,
西风且莫吹。

A Mountain in the River

Bright rosy clouds reddens the riversides,
Tied to the red branches is the rope tough.
"Oh, so charming is the scene," the guest sighs,
"West wind, please be gentle and not so rough."

柳絮

无风才到地，
有风还满空。
缘渠偏似雪，
莫近鬓毛生。

Willow Catkins

Swirling onto the ground on a calm day,
On a windy day in the air you play.
Covering ditches you are snowflakes white,
Stay off or my hair turns grey overnight.

残莺

花阑莺亦懒，
不语似含情。
何言百啭舌，
唯馀一两声。

Orioles in Late Spring

Lazy are orioles as flowers fade away,
Silent and their feelings are tender all day.
"They keep singing day and night", some people say,
But now only sing once or twice in a casual way.

秋蛩

雨绝苍苔地，
月斜青草阶。
蛩鸣谁不怨，
况是正离怀。

Autumn Crickets

Green is the mossy ground wet after rain,
The moon slants on the grassy steps again.
Chirps of crickets are annoying indeed,
What's more it is the time of parting pain.

赠苦行僧

幽深红叶寺，
清静白毫僧。
古殿长鸣磬，
低头礼昼灯。

To an Ascetic Monk

Deep and quiet is the temple amid maple trees,
Hoary-headed is the old monk calm and serene.
To strike the *qing** day and night his duty is,
To take care of the alter lamp he is so keen.

---

* *Qing* is a Buddhist percussion instrument made of bronze in the shape of an alms bowl.

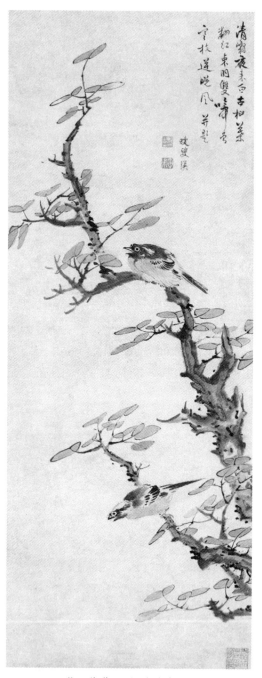

明　蓝瑛　《红叶秋禽图》

农家望晴

尝闻秦地西风雨,
为问西风早晚回。
白发老农如鹤立,
麦场高处望云开。

A Peasant Looking for the Fine Day

In northwest rain often follows the wind from the west,
But he wants to know the time the west wind comes to rest.
A hoary-headed peasant stands like a crane to fly,
At the top of thresh ground he prays for the sunny sky.

张　籍

张籍(767～830)，字文昌，和州乌江(今安徽和县)人。贞元十五年进士，曾任国子监助教，与韩愈、白居易等著名诗人交往甚密。其诗多反映社会矛盾和民生疾苦，诗风平易流畅。《全唐诗》存其诗五卷。

Zhang Ji (767～830), styled Wenchang, was born in Wujiang, Hezhou (He County, Anhui Province today). Zhang passed successfully the imperial examination in 800 and he was appointed a teaching assistant in the Directorate of Education. He was on intimate terms with Han Yu, Bai Juyi and some other famous poets then. Most of his poems mirrored the social crisis and the sufferings of the common people with simple language in smooth style. Five volumes of his poems are collected in *The Complete Collection of the Tang Poetry*.

寄西峰僧

松暗水涓涓，
夜凉人未眠。
西峰月犹在，
遥忆草堂前。

To the Monk on the West Peak

In the dark are pines by the trickling stream,
It's cool but I'm unable to sleep at night.
Atop the West Peak the moon is still bright,
Missing the monk it seems I'm in a dream.

梅溪

自爱新梅好,
行寻一径斜。
不教人扫石,
恐损落来花。

The Plum-flower Stream

I look for plum flowers in bloom fresh and fine,
Along the narrow path like a slanting line.
Nobody is told to sweep the pebble path,
Lest petals should be spoiled like weeds and grass.

惜花

山中春已晚，
处处见花稀。
明日来应尽，
林间宿不归。

Tender to Flowers

In the mountains spring is now fading away,
The slopes are sparsely dotted with flowers.
No more flowers in bloom if I come next day,
So I'll stay the night here into the small hours.

岸花

可怜岸边树,
红蕊发青条。
东风吹渡水,
冲着木兰桡。

Flowers by the Riverside

So lively are the trees by the riverside,
On the green branches and twigs red buds sprout.
With the east wind water flows round about,
Lashing the boat and paddle from side to side.

送元结

昔日同游漳水边,
如今重说恨绵绵。
天涯相见还离别,
客路秋风又几年。

Farewell to Yuan Jie

We cherish our tour to River Zhang in the past,
It's a pity that the past trip cannot long last.
Far away from home we meet but we have to part,
Bleak wind sees our parting we hope reunion comes fast.

与贾岛闲游

水北原南草色新,
雪销风暖不生尘。
城中车马应无数,
能解闲行有几人。

Sauntering with Jia Dao

On the outskirts of the capital grass is green,
Snow has thawed, breeze is vernal and the air clean.
So many people hustle and bustle in town,
Few of them can value the stroll free and serene.

忆故州

垒石为山伴野夫,
自收灵药读仙书。
如今身是他州客,
每见青山忆旧居。

Pining for My Former Abode in Hezhou

Piling up stones like a recluse I build a rock garden,
Reading Taoist classics I collect herbal medicine.
In a strange land today I'm often in a sorrow plight,
Pining for my former abode when green hill's in sight.

送客游蜀

行尽青山到益州,
锦城楼下二江流。
杜家曾向此中住,
为到浣花溪水头。

Sending Off a Friend to Chengdu

Having crossed green mountains Yizhou is in sight,
By the gate tower of Chengdu two rivers flow.
Du Fu once made his abode by the riverside,
Huanhua Stream was his haunt he used to come and go.

感春

远客悠悠任病身,
谢家池上又逢春。
明年各自东西去,
此地看花是别人。

Sighing over Spring

Pestered with illness I come here from afar in gloom,
Spring comes to the pond and all flowers are in bloom.
Next year each one will go his own way far and wide,
Some others will come for flowers from every side.

别客

青山历历水悠悠，
今日相逢明日秋。
系马城边杨柳树，
为君沽酒暂淹留。

Farewell to a Friend

Long is the river and green's the mountain in sight,
We meet today and the autumn tint is so bright.
Tie your steed to the willow by the city gate,
I'll buy a farewell cup of wine for you please wait.

寄故人

静曲闲房病客居,
蝉声满树槿花疏。
故人只在蓝田县,
强半年来未得书。

To an Old Friend

In a deep chamber in the strange land I kill days,
Cicadas buzz in trees and hibiscus are fading.
Faraway in Lantian County my friend still stays,
For a letter from him so long I've been yearning.

秋思

洛阳城里见秋风,
欲作家书意万重。
复恐匆匆说不尽,
行人临发又开封。

Autumn Thoughts

Bleak wind blows in Luoyang and autumn is at its height,
Writing a letter home but I have too much to say.
I'm afraid if there's something missing by oversight,
Open and check as the messenger's to go away.

玉仙馆

长溪新雨色如泥，
野水阴云尽向西。
楚客天南行渐远，
山山树里鹧鸪啼。

At a Guest House

Muddy is the water in the stream on the rainy day,
Brooks and clouds in the open country are all flowing west.
Visitors from the south walk farther and farther away,
In the mountain forest francolins' singing in the nest.

凉州词·其一

边城暮雨雁飞低,
芦笋初生渐欲齐。
无数铃声遥过碛,
应驮白练到安西。

Song of Liangzhou (1)

Raining at dusk on the frontier and swallows fly low,
Verdant are reed shoots by the river that quickly grow.
The jingle of caravan bells has long since died away,
Busy was the Silk Road in the past but slack today.

凉州词·其二

凤林关里水东流，
白草黄榆六十秋。
边将暂承主恩泽，
无人解道取凉州。

Song of Liangzhou (2)

In the lost territory eastwards the river flows,
In the deserted land for sixty years no crop grows.
Generals on the frontier do nothing in their posts,
Nobody wants to recover the lost land God knows.

华清宫

温泉流入汉离宫,
宫树行行浴殿空。
武帝时人今欲尽,
青山空闭御墙中。

Huaqing Palace

Warm spring flows into the imperial palace bright,
Flanked with trees but no figure at the bath place.
No maid of the former palace is now in sight,
Behind the palace walls only the green hill stays.

寻仙

溪头一径入青崖，
处处仙居隔杏花。
更见峰西幽客说，
云中犹有两三家。

Looking for the Fairyland

By the stream the path leads to the green cliff of great height,
The fairy court is amid the apricot blooms white.
From the west of the peak a hermit is drawing nigh,
He tells me there're some houses perched in the sky.

明 唐寅 《清溪松荫图》

春别曲

长江春水绿堪染，
莲叶出水大如钱。
江头橘树君自种，
那不长系木兰船。

Farewell to a Friend in Spring

Spring water in Yangtze River is green and crystalline,
Surfacing from water lotus leaves are like coins fine.
Planted yourself are the orange trees by the riverside,
Why for a long time only few boats to them have been tied.

寒塘曲

寒塘沉沉柳叶疏,
水暗人语惊栖凫。
舟中少年醉不起,
持烛照水射游鱼。

Song of Cold Pond

Cold is the pond and sparse are leaves of willow,
Startled by voices on the water wild ducks crow.
Drunk is the young lad on boat under the lamplight,
Spotlighting on the water shooting fish at night.

秋山

秋山无云复无风，
溪头看月出深松。
草堂不闭石床静，
叶间坠露声重重。

Mountains in Autumn

No cloud nor wind over the autumn mountains at night,
Beyond the pine grove by the stream the moon is in sight.
Sitting on the stone bed I keep my cottage open,
Pattering the leaves the dew drops drip quite often.

王 建

王建(约767～约830),字仲初,颍川(今河南许昌)人。出身寒微,曾在朝为官。其诗清新素雅,语言明快。《全唐诗》存其诗六卷。

Wang Jian (about 767～about 830), styled Zhongchu, was born of humble origin in Yingchuan (Xuchang City, Henan Province today). Wang once served as a government official and his poems were written in lucid style with simple fresh words, of which six volumes are collected in *The Complete Collection of the Tang Poetry*.

秋夜

夜久叶露滴,
秋虫入户飞。
卧多骨髓冷,
起覆旧绵衣。

An Autumn Night

Dew drops drip from the leaves in the dead of night,
Autumn insects fly into house towards the light.
Lying in bed for long I'm feeling very cold,
Getting up I wrap myself with a coat very old.

春意

去日丁宁别,
情知寒食归。
缘逢好天气,
教熨看花衣。

Aware of the Coming Spring

The moment we said parting words you went away,
I knew at heart you'd return on the Cold Food Day.
As it happens fine days for a long time stay,
It's the very time to iron my spring array.

夜闻子规

子规啼不歇，
到晓口应穿。
况是不眠夜，
声声在耳边。

A Cuckoo Calls at Night

Cuckoo, cuckoo, a cuckoo keeps calling,
Until its beak bleeds next morning.
I toss and turn all night without sleeping,
Cuckoo's calls in my ears keep lingering.

江馆

水面细风生，
菱歌慢慢声。
客亭临小市，
灯火夜妆明。

A Riverside Hotel

Blowing over the water is the breeze light,
Slow is the lotus-picking song soft at night.
The post house is close to the downtown street,
Ablaze with lights, it is a brilliant night sight.

赠谪者

何罪过长沙，
年年北望家。
重封岭头信，
一树海边花。

To a Banished Official

Banished beyond Changsha for what crime?
Year by year you gaze northward all the time.
Open and seal your letter time and again,
Homesick you are when flowers are at their prime.

新嫁娘

三日入厨下,
洗手作羹汤。
未谙姑食性,
先遣小姑尝。

A Bride

I became a bride three days ago,
It's time today to cook soup I know.
To cater for my mother-in-law's taste,
Let her daughter taste first it'll be best.

水精

映水色不别，
向月光还度。
倾在荷叶中，
有时看是露。

Crystal

Reflecting water it shines like water clear,
In the moonlight it casts no shadow at night.
Rolling in a lotus leave like a drop of tear,
It is a dew drop that is extremely bright.

落叶

陈绿尚参差,
初红已重叠。
中庭初扫地,
绕树三两叶。

Fallen Leaves

Degrees of greenness vary with autumn time,
Some are turning red with the advent of rime.
The yard ground is just swept and tidy enough,
But on the ground new fallen leaves are rough.

野菊

晚艳出荒篱，
冷香著秋水。
忆向山中见，
伴蛩石壁里。

Wild Chrysanthemums

Beautiful in the wilderness are late flowers,
Cold fragrance wafts over water in autumn hours.
In the mountains I saw you in my memory,
Among rocks playing with crickets you make merry.

荒园

朝日满园霜,
牛冲篱落坏。
扫掠黄叶中,
时时一窠薤。

The Deserted Garden

It's frosty at dawn all over the garden,
Trodden by cattle the wattle fence's fallen.
As the fallen leaves scatter with the wind,
From time to time you can see clusters of scallion.

晚蝶

粉翅嫩如水,
绕砌乍依风。
日高山露解,
飞入菊花中。

An Autumn Butterfly

Tender enough as water are the pink wings,
Around the steps to the wind it sometimes clings.
As the sun rises high and no more dew and rime,
To visit chrysanthemums it's the right time.

小松

小松初数尺，
未有直生枝。
闲即傍边立，
看多长却迟。

A Small Pine Tree

A small pine tree, only a few feet high,
No branch, no twig, but a rod well-nigh.
Idle it is, standing by the roadside,
If seen too often it would grow on the slide.

田家

啾啾雀满树，
霭霭东坡雨。
田家夜无食，
水中摘禾黍。

A Peasant's Family

Chirping are birds all over the clump of trees,
Gloomy over the east hill and raining it is.
The whole family are starving day and night,
They've to gather unripe crops in a bad plight.

长安别

长安清明好时节,
只宜相送不宜别。
恶心床上铜片明,
照见离人白头发。

Parting at Chang'an

The year's prime at Chang'an is the Pure Brightness Day,
It's nice for a farewell drink but "goodbye" never say.
I'm sick at the sight of the bronze mirror so bright,
Letting me see my hair turning grey overnight.

春词

良人朝早半夜起,
樱桃如珠露如水。
下堂把火送郎回,
移枕重眠晓窗里。

Song of Spring

My darling has to go to court at midnight,
Cherries are small as pearls and dew drops bright.
I get up and carry the lamp to the window,
To meet him back and sleep again on the pillow.

野池

野池水满连秋堤,
菱花结实蒲叶齐。
川口雨晴风复止,
蜻蜓上下鱼东西。

A Pool

Full to the brim the pool stretches to the autumn dyke,
Water plants start yielding and cattail in the neat array.
The rain stops at the river mouth and the wind dies away,
Dragonflies fly up and down and fishes swim as they like.

秋夜曲

秋灯向壁掩洞房,
良人此夜直明光。
天河悠悠漏水长,
南楼北斗两相当。

Song of Autumn Night

Facing the wall that shades the bedroom is the autumn light,
My darling is on duty in the bright palace tonight.
The Milky Way is long and the water clock ticks and ticks,
The South Building and the Big Dipper seem at the same height.

古谣

一东一西垄头水,
一聚一散天边霞。
一来一去道上客,
一颠一倒池中麻。

An Old Folk Song

To the east and west of the ridge the water flows,
Gather and part the clouds at the end of the sky.
Back and forth on the road are the passers-by,
Upside-down in the pool the hemp lushly grows.

镊白

总道老来无用处，
何须白发在前生。
如今不用偷年少，
拔却三茎又五茎。

Pulling Out Grey Hairs

It's often said the aged is of no avail,
But why my hair turned grey in my prime.
Now it's no use to follow the young like a tail,
As three pulled out five will turn grey in no time.

江馆对雨

鸟声愁雨似秋天,
病客思家一向眠。
草馆门临广州路,
夜闻蛮语小江边。

At a Riverside Hotel in the Rain

A bird's crying in the rain it looks like an autumn day,
Away from sleeping for a while I am pining away.
Close to the hotel in the open is the road to Guangzhou,
At night by the river the folk's talk sounds in a strange way.

雨过山村

雨里鸡鸣一两家,
竹溪村路板桥斜。
妇姑相唤浴蚕去,
闲着中庭栀子花。

Walking by a Mountain Village in the Rain

From one or two farmhouses come the cockcrows in the rain,
Across the bamboo stream a slanting plank is so plain.
For raising silkworms wench and mother-in-law come together,
Only the gardenias in the courtyard free from strain.

江陵使至汝州

回看巴路在云间，
寒食离家麦熟还。
日暮数峰青似染，
商人说是汝州山。

On the Mission from Jiangling to Ruzhou

Turning round, the road is hidden in the clouds so high,
Away from home in April I return when wheat is ripe.
In the twilight mountain peaks seem tinged with green dye,
A merchant tells me mountains of Ruzhou are of this type.

题禅师房

浮生不住叶随风,
填海移山总是空。
长向人间愁老病,
谁来闲坐此房中。

To a Buddhist Temple

It seems human life is a leave floating in the air,
To fill the sea with mountains always results in vain.
Senility is the main cause leading to despair,
Sitting in meditation they try to free from pain.

晓望华清宫

晓来楼阁更鲜明，
日出阑干见鹿行。
武帝自知身不死，
看修玉殿号长生。

The Huaqing Palace

At the crack of dawn splendid are the tall buildings bright,
The sunrise sees deer playing along the rails with delight.
Emperor Xuanzong thought he himself would be immortal,
He ordered to build the Palace entitled "Life's Eternal".

华清宫前柳

杨柳宫前忽地春,
在先惊动探春人。
晓来唯欠骊山雨,
洗却枝头绿上尘。

Willows in Front of the Palace

Spring comes to the palace willows all of sudden,
Looking for and alert to spring I'm the first person.
Pity is that no rain comes in the early morning,
But grime on the green twigs needs a complete washing.

留别张广文

谢恩新入凤凰城,
乱定相逢合眼明。
千万求方好将息,
杏花寒食的同行。

A Reluctant Parting with Zhang Guangwen

To show my gratitude I come to the capital,
It's nice to see your eyes bright after the upheaval.
Be sure to take good care of yourself without delay,
Let's enjoy apricot flowers on the Cold Food Day.

十五夜望月寄杜郎中

中庭地白树栖鸦,
冷露无声湿桂花。
今夜月明人尽望,
不知秋思落谁家。

The View of the Moon Festival to Minister Du

In the moonlit courtyard birds rest in the tree at night,
Wet with dew drops cold laurel flowers are sweet and still.
People all come out tonight to enjoy the moonlight,
No one knows to whom the autumn thought sends a slight chill.

山店

登登石路何时尽,
决决溪泉到处闻。
风动叶声山犬吠,
一家松火隔秋云。

An Overnight Stay at a Mountain Inn

Clip-clog they clack on the endless stone path in clogs,
Here and there you can hear brooks babble with delight.
Leaves rustling in the breeze startle mountain dogs,
Through the autumn clouds bright are pine torches at night.

夜看扬州市

夜市千灯照碧云,
高楼红袖客纷纷。
如今不似时平日,
犹自笙歌彻晓闻。

A Night View of Yangzhou

Night fair sees thousands of lights reddening the sky,
Singing girls and guests at night clubs are running high.
After the rebellion the country is not in peace,
But music and songs heard all night long are a scene of bliss.

秋夜对雨寄石瓮寺二秀才

夜山秋雨滴空廊,
灯照堂前树叶光。
对坐读书终卷后,
自铺衣被扫僧房。

To the Two Scholars in Shiweng Temple on a Raining Autumn Night

In the autumn mountains fine rain drips pit-a-pat at night,
Bare are the trees along the corridor lit in the light.
Sitting in company of the rain I finish reading,
And then cleaning the Buddhist room I arrange my bedding.

新晴后

住处近山常足雨,
闻晴晒曝旧芳茵。
立秋日后无多热,
渐觉生衣不著身。

A Sunny Day After Rain

Living near the mountains it rains more often than not,
I've to dry my bedding and mattress when the sun shines.
As the autumn comes it's getting more chilly than hot,
The summer clothes seems too thin I feel not so nice.

宫词

树头树底觅残红,
一片西飞一片东。
自是桃花贪结子,
错教人恨五更风。

Song from the Palace

Looking up and down for peach flowers in the garden,
Scattering here and there I find petals have fallen.
East wind is by no means the root cause for resentment,
Peach flowers long to yield more fruits that's the true reason.

听琴

无事此身离白云,
松风溪水不曾闻。
至心听著仙翁引,
今看青山围绕君。

Listening to an Ancient Melody

Since I made farewell to seclusion in the clouds white,
The scenic beauty of pines and streams are out of sight.
Deeply sincere I am lost in the sage's music play,
By and by the moving scene comes into sight today.

宋　李唐　《万壑松风图》

望夫石

望夫处,江悠悠,
化为石,不回头。
山头日日风复雨,
行人归来石应语。

A Stone Pining for Her Husband

Pining for her husband where the river flows away,
Turning into a stone she is gazing night and day.
The wind howls and the rain pours down atop the mountain,
The stone would talk to her darling back home for certain.

听雨

半夜思家睡里愁,
雨声落落屋檐头。
照泥星出依前黑,
淹烂庭花不肯休。

Raining While Sleeping

Homesick in midnight I'm sleeping in sorrow,
From the edge of eaves pit-a-pat rain drips low.
Some stars shine over the earth dark still at night,
Flowers flooded in the yard it's indeed a blight.

旧宫人

先帝旧宫宫女在,
乱丝犹挂凤凰钗。
霓裳法曲浑抛却,
独自花间扫玉阶。

The Former Palace Maids

The palace maids of the late emperor live on their own,
Hairs disheveled but held by the phoenix-shaped hair slide.
No dancing at all and its melody is cast aside,
Among flower shrubs they are sweeping the jade steps alone.

明　仇珠　《女乐图》

和门下武相公春晓闻莺

侵黑行飞一两声,
春寒啭小未分明。
若教更解诸余语,
应向宫花不惜情。

Heard Warbles in Early Spring with Wu

Sporadic warbles come before daybreak in flight,
Spring is chilly at the crack of dawn it chirps low.
About the other melodies if you know,
Sing heartily to palace flowers with delight.

寄广文张博士

春明门外作卑官,
病友经年不得看。
莫道长安近于日,
升天却易到城难。

To Zhang Ji a Learned Scholar

Outside the Chunming Gate you hold a humble position,
As invalids our visiting is out of the question.
Chang'an is the capital and imperial court so high,
A visit to town it is harder than climbing the sky.

新晴

夏夜新晴星校少，
雨收残水入天河。
檐前熟著衣裳坐，
风冷浑无扑火蛾。

A Nice Summer Night

The night after rain sees only a few stars in the sky,
The rain stops and remaining water flows farther away.
Sitting before the eaves I'm dressed in snug array,
No moth flits around the lamp as the cool wind blows nigh.

韩 愈

韩愈(768～824),字退之,河阳(今河南孟州)人。曾长期在朝为官,后遭贬。韩愈倡导古文运动,因散文造诣被列为唐宋八大家之首。其诗语言风格大胆创新,气势雄伟。《全唐诗》存其诗十卷。

Han Yu(768～824), styled Tuizhi, was born in Heyang (Mengzhou City, Henan Province today). Han served for a long time as a senior official in the court and was demoted later. He was the head of "Eight Prose Masters of the Tang-Song Period" (Han Yu, Liu Zongyuan, Ouyang Xiu, Su Xun, Su Shi, Su Zhe, Zeng Gong and Wang Anshi) as he championed the Classical Prose Movement. His poems were written with pithy language in unique style, of which ten volumes are collected in *The Complete Collection of the Tang Poetry*.

青青水中蒲

青青水中蒲,
下有一双鱼。
君今上陇去,
我在与谁居。

Cattails in the Pond

Green, green are cattails in the pond,
A couple of fish swim around.
For Lanzhou you leave me today,
With whom tonight can I stay?

花岛

蜂蝶去纷纷,
香风隔岸闻。
欲知花岛处,
水上觅红云。

A Flowery Island

Swarming are bees and butterflies,
Across the water waft of scent flies.
If you seek for the flowery island,
Red clouds on water wrap the fairyland.

柳溪

柳树谁人种？
行行夹岸高。
莫将条系缆，
著处有蝉号。

The Willow Stream

Who planted the willows along the stream?
Lining the banks in rows they are so high.
Don't tie your boat to the branches please,
As so many cicadas are chirping nigh.

荷池

风雨秋池上，
高荷盖水繁。
未谙鸣摵摵，
那似卷翻翻。

The Lotus Pond

It rains in the autumn wind in the pond,
Lotuses grow thick and dense all around.
Without the sound of rustling in the wind,
No sight of lotus leaves whirling round.

西山

新月迎霄挂，
晴云到晚留。
为遮西望眼，
终是懒回头。

The West Hill

Night falls and the new moon climbs up the sky,
It's a fine day and the white clouds hang high.
Blocking the view of the West Hill from my sight,
They refuse to fly away and stay the night.

月池

寒池月下明,
新月池边曲。
若不妒清妍,
却成相映烛。

The Moon-lit Pond

Cold is the pond glittering in the moonlight,
Mirrored on the pond is a gold crescent bright.
If not jealous of the beauty one another,
They can add to natural charm each other.

把酒

扰扰驰名者,
谁能一日闲。
我来无伴侣,
把酒对南山。

Drinking

Bustling are those who run after fame,
Day and night they try to be a big name.
I have no companion on the journey,
Cheers, the south mountain please drink with me.

清　王时敏　《南山积翠图》

题榴花

五月榴花照眼明，
枝间时见子初成。
可怜此地无车马，
颠倒青苔落绛英。

Pomegranate Blossoms

Pomegranate blossoms in May are a fiery glow,
Sometimes you find branches with new fruits hanging low.
Pity is that few people come for flowering day,
On the moss ground many blossoms have faded away.

盆池·其一

泥盆浅小讵成池，
夜半青蛙圣得知。
一听暗来将伴侣，
不烦鸣唤斗雄雌。

The Potted Flowers (1)

By no means a pond the pot is small and shallow,
Croaking at midnight it's the frog that makes me know.
He secretly passes on the code to its mate,
There's no need for her to make reply but to wait.

盆池·其二

池光天影共青青，
拍岸才添水数瓶。
且待夜深明月去，
试看涵泳几多星。

The Potted Flowers (2)

Ripples and the blue sky are spreading in the pot,
Full to the brim a few bottles will be the whole lot.
At the depth of night when the moon sinks in the west,
Let's see how many stars twinkle in the pot at best.

春雪

新年都未有芳华，
二月初惊见草芽。
白雪却嫌春色晚，
故穿庭树作飞花。

The Spring Snow

The New Year witnesses no flowers in bloom,
March sees grass in bud it's really a surprise.
Discontented with spring late snow is in gloom,
Through the tree branches in the courtyard it flies.

晚春

草树知春不久归,
百般红紫斗芳菲。
杨花榆荚无才思,
惟解漫天作雪飞。

The Fading Spring

Grass and trees are aware of spring fading away,
All flowers vie for beauty in glamorous array.
Catkins and elm seeds are not competitive in charm,
Like snowflakes they fly in the air meaning no harm.

遣兴

断送一生惟有酒,
寻思百计不如闲。
莫忧世事兼身事,
须著人间比梦间。

A True Realization of Life

Drinking is the only way to kill time all my life,
Pondering time and again I think leisure is best.
No need to worry about the world and your own time,
Just take life as a dream in which you have a good rest.

落花

已分将身着地飞,
哪羞践踏损光辉。
无端又被春风误,
吹落西家不得归。

Fallen Flowers

Petals drop onto the earth, scattering around,
Charm's lost, ashamed of being trodden on the ground.
Swept away by a gust of wind far and wide,
Over the west fence and left on the other side.

晚雨

廉纤晚雨不能晴,
池岸草间蚯蚓鸣。
投竿跨马蹋归路,
才到城门打鼓声。

The Evening Rain

It's overcast at dusk and drizzling the whole day,
In the thick grass by the pond earthworms were humming.
Mounting my horse for home I threw the rod away,
Through the city gate I heard the steady drumming.

晚春

谁收春色将归去，
慢绿妖红半不存。
榆荚只能随柳絮，
等闲撩乱走空园。

Spring on the Wane

Spring is on the wane, who makes it fading away,
Flowers are fading and plants dressed in verdant array.
Behind the willow catkins elm seeds follow around,
For nothing over the garden they give a dazzling play.

早春呈水部张十八员外

天街小雨润如酥,
草色遥看近却无。
最是一年春好处,
绝胜烟柳满皇都。

A Poem Composed for Mr. Zhang Ji in Early Spring

The royal streets are moistened with rainy air,
Grass is green from afar but if near still white.
It's the prime of the year and spring is so fair,
Misty willows in the capital are a charming sight.

薛 涛

薛涛(约 768~832),字洪度,长安(今陕西西安)人。自幼随父入蜀,后沦为歌伎。其诗多为赠人之作,情调伤感。《全唐诗》存其诗一卷。

Xue Tao (about 768~832), styled Hongdu, was born in Chang'an (Xi'an City, Shaanxi Province today). As a young girl Xue travelled to Sichuan with her father and was reduced to a singing girl, whose poems are sentimental and many of them were written as gifts presented to her friends. There is one volume collected in *The Complete Collection of the Tang Poetry*.

春望词 • 其一

花开不同赏,
花落不同悲。
欲问相思处,
花开花落时。

The Song of Spring View (1)

We cannot share together the flowers in bloom,
When flowers fall, either together we're in gloom.
If you ask me why I am lovesick and where,
When the flowers bloom and the petals scatter there.

春望词·其二

揽草结同心，
将以遗知音。
春愁正断绝，
春鸟复哀吟。

The Song of Spring View (2)

I knit the soft grass into a love knot,
Present it to my lover far apart.
I'm just rid of spring sorrow from my thought,
The sad cry of a bird gives me a start.

春望词·其三

风花日将老，
佳期犹渺渺。
不结同心人，
空结同心草。

The Song of Spring View (3)

Like flowers in wind I'm getting old day by day,
But our wedding date is still a long way away.
If our hearts cannot be tied like that of lovebirds,
A love knot of grass means nothing but hollow words.

池上双凫

双栖绿池上,
朝暮共飞还。
更忆将雏日,
同心莲叶间。

Double Wild Ducks on the Pond

A pair of wild ducks dwell on the green pond,
Side by side they come and go day and night.
Feeding their ducklings well is their strong bond,
Looking after their young with all their might.

送友人

水国蒹葭夜有霜，
月寒山色共苍苍。
谁言千里自今夕，
离梦杳如关塞长。

To a Friend

Along the waterside reeds are dyed with rime at night,
In the cold moonlight mountains and hills turn greyish white.
From this date, they say we'll be thousand miles apart,
Far beyond the Great Wall on my dream it casts a blight.

明　文徵明　《真赏斋图》(局部)

张仲素

张仲素(769～819),字绘之,符离(今安徽宿州)人。曾在朝为官,擅诗文,尤工绝句。《全唐诗》存其诗一卷。

Zhang Zhongsu (769～819), styled Huizhi, was born in Fuli (Suzhou City, Anhui Province today). Zhang passed successfully the palace examination in 788 and then began his official career. He was well versed in prose and poem, quatrains in particular. There is one volume of his poems collected in *The Complete Collection of the Tang Poetry*.

宫中乐

网户交如绮,
纱窗薄似烟。
乐吹天上曲,
人是月中仙。

Pleasures in the Palace

Lattice windows are ornamented with traceries,
The gauze for screening window is like a thin haze.
Celestial tunes are played by the palace fairies,
They are the nymphs living in the Moon Palace.

思君恩

紫禁香如雾,
青天月似霜。
云韶何处奏,
只是在朝阳。

Pining for Emperor's Overnight Stay

Misty scent wafts up from the Forbidden Palace,
Rime-bright in the blue sky is the moon that shines.
In which palace is the heavenly music played so nice,
It's nowhere to be heard but in Zhaoyang Palace*.

---

* Zhaoyang Palace refers to the residence of empress in the Tang Dynasty.

春游曲

烟柳飞轻絮,
风榆落小钱。
濛濛百花里,
罗绮竞秋千。

Song of Spring Outing

Willow catkins in mist are dancing with grace,
Elm pods like small coins floating with spring breeze.
Flowers are a riot of color all over the place,
Girls in spring garments are swinging in bliss.

春闺思

袅袅城边柳，
青青陌上桑。
提笼忘采叶，
昨夜梦渔阳。

Reverie in Boudoir

Around the city wall fresh willows are slender,
By the roadside mulberry leaves are tender.
Absent-minded under the tree basket in hand,
Missing her dear far away she's in dreaming land.

五代　荆浩　《渔乐图》

春江曲

家寄征河岸，
征人几岁游。
不如潮水信，
每日到沙头。

Song of the Spring River

Away from home I live by the riverside,
He's enlisted into army many years ago.
Trustworthy are the ebb and flow of the tide,
At the fixed time it's sure to come and go.

秋闺思 · 其一

碧窗斜月蔼深晖,
愁听寒螀泪湿衣。
梦里分明见关塞,
不知何路向金微。

Reverie in Boudoir in Autumn (1)

The moon slanted through the window screen with dim light,
I heard the chirping of autumn insects with dismay.
In my dream the frontier fortress was ready in sight,
But close to the destination I lost my way.

秋闺思·其二

秋天一夜静无云，
断续鸿声到晓闻。
欲寄征衣问消息，
居延城外又移军。

Reverie in Boudoir in Autumn (2)

Still is the autumn night and cloudless is the sky,
Now and then till dawn I can hear the wild geese cry.
To post him coat I ask about his information,
They've transferred again I know not his destination.

燕子楼·其一

楼上残灯伴晓霜,
独眠人起合欢床。
相思一夜情多少,
地角天涯未是长。

The Swallow Tower (1)

Waning is the lamp upstairs with the morning frost,
Rising from the nuptial bed but her bliss is lost.
Lovesick and pining away she's sleepless at night,
Never-ending is her lovesickness a fatal blight.

燕子楼·其二

北邙松柏锁愁烟,
燕子楼人思悄然。
自埋剑履歌尘散,
红袖香消已十年。

The Swallow Tower (2)

Pines around his grave are shrouded in the sad mist,
Lost in thought in the Swallow Tower she is on her own.
She sang no song since his name was on the death list,
Her dancing dress and rouge for ten years were left alone.

燕子楼·其三

适看鸿雁岳阳回,
又睹玄禽逼社来。
瑶瑟玉箫无意绪,
任从蛛网任从灰。

The Swallow Tower（3）

She saw wild geese flying southward from Yueyang,
And now she sees swallows return with spring again.
She's in no mood for instrument playing for long,
Shrouded in spider's webs and dusty as they remain.

秋夜曲

丁丁漏水夜何长,
漫漫轻云露月光。
秋逼暗虫通夕响,
征衣未寄莫飞霜。

Song of Autumn Night

Endless is the night and the water clock ticks away,
Now and then through the floating clouds appears the moonlight.
Forced by autumn the insects keep chirping all night,
Before the coat is sent I hope the frost could delay.

李 绅

李绅(772～846),字公垂,润州无锡(今江苏无锡)人。《全唐诗》存其诗四卷,以《悯农二首》最为有名。

Li Shen (772～846), styled Gongchui, was born in Wuxi, Runzhou (Wuxi City, Jiangsu Province today). There are four volumes of his poems collected in *The Complete Collection of the Tang Poetry*, of which the most famous are the two poems entitled *Compassion for Peasants*.

悯农·其一

春种一粒粟,
秋收万颗子。
四海无闲田,
农夫犹饿死。

Compassion for Peasants (1)

Every seed in spring they sow
Will yield in autumn a crop bumper.
Peasants allow no land lie fallow,
Still some of them die of hunger.

悯农·其二

锄禾日当午,
汗滴禾下土。
谁知盘中餐,
粒粒皆辛苦。

Compassion for Peasants (2)

Hoeing at noon during the dog days,
They're sweating in the fields always.
Although sweet is the food on the plate,
Each grain is the fruit of toiling late.

重到惠山

碧峰依旧松筠老，
重得经过已白头。
俱是海天黄叶信，
两逢霜节菊花秋。

Back to Huishan Hill Again

Covered with bamboos and pines is the green mountain,
My hair turns grey as soon as I come back again.
Yellow leaves by the sea floating in the sky,
Chrysanthemums bloom as Double Ninth Day draws nigh.

明　董其昌　《青弁图》

江亭

瘴江昏雾连天合，
欲作家书更断肠。
今日病身悲状候，
岂能埋骨向炎荒。

A Riverside Pavilion

Miasma and mist melt into the sky,
To write a letter home I want to cry.
Afflicted with illness I'm in a sad plight,
Buried in the wilderness how can I lie?

柳

千条垂柳拂金丝，
日暖牵风叶学眉。
愁见花飞狂不定，
还同轻薄五陵儿。

To Willow Trees

Thousands of willow twigs are dancing with grace,
Leaves unfold like eyebrows in the warm sunshine.
On seeing flowers blooming they are driven to craze,
Behaving frivolously like playboys drunk with wine.

白居易

白居易(772～846)，字乐天，号香山居士，祖籍太原，出生于河南新郑。贞元十六年(800年)进士，曾在朝为官，后遭贬谪。白居易是继杜甫之后的又一伟大的现实主义诗人。其绝句多即景寓情之作，语言通俗，格调清新。《全唐诗》存其诗三十九卷。

Bai Juyi (772～846), styled Letian, also known as "Hermit of Xiangshan", his literary name, was born in Xinzheng, Henan Province, but his ancestral home was Taiyuan, Shanxi Province. Bai Juyi passed successfully the imperial examination in 800, and served as a senior official in the court, but was demoted later. Bai was a great realistic poet next to nobody but Du Fu, whose quatrains were mainly extempore verses conveying his then feelings with simple language in fresh style. There are thirty-nine volumes of his poems collected in *The Complete Collection of the Tang Poetry*.

夜雨

早蛩啼复歇，
残灯灭又明。
隔窗知夜雨，
芭蕉先有声。

Night Rain

Crickets were crying and now they stop chirping,
The lamp was dying but now again it's bright.
Outside the window it is raining at night,
Pit-a-pat the plantain leaves are dripping.

秋夕

叶声落如雨，
月色白似霜。
夜深方独卧，
谁为拂尘床。

An Autumn Night

Leaves are dropping and it sounds like raining,
The moon light is bright and it seems rime shining.
In the dead of night I'm lying on bed alone,
I have to wipe dust off my bed on my own.

微雨夜行

漠漠秋云起，
稍稍夜寒生。
自觉衣裳湿，
无点亦无声。

Traveling at Night in Drizzle

A vast expanse of autumn clouds overhead,
There is a spell of nip in the depth of night.
Wet through I am aware only to myself,
No trace, no sound, but I'm in a sad plight.

夜雪

已讶衾枕冷，
复见窗户明。
夜深知雪重，
时闻折竹声。

Night Snow

Colder and colder are my quilt and pillow,
Brighter and brighter it's near the window.
It snows heavily in the depth of night,
From time to time bamboo snaps with snow.

昼卧

抱枕无言语，
空房独悄然。
谁知尽日卧，
非病亦非眠。

A Gloomy Day

Having nothing to say I hug my pillow,
Lonely in the room I'm a single shadow.
Nobody knows I'm lying in bed all day,
Neither ill nor sleepy just whiling time away.

南浦别

南浦凄凄别，
西风袅袅秋。
一看肠一断，
好去莫回头。

Parting by the Waterside

Heart-broken at parting by the waterside,
Desolate is the scene and autumn wind sighs.
I have to hide the tears that blur my eyes,
Go away quickly and get into your stride.

勤政楼西老柳

半朽临风树,
多情立马人。
开元一株柳,
长庆二年春。

An Old Willow Tree

Swaying in the wind is an old tree half rotten,
Sitting on a horse I'm a sentimental person.
The tree is a willow a hundred years old,
Every year it greets spring no matter warm or cold.

问刘十九

绿蚁新醅酒，
红泥小火炉。
晚来天欲雪，
能饮一杯无？

An Invitation to Mr. Liu

Newly brewed wine gleams green yellow,
My red clay stove gives warm glow.
Dusk gathers it looks like snow,
Come for a cup, why don't you?

醉中对红叶

临风杪秋树,
对酒长年人。
醉貌如霜叶,
虽红不是春。

Drinking to Red Leaves

Atop the autumn trees the wind sighs,
Drink and be merry all year round.
Like the maple leaves the frost dyes,
My face turns red but no spring comes around.

龙昌寺荷池

冷碧新秋水,
残红半破莲。
从来寥落意,
不似此池边。

Lotus Pond in Longchang Temple

Cold and clear is the water in early autumn,
Fading and withering are the lotus flowers.
Desolate and decaying is the autumn tint,
By lotus pond it evokes my gloomy hours.

闺怨词

朝憎莺百啭,
夜妒燕双栖。
不惯经春别,
谁知到晓啼。

Grievance in the Boudoir

I'm envious of orioles chirping in the morning,
Jealous of the swallows staying in pairs at night.
About the parting in spring they know nothing,
But keep singing all day long in the twilight.

池窗

池晚莲芳榭，
窗秋竹意深。
更无人作伴，
唯对一张琴。

A View from the Window by the Pond

Fading at dusk are the lotus flowers in the pond,
Tinged with autumn hues are bamboos by the window.
I'm alone in the room there is no one around,
The zither is the only mate besides my shadow.

池西亭

朱栏映晚树，
金魄落秋池。
还似钱唐夜，
西楼月出时。

A Pavilion by the Pond

Red railings and trees well match in the setting sun light,
Reflected on the autumn pond is the full moon bright.
It's similar still to the view of Qiantang River,
When the west pavilion is mirrored in the moonlight.

早秋独夜

井梧凉叶动，
邻杵秋声发。
独向檐下眠，
觉来半床月。

Alone at Night in Early Autumn

Leaves of phoenix tree in the courtyard are rustling,
From the neighbor comes the beating of washing.
Sleeping under the eaves I'm alone at night,
Woken up to find my bed half in the moonlight.

和友人洛中春感

莫悲金谷园中月,
莫叹天津桥上春。
若学多情寻往事,
人间何处不伤神。

Sentimental About the Spring in Luoyang

Don't grieve for the moon over the grand garden,
Across Tianjin Bridge don't sigh over the waning spring.
On the past if you're sentimentally lingering,
You'll be sad in the world and always grief-ridden.

惜牡丹花

惆怅阶前红牡丹,
晚来唯有两枝残。
明朝风起应吹尽,
夜惜衰红把火看。

Tenderness to the Fading Peonies

I'm sad to see the peonies by the steps still red,
Only two stems are left fading in the twilight.
They can't survive the wind next morning on the bed,
By the lamplight I've to have the last look tonight.

江上笛

江上何人夜吹笛,
声声似忆故园春。
此时闻者堪头白,
况是多愁少睡人。

A Flute Tune from the River

Who is playing flute on the river in the moonlight,
It evokes the memories of spring in my hometown.
On hearing this my hair should suddenly turn white,
Moreover I'm laden with sorrow and my sleep's gone.

燕子楼·其一

满窗明月满窗霜,
被冷灯残拂卧床。
燕子楼中霜月夜,
秋来只为一人长。

The Swallow Tower (1)

In the moonlight the window screen is laden with frost,
Cold is the quilt on the bed, lamp dying she feels lost.
In the Swallow Tower she's sad at the frosty night,
The endless autumn night for her is too long a blight.

燕子楼·其二

钿晕罗衫色似烟,
几回欲著即潸然。
自从不舞霓裳曲,
叠在空箱十一年。

The Swallow Tower (2)

Golden flower patterns fade from her silk dress like mist,
Trying it on, tears run down for reasons of her own.
Since *The Rainbow Cloak* was cut out from her dance list,
For years the dress has been left in the wardrobe alone.

燕子楼·其三

今春有客洛阳回，
曾到尚书墓上来。
见说白杨堪作柱，
争教红粉不成灰。

The Swallow Tower (3)

Some visitors returned this spring from Luoyang,
They paid homage to the tomb of her lord with pain.
They said the poplar by the tomb grew high and strong,
How could her rosy cheeks still charming remain?

大林寺桃花

人间四月芳菲尽,
山寺桃花始盛开。
长恨春归无觅处,
不知转入此中来。

Peach Blossoms in Dalin Temple

All flowers in late spring have already faded away,
Peach blossoms in the mountain temple just start to bloom.
Spring is gone with no trace left I'm often in dismay,
I have no idea about the temple a good place to roam.

赠江客

江柳影寒新雨地，
塞鸿声急欲霜天。
愁君独自沙头宿，
水绕芦花月满船。

To a Boatman

After rain willow shadows on the banks are cast afar,
Cries of the swans from the frontier fill the frosty sky.
My worry is that you sleep alone on the sandbar,
In the moon-lit boat I can see the reed catkins fly.

别草堂

三间茅舍向山开，
一带山泉绕舍回。
山色泉声莫惆怅，
三年官满却归来。

Farewell to the Thatched Cottage

My thatched cottages in the valley face the mountain,
Around my cottage is a stream of an endless fountain.
Mountains and spring, please don't be sad for parting today,
In three years when my term's over I'll be back for certain.

元　王蒙　《秋山草堂图》

后宫词

泪湿罗巾梦不成，
夜深前殿按歌声。
红颜未老恩先断，
斜倚熏笼坐到明。

Song of a Deserted Empress

Her silk scarf's wet with tears she cannot fall into sleep,
Strings are played in the front palace but night is deep.
Still young with rosy cheeks she is deserted by the king,
Leaning on the scented bed she waits in vain till birds sing.

长安春

青门柳枝软无力,
东风吹作黄金色。
街东酒薄醉易醒,
满眼春愁销不得。

Spring in the Capital

Soft and limp are the willow twigs beside the green gate,
With the vernal breeze into golden yellow they shade.
Easy to sober up as the wine down the street is weak,
Sorrow-laden I am but spring would certainly fade.

残春曲

禁苑残莺三四声,
景迟风慢暮春情。
日西无事墙阴下,
闲踏宫花独自行。

Song of the Waning Spring

In the imperial garden orioles are feebly singing,
Flowers are fading, breeze is breathing and spring waning.
The sun slants west and I am at leisure in the shade,
Amid the palace flowers alone I am walking.

忆江柳

曾栽杨柳江南岸,
一别江南两度春。
遥忆青青江岸上,
不知攀折是何人。

Recollection of the Riverside Willow

On the south bank of the river I planted the willow,
Having left the south of the Yangtze River two years ago.
Recollecting the person on the green bank from afar,
Who's the one plucking the willow twig then I don't know.

白云泉

天平山上白云泉,
云自无心水自闲。
何必奔冲山下去,
更添波浪向人间。

The White-cloud Spring

The white-cloud spring rises in the mountain kissing the sky,
Floating freely are the clouds and the spring is streaming.
No need for the water to gush down the mountain high,
Flooding the earth with waves and torrents galloping.

伤春词

深浅檐花千万枝,
碧纱窗外啭黄鹂。
残妆含泪下帘坐,
尽日伤春春不知。

Grief over the Waning Spring

Under the eaves there are various flowers in shade,
Orioles are singing outside the green frame of window.
Sitting by the screen her tears make her making-up fade,
Grieving over spring waning all day but it doesn't know.

醉后

醉后高歌且放狂，
门前闲事莫思量。
犹嫌小户长先醒，
不得多时住醉乡。

A Verse Composed in Drunkenness

Overwhelmed with wine I sing loudly wild with joy,
Free from cares and gossip I'm like a happy boy.
Easy to sober up if I'm not much of a drinker,
I would rather stay tipsy and always in a stupor.

立秋日登乐游园

独行独语曲江头,
回马迟迟上乐游。
萧飒凉风与衰鬓,
谁教计会一时秋。

A Visit to the Royal Paradise in Early Autumn

Riding alone around the Qujiang Pond I am chanting,
Turning round slowly I head for the Royal Paradise.
My hair grows grey and thin as autumn wind is coming,
Nobody but me cares that the bleak wind soughs and sighs.

暮江吟

一道残阳铺水中，
半江瑟瑟半江红。
可怜九月初三夜，
露似真珠月似弓。

A Twilight Scene on the River

The setting sun beams on the river pave a long way,
Half of the ripples shake and the other a red glow.
The third night of the ninth moon is a lively display,
The dew drops look like pearls and the new moon a bow.

思妇眉

春风摇荡自东来,
折尽樱桃绽尽梅。
惟余思妇愁眉结,
无限春风吹不开。

A Lady Knitting Her Brows in Gloom

From the east the vernal breeze is blowing,
Fading flowers in the wind are floating.
But the lady knits her brows in gloom,
No wind can sweep away with any broom.

采莲曲

菱叶萦波荷飐水,
荷花深处小船通。
逢郎欲语低头笑,
碧玉搔头落水中。

Song of Plucking Lotus Seeds

The wind ripples the ling leaves and lotus swaying,
To the depth of lotus flowers a small boat's sailing.
Meeting a nice lad she wants to talk but smiles instead,
Bowing shyly her green-jade hairpin falls off her head.

空闺怨

寒月沈沈洞房静，
真珠帘外梧桐影。
秋霜欲下手先知，
灯底裁缝剪刀冷。

Grievance from the Cold Boudoir

Dim is the cold moonlight and the chamber is still,
Outside the bead curtain is the phoenix tree's shadow.
It's time for frost to set in and my hand can feel,
When using scissors in the lamplight how cold I know.

村夜

霜草苍苍虫切切,
村南村北行人绝。
独出前门望野田,
月明荞麦花如雪。

An Overnight Stay in a Village

Wilted grass is frosted and insects chirp in sad plight,
Outside the village no figure can be seen in sight.
Walking out of the house alone I gaze far and wide,
Snow-white are the buckwheat flowers in the moonlight.

蓝桥驿见元九诗

蓝桥春雪君归日，
秦岭秋风我去时。
每到驿亭先下马，
循墙绕柱觅君诗。

Coming Across Yuan Zhen's Poem at Lanqiao Post House

When you got to Lanqiao it was snowing on a spring day,
The bleak wind blew from the capital when I went away.
No sooner had I got to the station and got off horse,
Than I looked for your poem everywhere on display.

舟中读元九诗

把君诗卷灯前读,
诗尽灯残天未明。
眼痛灭灯犹暗坐,
逆风吹浪打船声。

Reading Yuan Zhen's Poems on a Boat

Reading the collection of your poems in the lamplight,
Reading's over, the lamp's dying before the daybreak.
Blowing out the lamp with sore eyes I sat at night,
Against the wind I heard the waves beating the deck.

京路

西来为看秦山雪,
东去缘寻洛苑春。
来去腾腾两京路,
闲行除我更无人。

On the Way to the Capital

Westward I'm looking for snow in Qinling Mountain,
Eastward I try to find spring scenery in Luoyang.
To and fro between the two cities time and again,
Traveling on my own I'm at leisure all day long.

曲江有感

曲江西岸又春风，
万树花前一老翁。
遇酒逢花还且醉，
若论惆怅事何穷。

Lost in Thought by Qujiang Pond

To the west of the pond I'm basking in spring breeze,
Amid thousands of flowers I drink as I please.
Drinking to my heart's content I'd like to be tipsy,
To forget worry and sorrow is my idea of bliss.

邯郸冬至夜思家

邯郸驿里逢冬至，
抱膝灯前影伴身。
想得家中夜深坐，
还应说著远行人。

Homesickness on the Night of Winter Solstice in Handan

Winter solstice comes to Handan Post Station today,
With my shadow I sit alone killing night away.
I think of my family staying deep into the night,
They are concerned about me roaming in a sad plight.

秋游

下马闲行伊水头，
凉风清景胜春游。
何事古今诗句里，
不多说著洛阳秋。

An Excursion in Autumn

Off the steed by the river I'd like to walk along,
Cool wind, fresh scene, it's better than a spring outing.
Throughout the ages, poets love the autumn in Luoyang,
Many have lauded the autumn tint in the writing.

夜筝

紫袖红弦明月中，
自弹自感暗低容。
弦凝指咽声停处，
别有深情一万重。

An Ancient *Zheng** Melody Played at Night

In purple sleeves she plays red strings in the moonbeams bright,
Plucking alone she sighs with her looks hidden in dim light.
A sudden pause at her fingertips results in silence,
The implied meaning has to be read beyond the sentence.

---

* *Zheng* is an ancient plucked instrument with 18, 21 or 25 strings in ancient China.

小桥柳

细水涓涓似泪流,
日西惆怅小桥头。
衰杨叶尽空枝在,
犹被霜风吹不休。

Willows by a Tiny Bridge

Trickling like tears the brook is thin and slim,
By the tiny bridge I'm gloomy at dusk dim.
Willows are naked with all leaves fallen,
In the icy wind they're still frost-beaten.

问鹤

乌鸢争食鹊争窠，
独立池边风雪多。
尽日踏冰翘一足，
不鸣不动意如何。

A Question to Crane

Crows and hawks scramble for food and magpies for nest,
Standing alone in the pond you face wind in snow.
Standing on one leg and the other lifting for rest,
On the ice you stand motionless, why, let me know.

府西池

柳无气力枝先动,
池有波纹冰尽开。
今日不知谁计会,
春风春水一时来。

A Pond to the West of My Abode

Motionless is the willow trunk but twigs sway,
Ripples spread on the pond as ice melts away.
Who is so smart to work out the plan perfect?
Let spring breeze meets spring water on the same day.

衰荷

白露凋花花不残,
凉风吹叶叶初乾。
无人解爱萧条境,
更绕衰丛一匝看。

The Wilted Lotus

Dew drops are cool but no flowers wilt away,
Blown by chilly wind lotus leaves start to dry.
Few people love the desolate scene in decay,
Around the withered leaves you give a deep sigh.

病中

交亲不要苦相忧,
亦拟时时强出游。
但有心情何用脚,
陆乘肩舆水乘舟。

Suffering from Ailment

No need for my friends to worry so much for me,
Sometimes I'd like to go outing if need be.
If in a good mood I don't have to go on foot,
I can roam by sedan or travel by boat.

香山寺

空门寂静老夫闲,
伴鸟随云往复还。
家酝满瓶书满架,
半移生计入香山。

Xiangshan Temple

It's tranquil in the temple and I have spare time,
To and fro clouds and birds are good mates of mine.
Settling down in Xiangshan Mountain all my life,
I enjoy reading books and the home-made wine.

杨柳枝·其一

依依袅袅复青青，
勾引清风无限情。
白雪花繁空扑地，
绿丝条弱不胜莺。

Song of Willow Twigs (1)

Swaying in the breeze are weeping willows green,
Appealing to refreshing wind that is so keen.
Over the ground are willow catkins like snow white,
Green twigs are too slim to support the oriole light.

杨柳枝·其二

叶含浓露如啼眼,
枝袅轻风似舞腰。
小树不禁攀折苦,
乞君留取两三条。

Song of Willow Twigs (2)

Leaves are wet with dew drops like tears in eyes,
Slim twigs are swaying in breeze like dancing on ice.
Plucking its twigs is too much for a small tree to bear,
Would you be so kind as to have some twigs to spare?

岭上云

岭上白云朝未散,
田中青麦旱将枯。
自生自灭成何事,
能逐东风作雨无?

Clouds over the Mountain Ridge

Over the ridge in the morn white clouds freely pace,
Stricken by drought seedlings in the fields are wilting.
Emerging and perishing of yourself without trace,
Drifting with east wind but why do you grudge raining?

感月悲逝者

存亡感月一潸然,
月色今宵似往年。
何处曾经同望月,
樱桃树下后堂前。

Bereavement in the Moonlight

Sighing over life and death in the moonlight I shed tears,
Moonlight tonight is just the same as that in the past years.
Before long we enjoyed together the bright moonlight,
Under the cherry tree in the yard we chatted at night.

涧中鱼

海水桑田欲变时,
风涛翻覆沸天池。
鲸吞蛟斗波成血,
深涧游鱼乐不知。

Fishes in the Mountain Stream

When seas turned into mulberry fields that's a great change,
Wind howling, waves roaring and seas boiling out of range.
Sharks mauling, dragons fighting and waves were bleeding,
But in the mountain stream happy were the fishes swimming.

游赵村杏花

赵村红杏每年开,
十五年来看几回。
七十三人难再到,
今春来是别花来。

A Spring Outing to a Village for Apricot Blossoms

Apricot blossoms in the village year after year bloom,
For fifteen years I have spared little time to roam.
At the age of seventy three my chance is slight,
Spring outing this year is my farewell to the charming sight.

梨园弟子

白头垂泪话梨园,
五十年前雨露恩。
莫问华清今日事,
满山红叶锁宫门。

The Palace Actors

Talking of the palace actors I'm old often in tears,
Since the emperor favored them it's been fifty years.
No need to learn anything about Huaqing Palace today,
Red leaves cover the hill you cannot find the gateway.

刘禹锡

刘禹锡(772~842),字梦得,洛阳人,祖籍中山(今河北定县)。曾在朝为官,后因参与政治革新运动(805年)而遭贬。刘禹锡工诗文,尤以七绝见长,神韵隽永。《全唐诗》存其诗十二卷。

Liu Yuxi (772~842), styled Mengde, was born in Luoyang, but his ancestral home was Zhongshan (Dingxian County, Hebei Province today). Liu served as a senior official in the court for years, but was demoted later for his participation in political innovation (805). He was well versed in poetry and prose writing, quatrain in particular. His poems are pregnant with authentic essence in graceful style, of which twelve volumes are collected in *The Complete Collection of the Tang Poetry*.

庭竹

露涤铅粉节,
风摇青玉枝。
依依似君子,
无地不相宜。

Bamboo in the Courtyard

The powdered joints are wet with dewdrops,
Your green twigs sway in wind with easy grace.
Dancing with light steps you bow your slim tops,
East or west it can grows well in any place.

唐郎中宅与诸公同饮酒看牡丹

今日花前饮,
甘心醉数杯。
但愁花有语,
不为老人开。

Feasting My Eyes on Peonies While Drinking

Among flowers I am drinking today,
Willing to be drunk I'm carried away.
I'm afraid flowers have something to say,
But refuse to bloom for my hair turns gray.

秋风引

何处秋风至,
萧萧送雁群。
朝来入庭树,
孤客最先闻。

The Autumn Breeze

From where comes the autumn breeze?
Soughs and sighs it sends off wild geese.
At dawn it strokes the courtyard trees,
The lonely stranger first hears and sees.

柳花词

晴天阁阁雪,
来送青春暮。
无意似多情,
千家万家去。

Song of Willow Catkins

Like snowflakes you float slowly on a sunny day,
In company with spring when it's fading away.
Simple and innocent you seem sentimental,
Here, there and everywhere happily you play.

九日登高

世路山河险，
君门烟雾深。
年年上高处，
未省不伤心。

Climbing Mountains on the Double Ninth Festival

Life is a journey full of ups and downs,
In the royal court they scramble for crowns.
Year after year I ascend a height,
But all the time I'm in a sorrow plight.

别苏州

流水阊门外,
秋风吹柳条。
从来送客去,
今日自魂销。

Farewell to Suzhou

Outside the Changmen Gate a stream flows,
Willow twigs sway as autumn wind blows.
I've given send-off here to many friends,
But my soul today flies away with fiends.

再游玄都观

百亩庭中半是苔，
桃花净尽菜花开。
种桃道士归何处，
前度刘郎今又来。

The Second Tour to Xuandu Taoist Temple

Half of the temple courtyard is covered by moss,
No peach blossoms now but rape flowers are blooming.
Where to find the peach tree planter I'm at a loss,
For the second tour to the temple I'm coming.

望夫石

终日望夫夫不归,
化为孤石苦相思。
望来已是几千载,
只似当时初望时。

A Woman-like Stone Pining for Husband

Pining for her husband all day long but he's out of sight,
Reduced to a stone she is still missing day and night.
For thousands of years she's been yearning for his return,
Never giving up she keeps gazing afar upright.

石头城

山围故国周遭在，
潮打空城寂寞回。
淮水东边旧时月，
夜深还过女墙来。

The Ruins of the Stone Town

Around the ancient capital the mountains still stand high,
Crashing against the ancient walls tides ebb and fade away.
To the east of the Huai River the moon looms in the sky,
At dead of night on the parapet it still shines today.

乌衣巷

朱雀桥边野草花,
乌衣巷口夕阳斜。
旧时王谢堂前燕,
飞入寻常百姓家。

The Black-dress Street

Beside the Red-bird Bridge grass and flowers overgrow,
At the gate of Black-dress Street the setting sun slants low.
Swallows that used to nest in the mansions of the reach,
Now haunt the houses of the common folks to and fro.

台城

台城六代竞豪华，
结绮临春事最奢。
万户千门成野草，
只缘一曲后庭花。

The Ruins of the Former Capital

The most splendid was Taicheng Palace in the past,
Peerless are Jieyi and Linchun Palaces by contrast.
Thousands of old palaces are buried in weeds today,
It's *The Song of Backyard Flowers* that destroys them at last.

杨柳枝

春江一曲柳千条,
二十年前旧板桥。
曾与美人桥上别,
恨无消息到今朝。

Song of Willow Twigs

Thousands of willows see the winding river flow,
On the old wooden bridge a score of years ago.
A tearful parting from a belle on the bridge then,
No news from her and her whereabouts I don't know.

杏园花下酬乐天见赠

二十馀年作逐臣，
归来还见曲江春。
游人莫笑白头醉，
老醉花间有几人。

In the Apricot Garden for Letian*

I was demoted over twenty years ago,
Back to Chang'an spring is very much on the wane.
Don't laugh at a grey-haired man tipsy in this vein,
How many drunkards among flowers you don't know.

---

* Letian here refers to Bai Juyi, a great poet.

堤上行

江南江北望烟波,
入夜行人相应歌。
桃叶传情竹枝怨,
水流无限月明多。

Walking Along the Dike

Misty water in sight stretches far and vast,
Travelers start responding with songs at night.
Folk songs pour out the mixed feelings at last,
Water flows far away and the moon is bright.

踏歌行

春江月出大堤平,
堤上女郎连袂行。
唱尽新词看不见,
红霞影树鹧鸪鸣。

Song of Step Dance

The river dike in spring extends far at moonrise,
Hand in hand on the dike beauties are singing high.
At the end of new songs no gallant meets their eyes,
Crimson clouds tinge the trees and francolins cry.

宋　马远　《踏歌图》

秋词

自古逢秋悲寂寥，
我言秋日胜春朝。
晴空一鹤排云上，
便引诗情到碧霄。

To Autumn Season

Desolate autumn leads to poets' gloom for thousands of years,
But I don't think spring is nicer than autumn as it appears.
A beautiful crane flying freely across the clear sky,
Gives rise to poetic inspiration from the heaven high.

竹枝词·其一

山桃红花满上头,
蜀江春水拍山流。
花红易衰似郎意,
水流无限似侬愁。

Song of Bamboo Branches (1)

Peach blossoms bloom all over the mountain,
Lashing the rocks spring water quickly flows.
Like flowers fading fast his love's not certain,
My sorrow like an endless river grows and grows.

竹枝词·其二

日出三竿春雾消,
江头蜀客驻兰桡。
凭寄狂夫书一纸,
信在成都万里桥。

Song of Bamboo Branches (2)

The sun rises three poles high and spring mist slips away,
On the painted boat the businessmen from Chengdu stay.
I request a letter taken to my husband by them,
Wanli Bridge in Chengdu is the fixed address today.

竹枝词·其三

山上层层桃李花，
云间烟火是人家。
银钏金钗来负水，
长刀短笠去烧畲。

Song of Bamboo Branches (3)

On the mountain slopes peach and plum blossoms are in bloom,
Smoke curls up from the clouds and the roofs of cottages loom.
Gold-and-silver-adorned women draw water from spring,
Men in straw hats are busy burning weeds for farming.

竹枝词·其四

杨柳青青江水平，
闻郎江上唱歌声。
东边日出西边雨，
道是无晴却有晴。

Song of Bamboo Branches (4)

Flanked by green willows the river flows along,
I heard my darling aboard the ship sing a song.
It's sunny in the east but raining in the west,
Like weather he seems but I know he loves me best.

杨柳枝词·其一

金谷园中莺乱飞,
铜驼陌上好风吹。
城东桃李须臾尽,
争似垂杨无限时。

Song of Willow Twigs (1)

Freely flying are the orioles in the grand garden,
Gently blowing is the spring wind along the road side.
In the east of the town flowers have quickly fallen,
But it's the best time for willows to grow far and wide.

杨柳枝词·其二

城外春风吹酒旗，
行人挥袂日西时。
长安陌上无穷树，
唯有垂杨绾别离。

Song of Willow Twigs (2)

Outside the capital wine shop streamers flutter in breeze,
Travelers are waving farewell as the sun's slanting west.
The road to Chang'an is flanked by varieties of trees,
But only the willow branch can mark the sad parting best.

杨柳枝词 · 其三

轻盈袅娜占年华,
舞榭妆楼处处遮。
春尽絮花留不得,
随风好去落谁家?

Song of Willow Twigs (3)

In the prime of the year you lithely sway with grace,
Thick with leaves you cover halls all over the place.
Spring is on the wane and your catkins fly away,
Gone with wind I don't know where you finally stay.

浪淘沙·其一

九曲黄河万里沙，
浪淘风簸自天涯。
如今真上银河去，
同到牵牛织女家。

Song of Waves Sifting Sand（1）

The Yellow River winds through boundless sands beyond sight,
Slapping by wind and waves it flows forward from the sky.
Now it goes up to the Milky Way at a great height,
And helps the Cowherd and the Weaver Maid drawing nigh.

浪淘沙·其二

洛水桥边春日斜,
碧流轻浅见琼沙。
无端陌上狂风急,
惊起鸳鸯出浪花。

Song of Waves Sifting Sand (2)

Beside the Tianjin Bridge the spring sun slants west,
In the clear and shallow river the sand is bright.
All of sudden a high wind springs up the road,
Mandarin ducks startled from the waves take flight.

浪淘沙·其三

鹦鹉洲头浪飐沙,
青楼春望日将斜。
衔泥燕子争归舍,
独自狂夫不忆家。

Song of Waves Sifting Sand (3)

Waves slap the sand on the Parrot Sandbar,
Gazing in spring the sun slants from the boudoir.
On the way home swallows are busy nesting,
But no news about my darling from afar.

伤愚溪

溪水悠悠春自来,
草堂无主燕飞回。
隔帘惟见中庭草,
一树山榴依旧开。

A Sentimental Attachment to Yuxi Stream

The stream smoothly flows and the spring is ushered in,
No host in the hall but swallows home on the own.
Nothing but grass in the yard is seen through the screen,
A pomegranate tree blooms as usual alone.

和乐天春词

新妆宜面下朱楼,
深锁春光一院愁。
行到中庭数花朵,
蜻蜓飞上玉搔头。

A Song of Spring in Reply to Bai Juyi

Out of the mansion newly made-up she comes downstairs,
Locked in the courtyard she's sorrow-laden in spring.
In the middle of the yard she counts flowers in pairs,
Flying to her jade hairpin a dragonfly's to cling.

重答柳柳州

弱冠同怀长者忧，
临岐回想尽悠悠。
耦耕若便遗身老，
黄发相看万事休。

A Poem in Reply to Liu Zongyuan Again

At the age of twenty like the senior we're in sorrow,
At the parting of the ways the road was endless to go.
If we live to retire and return to our native land,
Ending up in nothing but our hair turns grey and yellow.

韩信庙

将略兵机命世雄,
苍黄钟室叹良弓。
遂令后代登坛者,
每一寻思怕立功。

Han Xin* Temple

As a commander of great strategy he's second to none,
Entrapped and killed in the court his credit's number one.
To those who will be appointed general that's a warning,
To make contribution or not that is really confusing.

---

* Han Xin (? ~196 BC), born in Huaiyin (Huaiyin City, Jiangsu Province today), was a military expert and one of the founding fathers of the Han Dynasty, who was entrapped and killed in Changle Palace as he was falsely charged with rebellion after Liu Bang came into power as the first emperor of the Han Dynasty.

尝茶

生拍芳丛鹰觜芽，
老郎封寄谪仙家。
今宵更有湘江月，
照出菲菲满碗花。

Sipping Tea

Picked from the fragrant bushes the tea is best,
An old monk sent to me at demotion to test.
Bright is the moon over the Xiang River tonight,
Tea buds in the cup like flowers in the moonlight.

望洞庭

湖光秋月两相和,
潭面无风镜未磨。
遥望洞庭山水翠,
白银盘里一青螺。

A Distant View of Dongting Lake

The lake is shimmering in the autumn moonlight,
Windless the lake water's like a big mirror bright.
The hill amid water adds charm to lake from afar,
Like a green conch in a large plate silver-white.

柳宗元

柳宗元(773~819),字子厚,河东(今山西永济)人。曾在朝为官,后遭贬谪。散文与韩愈齐名,诗歌与韦应物并称。诗风清新凄婉。《全唐诗》存其诗四卷。

Liu Zongyuan (773~819), styled Zihou, was born in Hedong (Yongji County, Shanxi Province today). Liu was a senior government official when he was young but demoted to a prefect later. He enjoyed equal fame with Han Yu in prose writing and with Wei Yingwu in poem. His quatrains were composed with plaintive voice in vigorous style. There are four volumes of his poems collected in *The Complete Collection of the Tang Poetry*.

江雪

千山鸟飞绝,
万径人踪灭。
孤舟蓑笠翁,
独钓寒江雪。

Angling in Snow

Over mountains no bird in flight,
Along paths no figure in sight.
A fisherman in straw rain coat,
Angling in snow in a lone boat.

登柳州峨山

荒山秋日午，
独上意悠悠。
如何望乡处，
西北是融州。

Climbing Mount E in Liuzhou

Climbing the mountain at noon on an autumn day,
Alone with no mate I'm in growing dismay.
For my native place I'm looking far and wide,
But Rongzhou in the northwest there's nothing beside.

清　龚贤　《木叶丹黄图》

重别梦得

二十年来万事同，
今朝歧路忽西东。
皇恩若许归田去，
晚岁当为邻舍翁。

Farewell to Liu Yuxi After the Last Parting

For a score and two years we are of the same fate,
To east and west different courses we'll take.
If the emperor allows to resign for farming,
We should be good neighbors for the years remaining.

柳州二月榕叶落尽偶题

宦情羁思共凄凄，
春半如秋意转迷。
山城过雨百花尽，
榕叶满庭莺乱啼。

Liuzhou in Mid-spring

Official life and nostalgia set me in sad plight,
Like autumn mid spring makes me give a gloomy sigh.
Too much rain to the flowers here is a fatal blight,
Banyan leaves cover the courtyard and orioles cry.

姚 合

姚合(约775～约846),陕州硖石(今河南陕县)人。元和十一年进士,曾在朝为官。其诗多反映日常生活和自然景色,风格与贾岛相似。《全唐诗》存其诗七卷。

Yao He (about 775～about 846), born in Xiashi Shanzhou (Shanxian County, Henan Province today), began his official career after he passed the palace examination in 816. His poems mainly mirror daily life and natural scenery, which are very much similar to Jia Dao's poems in style. Seven volumes of his poems are collected in *The Complete Collection of the Tang Poetry*.

古碑

荒田一片石,
文字满青苔。
不是逢闲客,
何人肯读来。

A Gravestone

A gravestone in the wasteland stands alone,
Moss-covered words are blurred on the stone.
Pay no attention to the stone you would,
Unless you are in a leisurely mood.

老马

卧来扶不起，
唯向主人嘶。
惆怅东郊道，
秋来雨作泥。

An Old Steed

Too weak to stand as it has lain for many days,
To its master the horse can do nothing but neighs.
Thinking of the road to the east suburb he's sad,
Rainy days in autumn make the roads muddy ways.

题鹤雏

羽毛生未齐,
嶙峭丑于鸡。
夜夜穿笼出,
捣衣砧上栖。

A Young Crane

Not yet fully fledged with its feathers white,
With a thin and ugly frame but it's of great height.
Passing through the hole of the cage every day,
It perches on the hammering block at night.

咏新菊

黄金色未足，
摘取且尝新。
若待重阳日，
何曾异众人。

To New Chrysanthemums

At the initial stage flowers are of light yellow,
I pick tender petals to try the taste in season.
On the Double Ninth Festival they will be sallow,
To taste the ordinary smell I have no reason.

春日游慈恩寺

年长归何处，
青山未有家。
赏春无酒饮，
多看寺中花。

A Spring Outing in an Old Temple

Advanced in age I wonder where to go,
Which mountain is my abode how can I know?
Having no wine even though spring is charming,
I can only feast my eyes on flowers blooming.

别杭州

醉与江涛别,
江涛惜我游。
他年婚嫁了,
终老此江头。

Farewell to Hangzhou

Tipsy I am to bid farewell to river waves,
Sad at the moment of parting is the big tide.
Some day when I'm over with my secular aims,
I'll make my final abode at the riverside.

秋中夜坐

疏散永无事,
不眠常夜分。
月中松露滴,
风引鹤同闻。

Stay Late at Mid-autumn Night

Totally relaxed I am free from care,
Oftentimes I stay awake at midnight.
Dew drips from pines in the moonlight so fair,
Cranes cry with the wind although it's light.

晦日送穷

送穷穷不去，
相泥欲何为。
今日官家宅，
淹留又几时。

Sending Away the Poverty Ghost on the Last Day of the First Lunar Month

To the ghost of poverty I've said goodbye,
But the poverty ghost lingers I don't know why.
In the official mansions up to this day,
How long I want to know you dare stay.

穷边词

将军作镇古汧州,
水腻山春节气柔。
清夜满城丝管散,
行人不信是边头。

Song of the Remote Frontier Town

The general garrisons the ancient town day and night,
Breeze is balmy with hill green, water clear and spring so bright.
In the dead of night strings are played all over the town,
Unbelieving the travelers are surprised with delight.

清　朱耷　《彩笔山水图》

杏园

江头数顷杏花开，
车马争先尽此来。
欲待无人连夜看，
黄昏树树满尘埃。

The Apricot Garden

By Qujiang Pond apricot blossoms are in full bloom,
In carriages tourists strive to be the first for the sight.
If you want to stay long enough for the view of night,
All the trees will be stained with dust in the dusk gloom.

对月

银轮玉兔向东流,
莹净三更正好游。
一片黑云何处起,
皂罗笼却水精球。

To the Moon

Bright is the moon floating eastward in the sky,
I'm in the mood for the soft shines at midnight.
But a mass of black cloud scuds quickly on high,
And soon the crystal ball is blocked from light.

杨柳枝词

叶叶如眉翠色浓,
黄莺偏恋语从容。
桥边陌上无人识,
雨湿烟和思万重。

Song of Willow Twigs

Like eyebrows are the vivid green willow leaves,
Fond of singing with ease are the orioles so proud.
By the roadside or bridge nobody takes notice,
In rain and mist willows seem deep in gloomy cloud.

夜期友生不至

忍寒停酒待君来，
酒作凌澌火作灰。
半夜出门重立望，
月明先自下高台。

Awaiting a Friend in Vain at Night

Stopping drinking I await you in the cold night,
Until wine is cold, fire goes out in the lamplight.
Outside my room I gaze far again at midnight,
In the dead of night slants to the west the moon bright.

元 稹

元稹(779~831),字微之,洛阳(今河南洛阳)人。元稹曾在朝为官,与白居易关系甚密,诗风相近。《全唐诗》存其诗二十八卷。

Yuan Zhen(779~831), styled Weizhi, was born in Luoyang (Luoyang City, Henan Province toady). Yuan once served as a senior government official and he was on good terms with Bai Juyi, a great realistic poet (772~846), even the style of his poems is similar to that of the latter. There are twenty-eight volumes of his poems collected in *The Complete Collection of the Tang Poetry*.

饮新酒

闻君新酒熟,
况值菊花秋。
莫怪平生志,
图销尽日愁。

Drinking Newly-brewed Wine

I'm informed you have brewed some wine,
It's time when chrysanthemums are so fine.
Don't blame me for drinking a huge swallow,
I want to be drunk and forget my sorrow.

雨后

倦寝数残更，
孤灯暗又明。
竹梢馀雨重，
时复拂帘惊。

After Rain

Staring at the hourglass I'm sick of sleep at night,
Now dim, now bright is the solitary lamp light.
Bent with rain drops the bamboo tops are hanging low,
Off rain drops they stroke the screen before I know.

行宫

寥落古行宫，
宫花寂寞红。
白头宫女在，
闲坐说玄宗。

The Imperial Palace

Deserted is the old palace in disrepair,
The pink palace flowers bloom alone in despair.
The palace maid of the old age with her hair white,
Gossips about the late emperor with delight.

菊花

秋丛绕舍似陶家,
遍绕篱边日渐斜。
不是花中偏爱菊,
此花开尽更无花。

Chrysanthemums

Autumn flowers around my cottage like that of Tao's house,
Along the twig fence until the sun slants I stroll for hours.
Not that I have a partiality for chrysanthemum,
But that it is the last flower blooming in late autumn.

晚春

昼静帘疏燕语频，
双双斗雀动阶尘。
柴扉日暮随风掩，
落尽闲花不见人。

Late Spring

Swallows are chirping in bliss through the thin screen,
Sparrows are fighting, their wings raising the dust.
Closed is the wicket gate with the wind at dusk,
Flowers are fading and no figure can be seen.

独醉

一树芳菲也当春,
漫随车马拥行尘。
桃花解笑莺能语,
自醉自眠那藉人。

Tipsy Alone

Fragrant flowers are blooming and grass green in spring,
Following the vehicles I'm in clouds of dust.
Peach blossoms are smiling and orioles muttering,
Drinking alone I'm drunk and sleeping is a must.

观心处

满座喧喧笑语频,
独怜方丈了无尘。
灯前便是观心处,
要似观心有几人。

A Deep Insight into the Mind

Filled to the brim with laughter and chat is the dome,
The abbot is the only one free from care in the room.
It is the very place to read your mind in the lamplight,
But few people among them can get the real insight.

使东川·江花落

日暮嘉陵江水东，
梨花万片逐江风。
江花何处最断肠，
半落江流半在空。

Visiting Dongchuan: Flowers Wafting over the River

Jialing River flows eastwards at sunset,
Thousands of pear petals with wind wafting.
The scene of heartbreaking most and upset,
Is that some petals are drifting and some floating.

使东川·梁州梦

梦君同绕曲江头，
也向慈恩院里游。
亭吏唤人排去马，
所惊身在古梁州。

Visiting Dongchuan: Dreaming in Liangzhou

Pacing with you around Qujiang Pond I'm in a dream,
Sightseeing in Ci'en Temple together we go.
The head of the posthouse sends for horse in the scheme,
Suddenly awaking to find that I'm in Liangzhou.

使东川·嘉陵驿

墙外花枝压短墙，
明月还照半张床。
无人会得此时意，
一夜独眠西畔廊。

Visiting Dongchuan: Jialing Post House

Over the short wall flowers are hanging low,
Half of the bed is bathed in the moonlight.
The implied meaning of the scene who can know?
In the West Chamber she sleeps alone at night.

使东川·嘉陵江

千里嘉陵江水声,
何年重绕此江行。
只应添得清宵梦,
时见满江流月明。

Visiting Dongchuan: The Jialing River

The sound of the Jialing River a thousand-mile long,
For river sight once more my desire is so strong.
Even if I have a dream in the dead of night,
At times I see the river bathed in the moonlight.

清　董邦达　《平湖秋月御题图》

岳阳楼

岳阳楼上日衔窗,
影到深潭赤玉幢。
怅望残春万般意,
满棂湖水入西江。

Yueyang Tower

Atop the Yueyang Tower the sun kisses the window,
Mirrored in the deep lake is a crimson jade rainbow.
Looking far into the distance spring is on the wane,
Into the Yangtze River I see the lake water flow.

离思

曾经沧海难为水，
除却巫山不是云。
取次花丛懒回顾，
半缘修道半缘君。

In Memory of My Dear Bereaved

Having sailed all seas I find no water is so vast,
Clouds over Mountain Wu are the grandeur of the past.
Charming enough are the flowers but I don't turn round,
For your grace rooted in my heart and Taoism will last.

远望

满眼伤心冬景和,
一山红树寺边多。
仲宣无限思乡泪,
漳水东流碧玉波。

A Distant Winter View

Gazing far and wide I'm sad with winter scene all my eyes,
All over the mountain red trees by the temple so nice.
Like Wang Can my heart is brimming over with homesickness,
Flowing eastwards Zhangshui River stretches to cloudless skies.

闻乐天授江州司马

残灯无焰影幢幢,
此夕闻君谪九江。
垂死病中惊坐起,
暗风吹雨入寒窗。

To Bai Juyi at His Demotion to an Assistant Prefect

Flickering are the flames and dim is the lamplight,
Informed of your demotion I'm surprised at night.
Dying on the sick leave I sit up all of sudden,
Chilly wind and rain beating the window cast a blight.

西归绝句

五年江上损容颜,
今日春风到武关。
两纸京书临水读,
小桃花树满商山。

Back to the Capital from the West

Demoted five years ago I was cast a heavy blight,
Good news comes today like the vernal breeze gentle and light.
Reading the letter from the capital by waterside,
Lifting my eyes I see peach blooms all over the hillside.

雨声

风吹竹叶休还动,
雨点荷心暗复明。
曾向西江船上宿,
惯闻寒夜滴篷声。

The Patter of Rain

Bamboo leaves are rustling gently in the wind.
The rain pats on the lotus leaves are soft and light.
Overnight stay on the river time and again,
I'm used to patter of rain on boat roof at night.

寒食日

今年寒食好风流,
此日一家同出游。
碧水青山无限思,
莫将心道是涪州。

On Cold Food Festival

I'm free and easy this year on the Cold Food Day,
The whole family go outing happy and gay.
Green hills and water evoke a long train of thought,
I think of the time I was on wedding array.

春词

山翠湖光似欲流,
蜂声鸟思却堪愁。
西施颜色今何在,
但看春风百草头。

A Spring Song

Verdant mountains mirrored in the lake brimming with charm,
Bees and birds seem in sorrow as they hum in alarm.
Gone are the days when Xi Shi the beauty was enchanting,
As the vernal breeze strokes plants flowers now are fading.

得乐天书

远信入门先有泪，
妻惊女哭问何如。
寻常不省曾如此，
应是江州司马书。

Reading the Letter from Bai Juyi

Reading the letter from afar I am in tears,
Very much surprised my family ask me why.
It's different from what's been usual in past years,
But for Letian's letter nothing can make him cry.

贾 岛

贾岛(779～843),字阆仙,范阳(今河北涿州)人。贾岛曾落拓为僧,还俗后,累试进士不第。其诗多苦寒之辞,注重词句锤炼,在晚唐、宋初颇有影响。《全唐诗》存其诗四卷。

Jia Dao(779～843), styled Langxian, was born in Fanyang (Zhuozhou City, Hebei Province toady). Frustrated and depressed, Jia once became a monk, but resumed secular life later and failed in the imperial examinations time and again. Jia spared no effort to whet the words of his poems which exerted a great influence on the poets of the late Tang Dynasty and early Song Dynasty. Four volumes of his poems are collected in *The Complete Collection of the Tang Poetry*.

剑客

十年磨一剑,
霜刃未曾试。
今日把示君,
谁有不平事。

To a Swordsman

I have whetted my sword for ten years,
I wonder if it's sharp enough to pierce.
To you I'd like to show its blade today,
For justice I can ensure fair play.

宿悬泉驿

晓行沥水楼,
暮到悬泉驿。
林月值云遮,
山灯照愁寂。

An Overnight Stay at Xuanquan Post House

From Lishui Tower I start off in the morning,
At Xuanquan post house I lodge for the night.
The moon over the woods is hidden in the clouds,
Mountain lights loom and I am in a lonely plight.

元　王蒙　《具区林屋图》

壮士吟

壮士不曾悲，
悲即无回期。
如何易水上，
未歌先泪垂。

The Song of a Hero

"I am not sad," the hero said, "never",
Once he starts he has no return chance.
But why? By the side of Yishui River,
Tears run down his cheeks before he chants.

绝句

海底有明月，
圆于天上轮。
得之一寸光，
可买千里春。

A Quatrain

At the bottom of the sea the moon is bright,
Which is more round than the moon in the sky.
Precious are its beams, with an inch of the light,
Even a thousand miles of spring you can buy.

口号

中夜忽自起，
汲此百尺泉。
林木含白露，
星斗在青天。

An Extempore Verse

I get up all of sudden at midnight,
My poetic mood flows like spring from on high.
Wet are the trees with sparkling dew drops white,
Thousands of stars are twinkling in the sky.

送别

丈夫未得意，
行行且低眉。
素琴弹复弹，
会有知音知。

Send-off to a Friend

Frustrated but you're a man of ambition,
Walking, bowing your head in meditation.
Playing your zither time and again in sorrow,
As your close friend the implied meaning I know.

雨中怀友人

对雨思君子，
尝茶近竹幽。
儒家邻古寺，
不到又逢秋。

Good Memories of My Friend in Rain

The misty rain brings back my memories of you,
Sipping tea near green bamboos that lushly grow.
Near an old temple your home is of scholar-style,
How time flies the autumn comes before I know.

寄远

家住锦水上，
身征辽海边。
十书九不到，
一到忽经年。

A Letter from Afar

By the river near Chengdu is my abode,
I'm fighting on the battlefield far away.
Nine letters out of ten fail to reach me,
A letter usually comes on a long delay.

访隐者不遇

松下问童子，
言师采药去。
只在此山中，
云深不知处。

A Vain Visit to a Recluse

Under the pine tree I asked the lad,
"My master is out for herbs," he said.
"Somewhere in the mountains," he told me,
"But deep in clouds nobody could see."

昆明池泛舟

一枝青竹榜，
泛泛绿萍里。
不见钓鱼人，
渐入秋塘水。

Boating on Kunming Lake

I'm pulling on an oar of bamboo green,
Rippling through the duckweed the boat comes in.
The angler now is nowhere to be seen,
On and on the boat enters the pond serene.

哭孟东野

兰香无气鹤无声,
哭尽秋天月不明。
自从东野先生死,
侧近云山得散行。

An Elegy to Meng Jiao

No fragrance wafts from orchids and cranes stop singing,
Weeping through autumn the moon is by no means bright.
Before your death I had no courage to write poem,
But now I dare to write poems on the autumn sight.

送僧

池上时时松雪落，
焚香烟起见孤灯。
静夜忆谁来对坐，
曲江南岸寺中僧。

To a Monk

Falling into pond is the snow from pines from time to time,
Through the smoke of incense I see a solitary light.
Often sitting face to face with me at the dead of night,
Is the monk from the lakeside temple whose bearing's sublime.

崔卿池上鹤

月中时叫叶纷纷，
不异洞庭霜夜闻。
翎羽如今从放长，
犹能飞起向孤云。

A Crane on the Pond

Leaves are falling with your singing when the moon is bright,
It is a commonplace on Donting Lake at frosty night.
Fully-fledged are your plumes if they are well-preserved,
You'd be strong enough to fly to the lone cloud at great height.

渡桑干

客舍并州已十霜,
归心日夜忆咸阳。
无端更渡桑干水,
却望并州是故乡。

Crossing Sanggan River

I took up my abode in Bingzhou ten years ago,
Desire to return to Xianyang is itching day and night.
Crossing Sanggan River for the reason I don't know,
Pining for my home but only Bingzhou is in sight.

夜期啸客吕逸人不至

逸人期宿石床中，
遣我开扉对晚空。
不知何处啸秋月，
闲著松门一夜风。

A Vain Wait for a Hermit at Night

The hermit covets a stone bed for an overnight stay,
He asks me to leave the gate open at night today.
Somewhere he must be sighing over the autumn moonlight,
Leave the door wide open and the wind blowing all night.

题兴化园亭

破却千家作一池,
不栽桃李种蔷薇。
蔷薇花落秋风起,
荆棘满庭君始知。

A Prime Minister's Garden

Thousands of homes levelled for a pond in his garden,
No fruit trees planted only wild roses can be seen.
When bleak wind blows in autumn and roses fade away,
Thorny bushes all over the yard what would you say?

竹

篱外清阴接药栏,
晓风交戛碧琅玕。
子猷没后知音少,
粉节霜筠漫岁寒。

To Bamboo

Outside the fence fresh shade stretches to the herb garden,
Beating each other in the dawn wind are your poles clean.
You have no alter ego since Ziyou* passed away,
Throughout the cold winter white with rime your joints turn grey.

---

* Ziyou refers to Wang Huizhi (about 303~about 361), born in Linyi (Linyi City, Shandong Province today) in the Eastern Jin Dynasty, who is the son of Wang Xizhi, a famous calligrapher, and fond of bamboo exceptionally.

客思

促织声尖尖似针,
更深刺著旅人心。
独言独语月明里,
惊觉眠童与宿禽。

Homesickness

Chirping, chirping, crickets' peep is really annoying,
For the travelers in a strange land it's so grating.
Muttering to no one but myself in the moonlight,
Waking up from sleep are the boy and fowl at night.

题隐者居

虽有柴门长不关,
片云孤木伴身闲。
犹嫌住久人知处,
见拟移家更上山。

A Verse to a Hermit

To his cottage often left ajar is the wicket gate,
With floating clouds and a lone tree he has more leisure time.
Considering dwelling long he would be known sometime late,
He plans to move to a mountain higher for a life prime.

经苏秦墓

沙埋古篆折碑文,
六国兴亡事系君。
今日凄凉无处说,
乱山秋尽有寒云。

A Verse to Su Qin's Tomb

Buried in sand is the inscription on your tombstone old,
Rise and fall of six states are due to your implication.
All over your graveyard is a scene of desolation,
In late autumn the wild mountains are shrouded in clouds cold.

夏夜登南楼

水岸寒楼带月跻,
夏林初见岳阳溪。
一点新萤报秋信,
不知何处是菩提。

A Summer Night View atop the South Tower

Climbing the waterside tower in the moonlight,
By the summer woods Yueyang Stream is just in sight.
A dot of new firefly signals the fresh autumn,
To attain Bodhi I'm looking around at night.

唐人绝句精粹
中英文版
A Translation of the Choice Tang Quatrains

下卷
Volume Three

献给共和国七十华诞

周方珠 编译

By Zhou Fangzhu

北京师范大学出版集团
BEIJING NORMAL UNIVERSITY PUBLISHING GROUP
安徽大学出版社

下卷目录
Catalogue of Volume Three

施肩吾 …… 1	李商隐 …… 236
张　祜 …… 35	李群玉 …… 267
李德裕 …… 58	卢　肇 …… 289
李　贺 …… 63	罗　隐 …… 292
徐　凝 …… 78	韦　庄 …… 296
许　浑 …… 99	司空图 …… 298
卢　仝 …… 120	陆龟蒙 …… 309
马　戴 …… 125	皮日休 …… 324
崔道融 …… 129	雍　陶 …… 328
杜　牧 …… 151	韩　偓 …… 335
赵　嘏 …… 201	王　驾 …… 345
陈　陶 …… 219	杜荀鹤 …… 347
温庭筠 …… 226	黄　巢 …… 350

译后记 …………………………… 352

施肩吾

施肩吾(780~861),字希圣,号东斋,睦州分水(今浙江桐庐)人。好诗酒,重仙道,元和十五年(820年)登进士第后,便隐居于洪州西山。诗作奇丽,善于言情。《全唐诗》存其诗一卷。

Shi Jianwu(780~861), styled Xisheng, also known as Dongzhai, his courtesy name, was born in Fenshui, Muzhou (Tonglu City, Zhejiang Province today). Shi lived in seclusion after he successfully passed the imperial examination in 820 during the reign of Emperor Xianzong and he was very much fond of drinking and keen on immortality. His poems are lyric and romantic with well-chosen words in unique style, of which one volume is collected in *The Complete Collection of the Tang Poetry*.

秋山吟

夜吟秋山上,
袅袅秋风归。
月色清且冷,
桂香落人衣。

Song in the Autumn Mountain

I'm singing in the autumn mountain at night,
Gentle is the autumn wind soft and light.
Sweet scent of laurel flowers waft around,
Chilly are the beams of the moon so bright.

惜花

落尽万株红，
无人解系风。
今朝芳径里，
惆怅锦机空。

Tender Feeling for Flowers

All flowers have fallen into decay,
Who knows it's the wind that blows them away.
Walking along the fragrant path today,
Nowhere in sight is the charming array.

夜愁曲

歌者歌未绝,
愁人愁转增。
空把琅玕枝,
强挑无心灯。

Song of Sorrow at Night

Of their singing the singers are at the height,
Pacing to and fro my sorrow grows at night.
Holding a needle of jade in my fingers,
I try to pick the hollow lamp wick more bright.

湘竹词

万古湘江竹，
无穷奈怨何。
年年长春笋，
只是泪痕多。

Song of Mottled Bamboos

Oh, throughout ages mottled bamboos grow,
Alas, always growing up in sorrow.
Year after year bamboo shoots grow in spring,
But many tear stains mark the mottled skin.

湘川怀古

湘水终日流，
湘妃昔时哭。
美色已成尘，
泪痕犹在竹。

Meditations by the Xiang River

The Xiang River flows and flows day and night,
By the river Concubine Xiang wept in the past.
The beauty passed away and turned to dust,
But the tear stains on bamboos forever last.

及第后夜访月仙子

自喜寻幽夜，
新当及第年。
还将天上桂，
来访月中仙。

A Night Visit to the Moon Nymph After Passing the Imperial Examination

Joy at passing the imperial exam,
I'm roaming around at the still night.
To present my laurel wreath I am,
To the nymph in the moon with delight.

瀑布

豁开青冥颠,
泻出万丈泉。
如裁一条素,
白日悬秋天。

To Cataract

Splitting the mountain peak extremely high,
The cataract pours out from the sky.
Hanging like a long and wide ribbon white,
From the autumn sky of a great height.

幽居乐

万籁不在耳，
寂寥心境清。
无妨数茎竹，
时有萧萧声。

Song of a Secluded Life

All sounds are hushed and I can hear nothing,
It's quiet and still I am in a peace of mind.
Numbering bamboo stems I enjoy counting,
From time to time there's rustle of every kind.

春日美新绿词

前日萌芽小于粟，
今朝草树色已足。
天公不语能运为，
驱遣羲和染新绿。

Song of Fresh Green in Charming Spring

Like seeds of millet were the buds the other day,
But grass and trees are verdantly dressed today.
Heaven keeps silent yet it works in His own way,
It sends the God of Day for a fresh green array.

帝宫词

自得君王宠爱时,
敢言春色上寒枝。
十年宫里无人问,
一日承恩天下知。

Song of the Imperial Palace

Since I find favor in emperor's eyes,
He makes a pet of me at any price.
I was nobody in the court for ten years,
But well-known as the king to me is so nice.

海边远望

扶桑枝边红皎皎,
天鸡一声四溟晓。
偶看仙女上青天,
鸾鹤无多采云少。

A Distant View from the Seaside

Near the super-tree is the vermilion-tinted sky,
As the cock crows in the Heaven it dawns far and wide.
By chance I see the fairy dancing freely on high,
Riding a phoenix in the blue sky sitting astride.

望晓词

揽衣起兮望秋河,
濛濛远雾飞轻罗。
蟠桃树上日欲出,
白榆枝畔星无多。

Gazing at Dawn

Putting on my gown I gaze at the Milky Way,
Mist floating at distance looks like fine gauze at play.
At the top of flat peach tree the sun is to rise,
Near the huge elm tree few stars twinkle like bright eyes.

杜鹃花词

杜鹃花时夭艳然,
所恨帝城人不识。
丁宁莫遣春风吹,
留与佳人比颜色。

Song of Azaleas

Bright and enchanting are azaleas when they're blooming,
It's a pity people in the capital know nothing.
I pray spring wind again and again to stop blowing,
To match the beauty with scarlet color so charming.

叹花词

前日满林红锦遍，
今日绕林看不见。
空馀古岸泥土中，
零落胭脂两三片。

A Sigh over Fallen Flowers

There was a riot of color in the woods the other day,
But here and there flowers are nowhere to be seen today.
They are mixed into the soil along the ancient bank,
Only a few petals like rouge are still dancing away.

秋夜山居

去雁声遥人语绝，
谁家素机织新雪。
秋山野客醉醒时，
百尺老松衔半月。

An Autumn Night Stay in the Mountain

Silence prevails as the wild geese fly out of sight,
Mountains and fields are shrouded in frost at night.
Sobering up from the drunken stupor at last,
I see branches of an old pine grip the moon bright.

山中送友人

欲折杨柳别恨生,
一重枝上一啼莺。
乱山重叠云相掩,
君向乱山何处行。

Farewell to a Friend in the Mountain

Grief grows in my bosom at the time of parting,
An oriole's crying at the top of the willow.
Rolling hills and mountains are wrapped in the clouds,
My friend, you have to decide which course to follow.

宋　王诜　《烟江叠嶂图》(局部)

春日餐霞阁

洒水初晴物候新，
餐霞阁上最宜春。
山花四面风吹入，
为我铺床作锦茵。

The Fairy Pavilion in Spring

Warm is the sunshine after rain and new season fresh,
Through the Fairy Pavilion spring breeze kisses my flesh.
Petals of the mountain flowers wafting from all sides,
Make the bed for me a snug flower mattress so nice.

喜友再相逢

三十年前与君别，
可怜容色夺花红。
谁知日月相催促，
此度见君成老翁。

A Happy Reunion with a Friend

We parted from each other thirty years ago,
In your prime you looked sweet with a rosy glow.
But how time flies and years slip before we know,
This time as we meet old you are wan and sallow.

观舞女

缠红结紫畏风吹,
袅娜初回弱柳枝。
买笑未知谁是主,
万人心逐一人移。

Watching a Dancing Girl's Performance

Gorgeously dressed she is delicate enough,
Graceful and slim she looks like a twig of willow.
Sparing no effort to flirt, with whom she dallies,
Her steps of dancing cause the audience to follow.

山居乐

鸾鹤每于松下见，
笙歌常向坐中闻。
手持十节龙头杖，
不指虚空即指云。

Joys of a Secluded Life

Swans and cranes are often seen under the pine trees,
Music and singing are the daily items of ours.
A dragon-shaped walking stick in hand I'm of bliss,
Towards the sky I can touch the clouds at all hours.

归将吟

百战放归成老翁,
馀生得出死人中。
今朝授敕三回舞,
两赐青娥又拜公。

Song of a General on His Return with Glory

Permitted to return from battlefield my hair turns white,
I'm old but surviving all the battles by a hair breadth.
The imperial decree in hand I go wild with delight,
Duke is bestowed on me and the award of palace maids.

少妇游春词

簇锦攒花斗胜游,
万人行处最风流。
无端自向春园里,
笑摘青梅叫阿侯。

A Young Lady on Her Spring Outing

Gorgeously dressed is the lady with lots of glamour,
Like a crane among chickens she is full of flavor.
Heading for the spring garden in spite of herself,
Picking plum with a smile she calls her son to come over.

惜花词

千树繁红绕碧泉，
正宜尊酒对芳年。
明朝欲饮还来此，
只怕春风却在前。

A Tender Love for Flowers

Around the clear spring are the flowers in full bloom,
It's the very time for the young to drink in their prime.
Tomorrow I'll come here to drink again if I roam,
But I'm afraid spring wind will blow them off in no time.

长安早春

报花消息是春风,
未见先教何处红。
想得芳园十馀日,
万家身在画屏中。

Early Spring in Chang'an

Spring breeze is the harbinger of flowers blooming,
But flowers are nowhere to be seen as spring's coming.
The imperial garden will be a sweet spot in ten days,
All courtyards then will be dressed in charming arrays.

春霁

煎茶水里花千片，
候客亭中酒一樽。
独对春光还寂寞，
罗浮道士忽敲门。

A Fine Day After the Spring Rain

Thousands of sweet buds in the spring water of tea pot,
A jar of wine ready for guests at the scenic spot.
All alone in the scene of spring I feel quite lonely,
A sudden knock at the door but I find a Taoist only.

寄隐者

路绝空林无处问,
幽奇山水不知名。
松门拾得一片屐,
知是高人向此行。

To a Recluse

Cut off from the world no path in the woods can be found,
Wonderful mountains and still streams are nameless to me.
Through the pine woods I pick up a piece of clog from the ground,
I know it's a noble recluse the visitor must be.

观美人

漆点双眸鬓绕蝉,
长留白雪占胸前。
爱将红袖遮娇笑,
往往偷开水上莲。

To a Belle

Between hairs on her temples are shining eyes bright,
Beneath the neck is her delicate bosom snow-white.
Smiles on her face are often screened with sleeves,
So charming is the belle with a chuckle of delight.

佳人览镜

每坐台前见玉容,
今朝不与昨朝同。
良人一夜出门宿,
减却桃花一半红。

A Belle Looking at Herself in the Mirror

Wherever I look at myself in the mirror,
I can find something different than ever.
If my love leaves home for an overnight stay,
Like a flower I would be soon fading away.

下第春游

羁情含蘖复含辛，
泪眼看花只似尘。
天遣春风领春色，
不教分付与愁人。

Spring Outing After Failure in the Imperial Examination

Homesick in a strange land I'm living in misery,
In my eyes filled with tears flowers are dust and grime.
Coming with the vernal breeze is the spring scenery,
But to me stricken by failure it's nothing but rime.

宿兰若

听钟投宿入孤烟，
岩下病僧犹坐禅。
独夜客心何处是，
秋云影里一灯然。

An Overnight Stay in a Temple

The bell leads me to the temple where smoke curls up,
In meditation under the rock a sick monk sits up.
Quite lonely I feel my mind seems wandering at night,
Flickering in autumn clouds looms a solitary light.

赠施仙姑

缥缈吾家一女仙，
冰容虽小不知年。
有时频夜看明月，
心在嫦娥几案边。

To Nymph Shi

Graceful and sweet is the nymph of my clan,
At a tender age she is so pure and fair.
Staring at the bright moon as long as she can,
On the Goddess of the Moon her mind is there.

秋夜山中赠别友人

何处邀君话别情，
寒山木落月华清。
莫愁今夜无诗思，
已听秋猿第一声。

Farewell to a Friend at Autumn Night in the Mountain

Where is the proper spot to bid farewell to you?
In the cold mountain leaves fall and the moon's bright.
No need to worry about poetic mood tonight,
The first yelp meets my ear and autumn is on view.

禁中新柳

万条金线带春烟，
深染青丝不直钱。
又免生当离别地，
宫鸦啼处禁门前。

New Willows in the Imperial Palace

Thousands of willow twigs are swaying in the spring mist,
Green hairs of willows are not valuable in the least.
Removed from my position at the spot of parting,
At the gate of the palace I hear a crow crying.

张 祐

张祐(785～852),字承吉,南阳(今河南南阳)人。其诗清幽淡雅,情致婉约。《全唐诗》存其诗两卷。

Zhang Hu (785～852), styled Chengji, was born in Nanyang (Nanyang City, Henan Province today). Grace and appeal are characteristics of his poems which are simple but elegant in style, two volumes of which are collected in *The Complete Collection of the Tang Poetry*.

宫词

故国三千里,
深宫二十年。
一声何满子,
双泪落君前。

An Elegy Poured out

Oh, my native land, a thousand miles away,
In the deep court I'm caged for a score of years.
An elegy is poured out with dismay today,
Before the king how can I hold back my tears?

昭君怨

万里边城远，
千山行路难。
举头唯见日，
何处是长安？

Wang Zhaojun's Grievance

The border town is ten thousand miles away,
Rough is the mountain path she's plodding her way.
Looking up she sees nothing but the sun in the sky,
Where is Chang'an the capital she gives a deep sigh.

明　戴进　《关山行旅图》

苏小小歌

新人千里去，
故人千里来。
剪刀横眼底，
方觉泪难裁。

A Song to Su Xiaoxiao, a Famous Singing Girl

New playboys left and they went far away,
The old ones came from afar day after day.
Before her very eyes there's a pair of shears,
But she could hardly use it to cut her tears.

襄阳乐

大堤花月夜,
长江春水流。
东风正上信,
春夜特来游。

A Song of Xiangyang

Flowers bloom along the banks in the moonlight,
Spring tide in Yangtze River is just at its height.
Vernal breeze comes into season mild and gentle,
I'm carried away with the charming scene at night.

梦江南

行吟洞庭句,
不见洞庭人。
尽日碧江梦,
江南红树春。

Dreaming of the South of Yangtze River

Chanting his poem lines I'm strolling along,
Yearning to see the poet for whom I long.
Dreaming of the limpid water day and night,
Looking for spring dyed with flowers red and bright.

集灵台

虢国夫人承主恩,
平明骑马入宫门。
却嫌脂粉污颜色,
淡扫蛾眉朝至尊。

The Longevity Palace

Summoned to the palace was the imperial grace,
The Duchess of Guo State rode the gate of palace.
Too much rouge and powder might spoil her beauty,
With light make-up on brows she met His Majesty.

题金陵渡

金陵津渡小山楼，
一宿行人自可愁。
潮落夜江斜月里，
两三星火是瓜洲。

At Jinling Ferry Crossing

In the small hotel at Jinling Ferry Crossing,
Lonely and sad at night but I can do nothing.
The moon slants on the river with tide going out,
Two or three lights on the sandbar flicker about.

瓜洲闻晓角

寒耿稀星照碧霄，
月楼吹角夜江遥。
五更人起烟霜静，
一曲残声遍落潮。

Harbinger of Dawn on Guazhou Sandbar

Cold are a few stars flickering in the blue sky,
The horn blare goes far from the moon-lit tower high.
Getting up at dawn I find the haze and rime white,
The lingering music sends off the ebbing tide.

折杨柳枝

莫折宫前杨柳枝,
玄宗曾向笛中吹。
伤心日暮烟霞起,
无限春愁生翠眉。

The Song of Willow Twigs

Snap no twigs from the willows before the palace,
The emperor* once played the flute in the right place.
Heart-broken at dusk as mist and clouds come into sight,
Knitting her eyebrows as she is in a sad plight.

---

* "The emperor" here refers to Emperor Xuanzong (685~762), the seventh emperor of the Tang Dynasty.

华清宫

水绕宫墙处处声,
残红长绿露华清。
武皇一夕梦不觉,
十二玉楼空月明。

The Huaqing Palace

Murmuring around the palace wall is a clear stream,
Dotted with red petals are evergreens with dew cream.
Emperor Xuanzong is dreaming throughout the night,
The imperial palace lies idle in the moonlight.

长门怨

日映宫墙柳色寒,
笙歌遥指碧云端。
珠铅滴尽无心语,
强把花枝冷笑看。

Grievance of a Deserted Empress

The sun shines on the palace but chilly is the willow,
The strains of music and singing echo to the sky.
Tears spoil the rouge and powder she's silent in sorrow,
With the forced smile at flowers her tears now are dry.

邮亭残花

云暗山横日欲斜，
邮亭下马对残花。
自从身逐征西府，
每到花时不在家。

Faded Flowers near the Posthouse

Gloomy clouds over the mountains as the sun slants west,
Off my horse at the posthouse flowers are past their best.
Since I was sent into battle beyond the great wall,
Whenever flowers in bloom I'm not at home at all.

宿武牢关

行人候晓久裴徊,
不待鸡鸣未得开。
堪羡寒溪自无事,
潺潺一夜宿关来。

An Overnight Stay at Wulao Pass

Waiting for dawn travelers are pacing to and fro,
The gate of pass won't be open until the cockcrow.
I envy the cold stream for its true leisure indeed,
And murmuring through the pass so gentle is the flow.

感归

行却江南路几千，
归来不把一文钱。
乡人笑我穷寒鬼，
还似襄阳孟浩然。

Thoughts on Homecoming

Travelling all over the south far and wide,
Having no penny left I get home at last.
Folks laugh at me a poor pedantic scholar,
Like Meng Haoran who had a secluded past.

峰顶寺

月明如水山头寺,
仰面看天石上行。
夜半深廊人语定,
一枝松动鹤来声。

A Temple atop the Mountain

A temple atop the mountain in the clear moonlight,
Towering into sky over the rock the clouds fly.
Through the deep corridor nobody's seen at night,
With the rustle of the pine trees comes the crane's cry.

塞上闻笛

一夜梅花笛里飞,
冷沙晴槛月光晖。
北风吹尽向何处,
高入塞云燕雁稀。

Fluting Heard at the Frontier

The flute tune of *Plum Petals* is heard at dead of night,
Cold desert and railings are bathed in the moonlight.
Cold is the north wind howling and sweeping far away,
Few wild geese across the clouds on the border are in flight.

赠内人

禁门宫树月痕过，
媚眼唯看宿燕窠。
斜拔玉钗灯影畔，
剔开红焰救飞蛾。

To a Palace Maid

Shadowed by trees is the palace in the moonlight,
Her charming eyes fix on a nest of birds at night.
Removing her jade hairpin to the candle-stick,
To save a moth from the wick she's about to pick.

纵游淮南

十里长街市井连,
月明桥上看神仙。
人生只合扬州死,
禅智山光好墓田。

Sightseeing all over Yangzhou

The long street is flanked by marketplace on both sides,
From the bridge many street girls are walking in the moonlight.
Living in Yangzhou as if dreaming in paradise,
Chanzhi Mountain in the suburbs is the best grave site.

杨花

散乱随风处处匀，
庭前几日雪花新。
无端惹著潘郎鬓，
惊杀绿窗红粉人。

Willow Catkins

Dancing with wind here, there, everywhere,
Covering the courtyard like snowflakes so fair.
When sticking to the hair of her sweetheart,
By the window the pink lady was given a start.

散花楼

锦江城外锦城头,
回望秦川上轸忧。
正值血魂来梦里,
杜鹃声在散花楼。

Flower-strewing Tower

At the top of gate tower by Jinjiang river,
Gazing east to the emperor* it's a cold shiver.
The deceased** in his dream was about to loom,
Cuckoos' cry at the tower filled him with gloom.

---

* "The emperor" here refers to Emperor Xuanzong.
** The deceased refers to Yang Yuhuan, Li Longji's concubine who was forced to kill herself at Mawei Slope on the way of seeking refuge to Sichuan.

杭州开元寺牡丹

浓艳初开小药栏，
人人惆怅出长安。
风流却是钱塘寺，
不踏红尘见牡丹。

Peonies in Kaiyuan Temple in Hangzhou

In the herb bed peonies begin to burst into bloom,
Going outing from Chang'an travelers are in gloom.
Graceful and charming are the flowers in the temple,
Free from mortals peonies here are a prime example.

晚秋潼关西门作

日落寒郊烟物清,
古槐阴黑少人行。
关门西去华山色,
秦地东来河水声。

A Verse Composed at the West Gate of Tongguan in Late Autumn

The sunset in the cold suburbs presents a view bright,
The old tree casts its shadow and few figures in sight.
To the west of the gate Mountain Hua towers to the sky,
From the east of the town waves in the river rise high.

李德裕

李德裕(787～850),字文饶,赵郡(今河北赞皇)人。出身世家,曾官拜宰相。为政六年,史称名相,后遭贬,卒于崖州(今海南三亚市)。《全唐诗》存其诗一卷。

Li Deyu (787～850), styled Wenrao, was born into a noble family in Zhaojun (Zanhuang County, Hebei Province today). Li had served Emperor Wuzong (814～846) as a famous prime minister for six years before he was demoted and banished to Yazhou (Sanya City, Hainan Province today) and finally died there. There is one volume of his poems collected in *The Complete Collection of the Tang Poetry*.

题罗浮石

清景持芳菊,
凉天依茂松。
名山何必去,
此地有群峰。

To Stones in Luofu Mountain

Sweet chrysanthemums add much to the fresh scene nice,
Autumn is cooler with pine trees touching the sky.
No need to go to the famous mountains for sights,
Chains of the peaks here tower into air so high.

雪霁晨起

雪覆寒溪竹,
风卷野田蓬。
四望无行迹,
谁怜孤老翁。

A Clear Morning After Snow

Along the cold stream are bamboos coated with snow,
Swaying with the wind weeds in the wilds overgrow.
No figure in sight in the open country vast,
Who shows compassion for the old one lonely cast?

题奇石

蕴玉抱清辉,
闲庭日潇洒。
块然天地间,
自是孤生者。

To the Grotesque Stone

Containing jade it shines with brilliant light,
In the quiet garden it stands with easy grace.
All on its own it towers into the sky,
Solitary but nothing can take its place.

长安秋夜

内官传诏问戎机,
载笔金銮夜始归。
万户千门皆寂寂,
月中清露点朝衣。

An Autumn Night in Chang'an

Summons from the emperor for military affairs,
Hurrying to the golden court with pens I return at night.
It's tranquil on the way and people seem free from cares,
Wet with dew drops clear is my costume in the moonlight.

登崖州城作

独上高楼望帝京，
鸟飞犹是半年程。
青山似欲留人住，
百匝千遭绕郡城。

A Poem Composed atop the Gate Tower of Yazhou

Atop the tower I gaze the capital on my own,
Too far away it takes a bird half a year to fly there.
It seems green mountains want me to stay there to do my share,
Range upon range on all sides the town's surrounded alone.

李 贺

李贺(790~816),字长吉,福昌(今河南宜阳)人。早年多病,生活困顿,诗中时有反映。其诗辞采瑰丽,意境奇崛,在诗史上独树一帜。《全唐诗》存其诗五卷。

Li He (790~816), styled Changji, was born in Fuchang (Yiyang County, Henan Province today). Afflicted with a lingering illness in his early years, Li He was frustrated and poverty-stricken, which was manifested time and again in his poems. Splendor of well-whetted words and unusual ingenuity of artistic mood are characteristics of his poetry, which constitute a unique school in history of Chinese poetry. There are five volumes of his poems collected in *The Complete Collection of the Tang Poetry*.

马诗·其一

龙脊贴连钱,
银蹄白踏烟。
无人织锦韂,
谁为铸金鞭。

Horse Poem (1)

Like string of coins the spots are dotted on your back,
While galloping four silver hoofs leave a white track.
But now you have no saddle nor pad of brocade,
And no one knows where the golden whip can be made.

马诗·其二

此马非凡马，
房星本是星。
向前敲瘦骨，
犹自带铜声。

Horse Poem（2）

This is by no means an ordinary steed,
It's the incarnation of a constellation indeed.
Tap the bony frame to gallop forward,
As if the metallic sound can be heard.

马诗·其三

大漠沙如雪，
燕山月似钩。
何当金络脑，
快走踏清秋。

Horse Poem（3）

Sands of vast desert gleam white as snow,
The moon in the sky looks like a bow.
If the golden halter is around your head,
You can gallop thousands of miles at one go.

清　郎世宁　《百骏图》(局部)

马诗·其四

催榜渡乌江，
神骓泣向风。
君王今解剑，
何处逐英雄？

Horse Poem (4)

The sentry-box head crosses the river in a hurry,
But the mighty horse against the wind weeps with worry.
If you draw out your sword and kill yourself today,
To follow and accompany you I can't find my way.

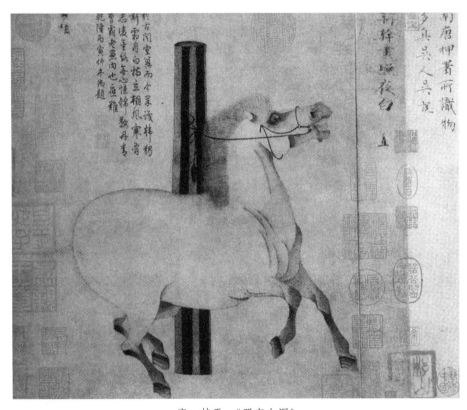

唐 韩干 《照夜白图》

塞下曲

秋静见旄头,
沙远席羁愁。
帐北天应尽,
河声出塞流。

A Frontier Song

Calm is the autumn but the enmity star is bright,
Vast is the desert with wild reeds indeed a blight.
To the north of the camp the earth kisses the sky,
Beyond the Great Wall the Yellow River flows on high.

塘上行

藕花凉露湿，
花缺藕根涩。
飞下雌鸳鸯，
塘水声溘溘。

Walking Around the Lotus Pond

Lotus flowers are fading and wet with cold dew,
Acerbic are roots and flowers only a few.
A flying mandarin duck splatters on the pond,
The water is suddenly splashed all around.

京城

驱马出门意,
牢落长安心。
两事向谁道,
自作秋风吟。

The Capital City

Spurring on the horse I'm leaving the capital,
Feeling lonely in Chang'an I'm sentimental.
My worry about fame and fortune no one knows,
I cannot but chant myself as autumn wind blows.

南园·其一

花枝草蔓眼中开,
小白长红越女腮。
可怜日暮嫣香落,
嫁与春风不用媒。

The South Garden（1）

In full bloom are herbaceous and woody flowers in sight,
Like dimples of a beauty are the flowers red and white.
Pity is that sweet flowers at dusk are fading away,
Married spring breeze with no matchmaker like children at play.

南园·其二

男儿何不带吴钩,
收取关山五十州。
请君暂上凌烟阁,
若个书生万户侯。

The South Garden(2)

Armed with a sword, to be a valiant man, why not,
Recover the lost fifty states you can do a lot.
Climb the memorial tower to learn the heroes' merits,
You will be aware that no pedant can be a marquis.

南园·其三

寻章摘句老雕虫，
晓月当帘挂玉弓。
不见年年辽海上，
文章何处哭秋风？

The South Garden(3)

Culling while reading is nothing but a trifling skill,
Studying till dawn the moon in the sky is like a jade bow.
Year in year out the frontier war news is a big thrill,
Combat needs warriors while pedants can do nothing but sorrow.

南园·其四

春水初生乳燕飞，
黄蜂小尾扑花归。
窗含远色通书幌，
鱼拥香钩近石矶。

The South Garden（4）

Fresh is spring water and young swallows are in flight,
Wrapped with pollen small bees around the hive wait.
Through the screen distant view from window is in sight,
Near the rock are the fishes around the sweet bait.

昌谷北园新笋

斫取青光写楚辞,
腻香春粉黑离离。
无情有恨何人见,
露压烟啼千万枝。

To the New Bamboo Shoots in the North Garden

To write poems on bamboo slips I scrape them clean,
Poems on the fragrant slips can be vividly seen.
Unfeeling are bamboos but their resentment who knows,
Bent with dew in mist they weep as their sorrow grows.

三月过行宫

渠水红繁拥御墙，
风娇小叶学娥妆。
垂帘几度青春老，
堪锁千年白日长。

Visiting an Imperial Palace in Late Spring

Wormwood in the ditch clusters around the imperial wall,
Tender leaves in spring breeze are very charming but small.
Behind the curtains the palace maids are long past their prime.
Deep in the court each day's like a year they've to kill the time.

徐　凝

徐凝(792～853),睦州(今浙江建德)人。诗歌以七绝见长,语言洗练,风格简朴。《全唐诗》存其诗一卷。

Xu Ning (792～853), born in Muzhou (Jiande County, Zhejiang Province today), was famous for quatrains of seven characters per line, which are characterized by terse language in plain style. There is one volume of his poems collected in *The Complete Collection of the Tang Poetry*.

问渔叟

生事同漂梗,
机心在野船。
如何临逝水,
白发未忘筌。

A Question to Fisherman

Your life seems like duckweed floating,
And your mind is focused on fishing.
How can you float here, there, everywhere,
But you never forget your fishing snare?

春寒

乱雪从教舞,
回风任听吹。
春寒能作底,
已被柳条欺。

A Cold Spell in Spring

Reckless are snowflakes whirling,
Wilful is the whirlwind blowing.
Spring chill, what does it mean,
The willow twigs must turn green.

庐山独夜

寒空五老雪,
斜月九江云。
钟声知何处,
苍苍树里闻。

A Lonely Overnight Stay in Lushan Mountain

Snow-capped five peaks tower very high,
Slanting is the moon through the clouds in the sky.
A peal of bells comes from where I don't know,
But they can be heard from the woods nearby.

明 沈周 《庐山高图》

天台独夜

银地秋月色，
石梁夜溪声。
谁知屐齿尽，
为破烟苔行。

A Lonely Overnight Stay in Tiantai Mountain

Silvery is the ground in the autumn moonlight,
Over the stone dam the stream gurgles at night.
My clogs have been worn smooth before I know,
Along the mossy path in mist I come and go.

武夷山仙城

武夷无上路,
毛径不通风。
欲共麻姑住,
仙城半在空。

The Fairy Town in Wuyi Mountain

There is no path leading up to Wuyi Mountain,
Even the trail is blocked by vegetation.
I want to be the neighbor of the fairy maiden,
But the fairy town is halfway in the heaven.

香炉峰

香炉一峰绝,
顶在寺门前。
尽是玲珑石,
时生旦暮烟。

The Censer Peak

Extremely unique is the shape of Censer Peak,
Before a temple's gate it seems a huge beak.
Its rocks are vivid as if they're carved with knife,
Hazy at dawn, misty at dusk they're true to life.

忆扬州

萧娘脸薄难胜泪，
桃叶眉头易得愁。
天下三分明月夜，
二分无赖是扬州。

Recollection of the Past in Yangzhou

A drop of tear will spoil her face as it's so fair,
Her eyebrows are slim enough no grief can it bear.
Of all the moonlit nights lingering in my mind,
Two thirds of the nights spent in Yangzhou are so kind.

观浙江涛

浙江悠悠海西绿,
惊涛日夜两翻覆。
钱塘郭里看潮人,
直至白头看不足。

Enjoying the View of Qiantang Tide

Qiantang River flows into the sea blue and vast,
Towering waves surge to and fro day and night.
To have the view of tide people in town stand fast,
Even to the grey hairs it's always a delight.

庐山瀑布

虚空落泉千仞直,
雷奔入江不暂息。
今古长如白练飞,
一条界破青山色。

Waterfall in Mount Lu

Pouring down thousand feet the waterfall hangs from the sky,
Dashing into river without stop it roars at its height.
Through the ages like silk ribbon long enough it flies from high,
The green mountain is split apart by the white ribbon bright.

八月十五夜

皎皎秋空八月圆，
常娥端正桂枝鲜。
一年无似如今夜，
十二峰前看不眠。

The Mid-autumn Night

In the mid-autumn the moon is full in the sky,
Fair is the fairy in the moon that hangs so high.
Throughout the year it is the obvious choice tonight,
Gazing at the twelve peaks I have a sleepless night.

七夕

一道鹊桥横渺渺,
千声玉佩过玲玲。
别离还有经年客,
怅望不如河鼓星。

The Double Seventh Evening

A long magpie bridge spans over the Milky Way,
Thousand jade pendants twinkle on the very day.
I parted from my family many years ago,
Lucky is the cowherd but I envy in dismay.

读远书

两转三回读远书,
画檐愁见燕归初。
百花时节教人懒,
云鬓朝来不欲梳。

Reading a Letter from Afar

I read the letter from afar time and again,
Seeing swallows return to eaves I'm in pain.
At flowering time in low spirits I'm lazy,
In no mood for making up at dawn I'm drowsy.

喜雪

长爱谢家能咏雪，
今朝见雪亦狂歌。
杨花道即偷人句，
不那杨花似雪何。

Timely Snow

I admire Xie Daoyun for her poem *Ode to Snow*,
Why I sing of snow with wild joy now I come to know.
"Like catkins dancing with wind" all poets like to cite,
They have no choice but to say "snow like catkins white".

古树

古树欹斜临古道，
枝不生花腹生草。
行人不见树少时，
树见行人几番老。

An Ancient Tree

By the ancient road an old tree grows on the slant,
No flowers on the twigs but on its trunk grass grows.
Passers-by have not seen the tree as a young plant,
But how many passers-by grow old the tree knows.

玩花

一树梨花春向暮，
雪枝残处怨风来。
明朝渐校无多去，
看到黄昏不欲回。

A Feast of Pear Flowers

Pear blossoms in late spring are fully blooming,
Off some branches with wind flowers are blowing.
More of them tomorrow will be fading away,
Feasting my eyes on them till the dusk I stay.

春雨

花时闷见联绵雨,
云入人家水毁堤。
昨日春风源上路,
可怜红锦枉抛泥。

Spring Rain

Rainy days in the flowering seem never-ending,
Clouds are low and dams damaged by flooding.
On the tableland spring wind blew yesterday,
Mixed with mud red silk fabrics shade into grey.

牡丹

何人不爱牡丹花,
占断城中好物华。
疑是洛川神女作,
千娇万态破朝霞。

To Peony

Who can say he has no love for peony flower,
When the queen of flowers is at the finest hour?
Displaying its ravishing beauty at rosy dawn,
I wonder if the river goddess shows its power.

上阳红叶

洛下三分红叶秋，
二分翻作上阳愁。
千声万片御沟上，
一片出宫何处流。

Red Leaves Outside Shangyang Palace

Maple leaves by the riverside turn red in autumn,
To the maids of Shangyang Palace it's time of sorrow.
On the imperial moat many leaves form a column,
If one flows out of the palace what can it follow?

览镜词

宝镜磨来寒水清,
青衣把就绿窗明。
潘郎懊恼新秋发,
拔却一茎生两茎。

Song of Mirror

Smoothly ground the mirror is clear and bright,
Dressed in black gown standing by the window.
Looking himself in the mirror he's in sorrow,
Plucking out a grey hair but more turn white.

语儿见新月

几处天边见新月，
经过草市忆西施。
娟娟水宿初三夜，
曾伴愁蛾到语儿。

The New Moon Seen in Yu'er

Over the horizon the new moon hangs in the sky,
Through the country fair I think of Xi Shi like Helen.
Fair and bright is the Plough twinkling in the heaven,
Accompanying Xi Shi to Yu'er with a deep sigh.

许 浑

许浑(793~858),字用晦,一作仲晦,润州丹阳(今江苏丹阳)人。许浑自幼劳心苦学,曾在朝为官。尤钟情山水,晚年隐居山林。其诗深沉含蓄,多怀古之作。《全唐诗》存其诗十一卷。

Xu Hun(793~858), styled Yonghui, also Zhonghui his alias, was born in Danyang, Runzhou (Danyang County, Jiangsu Province today). From the early childhood, Xu Hun was fond of learning and once served as a government official. He had a great love of woods and streams, so he withdrew from active service and led a secluded life in the country when he was advanced in age. His poems, full of meditations on the past, are meaningful with implications, of which eleven volumes are collected in *The Complete Collection of the Tang Poetry*.

雨后思湖上居

前山风雨凉,
歇马坐垂杨。
何处芙蓉落,
南渠秋水香。

Thinking of My Lake Dwelling After Rain

It is cold after the storm from the front mountain,
Off the steed I sit in the shade of a willow.
From where wafts the scent of lotus flowers fallen?
Autumn water from the south ditch is sweet and mellow.

闻歌

新秋弦管清，
时转遏云声。
曲尽不知处，
月高风满城。

Listening to Music

Sweet is the orchestral music in early autumn,
Melodious enough to lure clouds in a long column.
When and where the music ends I really don't know,
With the moon in the sky I only hear the wind blow.

思天台

赤城云雪深,
山客负归心。
昨夜西斋宿,
月明琪树阴。

Fond Memories of Tiantai Mountain

Capped with snow the Red Mountains deep in the clouds loom,
Failing to return to the mountain I'm deep in gloom.
In the West Chamber yesterday I put up for the night,
Splendid are the trees of fairy land in the moonlight.

塞下

夜战桑干北,
秦兵半不归。
朝来有乡信,
犹自寄征衣。

The Frontier Song

Beyond the Sanggan River soldiers went on fight,
Brave during the day but half of them died at night.
From the battlefield in the morn came the sad news,
Their coats were still posted as if nobody knows.

寄桐江隐者

潮去潮来洲渚春,
山花如绣草如茵。
严陵台下桐江水,
解钓鲈鱼能几人。

To the Hermit on Tongjiang River

The ebb and flow of the tides greet the spring on the sandbar,
Flowers bloom and grass like a green carpet stretches far.
Yan Guang is a true hermit angling on Tongjiang River,
Lead a secluded life how many people can ever?

重别

泪沿红粉湿罗巾,
重系兰舟劝酒频。
留却一枝河畔柳,
明朝犹有远行人。

Parting Again

Down her pink cheeks the silk handkerchief is wet with tears,
With the painted boat tied I'm urged to drink with cheers.
Reserving a willow twig plucked from the riverside,
For those who will take a trip tomorrow far and wide.

湖上

仿佛欲当三五夕,
万蝉清杂乱泉纹。
钓鱼船上一尊酒,
月出渡头零落云。

On the Lake

It seems in the middle of the month the moon shines at night,
Breeze ripples the lake water gleaming in the moonlight.
With a cup of wine in hand I'm angling on the boat,
Over the crossing the moon through the clouds looms in sight.

谢亭送别

劳歌一曲解行舟,
红叶青山水急流。
日暮酒醒人已远,
满天风雨下西楼。

Parting at the Riverside Tower

At the end of farewell song your boat sails away,
Between mountains and red leaves strong rapids flow.
Sobering from wine I see no one at dusk of the day,
Storm comes and downstairs the tower I slowly go.

蝉

噪柳鸣槐晚未休，
不知何事爱悲愁。
朱门大有长吟处，
刚傍愁人又送愁。

To Cicada

In willow or locust trees you buzz day and night,
Why in autumn you're always in a sorrow plight?
By the gates of peers there's many right spots for singing,
Just pestered with sorrow but sorrow is coming.

陈宫怨

地雄山险水悠悠，
不信隋兵到石头。
玉树后庭花一曲，
与君同上景阳楼。

Grief of a Chen Palace Maid

Surrounded with mountains steep and waters long and vast,
Who believes the Sui troops can capture the town so fast?
Enchanting are the tune and dancing steps graceful and light,
Upstairs with the emperor enjoying the dreamy night.

途经秦始皇墓

龙盘虎踞树层层，
势入浮云亦是崩。
一种青山秋草里，
路人唯拜汉文陵。

Meditations on the Mausoleum of the First Emperor of the Qin Dynasty

Guarded by dragon and tiger with trees touching the sky,
Collapsed in the end though it's imposingly high.
Shrouded in autumn weeds the tomb is a green hill now,
Only before Liu Heng's* Tomb the passers-by like to bow.

---

* Liu Heng(203～157), the fifth Emperor of the West Han Dynasty(202BC～AD8), was famous for his policy of "Relaxing the Ban on Civilians", which turned out to be popular with people then.

缑山庙

王子求仙月满台，
玉箫清转鹤裴徊。
曲终飞去不知处，
山下碧桃春自开。

Goushan Temple

For immortality in the moonlight the prince prays,
Melodious is the flute tune and up and down cranes pace.
At the end of the tune the birds are nowhere to be seen,
Peach blossoms bloom in spring and the new leaves are green.

鸿沟

相持未定各为君,
秦政山河此地分。
力尽乌江千载后,
古沟芳草起寒云。

Meditations on Honggou Chasm

Reaching a stalemate each side fought for its own kingdom,
Cut apart by the chasm the Qin Dynasty met its doom.
Xiang Yu killed himself near Yangtze River thousand years ago,
But cold clouds float over the chasm now and green plants grow.

韩信庙

朝言云梦暮南巡,
已为功名少退身。
尽握兵权犹不得,
更将心计托何人。

Meditations on Han Xin Temple

Talking of lake at dawn the emperor inspects there at dusk,
Refusing to retire Han Xin covets more fame, rank and gain.
Military power in hand, that is nothing but the husk,
A nice scheme presented to him which finally ends in vain.

楚宫怨

十二山晴花尽开，
楚宫双阙对阳台。
细腰争舞君王醉，
白日秦兵天上来。

Grief of a Chu Palace Maid

In full bloom are flowers at twelve peaks on a fine day,
Facing balcony are two towers of the palace gate.
Slim belles dancing make the emperor carried away,
But sudden attack by the Qin troops is a hapless fate.

秋思

琪树西风枕簟秋，
楚云湘水忆同游。
高歌一曲掩明镜，
昨日少年今白头。

Autumn Thoughts

Autumn wind strokes fine trees and on bamboo mat I lie,
Thinking of sightseeing with my friends in my prime.
Covering the bright mirror I sing a song and sigh,
Yesterday I was young but now my hair's dyed with rime.

宋　刘松年　《四景山水图·秋》

听琵琶

欲写明妃万里情，
紫槽红拨夜丁丁。
胡沙望尽汉宫远，
月落天山闻一声。

Enjoying the *Pipa* Melody

To vent my gloomy mood of Zhaojun's marriage far away,
I play the tune on the strings again and again at night.
The Han Palace is out of sight she is in a sad plight,
The moon sets beyond Mount Tian and the tune causes dismay.

鹭鸶

西风澹澹水悠悠，
雪点丝飘带雨愁。
何限归心倚前阁，
绿蒲红蓼练塘秋。

To Egrets

Soft is the west wind and ripples on the water are light,
Gloomy in rain are the egrets like silk ribbons snow-white.
Leaning on the garret you're homesick in your bosom,
Cattail is green and knotweed red on the lake in autumn.

清　恽冰　《蒲塘秋艳图》

紫藤

绿蔓秾阴紫袖低,
客来留坐小堂西。
醉中掩瑟无人会,
家近江南罨画溪。

To Wisteria

Green vines with many clusters of purple flowers are drooping,
Guests are warmly entertained in the small hall drinking.
Tipsy I play zither but the true meaning no one knows,
Along the stream near my hometown wisteria also grows.

卢 仝

卢仝(795～835),号玉川子,范阳(今河北涿州)人。幼时家境贫困,刻苦读书;曾隐居少室山,不愿仕进。其诗风格奇警,近于散文,多为针砭时弊之作。《全唐诗》存其诗三卷。

Lu Tong (795～835), styled Yu Chuanzi, was born in Fanyang (Zhuozhou County, Hebei Province today). His family was in straitened circumstances when he was a child, but he was studious and diligent. However, instead of entering into officialdom Lu Tong withdrew from society and lived in seclusion in Shaoshi Mountain. Composed in singular style of prose, most of his poems are allegorical verses of the time, of which three volumes are collected in *The Complete Collection of the Tang Poetry*.

新月

仙宫云箔卷,
露出玉帘钩。
清光无所赠,
相忆凤凰楼。

The Crescent Moon

Rising is the cloud curtain of the fairy palace,
The crescent moon like a hook of white jade shows its face.
Pity is that I can't present you the bright moonlight,
The past time in Phoenix Tower gnaws at me at night.

解闷

人生都几日，
一半是离忧。
但有尊中物，
从他万事休。

Relief of Boredom

Life is a journey that is too short to go,
But half of life is full of parting sorrow.
Drink and drink so long my cup is full of wine,
Free from care and everything will be fine.

新蝉

泉溜潜幽咽,
琴鸣乍往还。
长风翦不断,
还在树枝间。

To Newborn Cicadas

Low and deep is your voice of murmuring spring,
Rising and falling like the music of string.
Wind cannot stop you from chirping though it's strong,
Perched in branches you keep on singing long.

村醉

昨夜村饮归，
健倒三四五。
摩挲青莓苔，
莫嗔惊著汝。

Drunk in the Village

Getting drunk I returned from the village last night,
On the way back I slipped and fell time and again.
Groping my way with green moss slippery and slight,
Having frightened you I hope you won't complain.

喜逢郑三游山

相逢之处花茸茸,
石壁攒峰千万重。
他日期君何处好,
寒流石上一株松。

Coming Across Zheng San with Delight While Touring Mountains

At the place of meeting soft flowers thickly grow,
Mountain peaks on the stony precipice touch the blue sky.
Where's the right spot for future meeting I don't know,
On the huge stone by the cold stream a pine stands high.

马 戴

马戴(799~869),字虞臣,华州(今陕西华县)人。曾在朝为官,后因直言遭贬。其诗语言平实,风格自然。《全唐诗》存其诗两卷。

Ma Dai(799~869), styled Yuchen, was born in Huazhou (Huaxian County, Shaanxi Province today). Ma once served as a government official, but he was late demoted for talking straight. His poems were composed with plain and unadorned language in natural style, of which two volumes are collected in *The Complete Collection of the Tang Poetry*.

白鹿原晚望

浐曲雁飞下,
秦原人葬回。
丘坟与城阙,
草树共尘埃。

An Evening View of Bailu Wilderness

At the turn of Chanhe River swan geese alight,
Back from funeral are people on the way home.
Watch towers and grave mounds cast a deep gloomy sight,
Covered with dust are plants and grass around the tomb.

秋思

万木秋霖后，
孤山夕照馀。
田园无岁计，
寒近忆樵渔。

Autumn Thoughts

Freshly bathed are the trees in the autumn rain,
Standing alone is the mountain in the dusk glow.
Crops are gathered in they have nothing on the brain,
Fishing and wood-cutting are the things that follow.

元　吴镇　《渔父图》

赠道者

深居白云穴,
静注赤松经。
往往龙潭上,
焚香礼斗星。

To a Taoist Priest

You lead a secluded life in the white-cloud cave,
Lost in the classical scripture you spare no time.
Often standing by an abyss you are so brave,
To worship the Plough you burn incense that is prime.

崔道融

崔道融(生卒年不详),荆州江陵(今湖北江陵)人。绝句语言平实,行文流畅,风格多变。《全唐诗》存其诗一卷。

Cui Daorong, was born in Jiangling, Jingzhou(Jiangling County, Hubei Province today). Cui was well versed in quatrain characterized by smooth and plain language in varied style. Of his poems one volume is collected in *The Complete Collection of the Tang Poetry*.

春闺·其一

寒食月明雨,
落花香满泥。
佳人持锦字,
无雁寄辽西。

Boudoir Reverie in Spring(1)

After rain on the Cold Food Festival the moon's bright,
Fallen petals on the muddy ground smell sweet at night.
A letter to her darling in hand she pines away,
No swan geese can take her letter to him she looks grey.

春闺·其二

欲剪宜春字，
春寒入剪刀。
辽阳在何处，
莫忘寄征袍。

Boudoir Reverie in Spring (2)

I try to cut a mascot of the new spring,
But the nip of my scissors is lingering.
Far away in Liaoyang it is freezing cold,
What he needs badly is a long winter coat.

月夕

月上随人意，
人闲月更清。
朱楼高百尺，
不见到天明。

Mid-autumn Night

Catering to people's wish the moon rises in the sky,
Enjoying autumn at leisure the moon is so bright.
Wild with joy in the red chamber a hundred feet high,
They have lost the chance to enjoy the tender moonlight.

槿花

槿花不见夕，
一日一回新。
东风吹桃李，
须到明年春。

Hibiscus Flowers

Blooming at dawn they fade in the twilight,
Once a day their color is fresh and bright.
The east wind makes peach and plum flowering,
But you have to wait till breeze blows next spring.

西施滩

宰嚭亡吴国,
西施陷恶名。
浣纱春水急,
似有不平声。

Xi Shi Shoal

Zai Pi resulted in the downfall of the Wu Kingdom,
Pity is that in history Xi Shi* bears the blame.
Near her washing stone the river has a rapid flow,
It seems to redress the injustice to restore her fame.

---

* Xi Shi, a famous beauty in the late Spring-Autumn Period, was presented to Fu Chai, the king of the Wu State by Gou Jian, the king of the Yue State as a beauty trap, which resulted in the fall of the Wu State.

过农家

欲羡农家子，
秋新看刈禾。
苏秦无负郭，
六印又如何。

Passing by a Farmyard

Admiring the farming family and the idyll life,
Go and see them reap in autumn with sickle and knife.
Su Qin*, though an official of eminent rank and fame,
Without farmland he hasn't a penny to his name.

---

* Su Qin (？～284BC) was a politician and a strategist of the Warring States, who sought to unite all the other Warring States against the Qin Empire and was appointed the leader of alliance, later wrecked by the stratagem of Qin as well as the selfish intrigues among the allies.

春墅

蛙声近过社，
农事忽已忙。
邻妇饷田归，
不见百花芳。

Farming Cottage in Spring

Frogs start to croak after the spring sacrifice,
All day in the fields farmers are busy twice.
Back from the fields women send meals sweet and nice,
They find no flowers blooming along roadsides.

江村

日暮片帆落，
江村如有情。
独对沙上月，
满船人睡声。

A Riverside Village

The lonely sail lowers in the sunset glow,
The riverside village seems to be in the know.
Facing the moon alone over the sandbar,
Snoring from the boat can be heard from afar.

寄人

澹澹长江水，
悠悠远客情。
落花相与恨，
到地一无声。

A Verse to a Friend

The water of the Yangtze River flows in peace,
Like my affection for you long as it is.
Much to my regret petals fall onto the ground,
No farewell to the flower you can hear no sound.

病起

病起春已晚，
曳筇伤绿苔。
强攀庭树枝，
唤作花未开。

Recovery from Illness

Recovered from illness spring has faded away,
Walking with a bamboo stick I step on the moss.
Off the courtyard tree I pull down a branch by force,
Take it as a flowery twig and make a spray.

春晚

三月寒食时,
日色浓于酒。
落尽墙头花,
莺声隔原柳。

An Evening View in Spring

The Cold Food Festival comes and spring takes a call,
Sweet is the breeze and warm enough is the sunlight.
Fading away are all flowers atop the wall,
In the willow foliage orioles sing with delight.

长安春

长安牡丹开,
绣毂辗晴雷。
若使花长在,
人应看不回。

Spring in Chang'an the Capital

Peonies in Chang'an are blooming in their prime,
The painted wheels are thundering on a fine day.
If flowers are in full blossom all the time,
Visitors will linger there for a long stay.

寒食夜

满地梨花白，
风吹碎月明。
大家寒食夜，
独贮望乡情。

Night of the Cold Food Festival

All over the ground are pear petals white,
From behind floating clouds the moon is bright.
On the night of the Cold Food Festival,
We stand homesick for long in the moonlight.

銮驾东回

两川花捧御衣香，
万岁山呼辇路长。
天子还从马嵬过，
别无惆怅似明皇。

Imperial Carriage on the Way Back to the Capital

Aromatic are imperial costumes and sprays of flowers,
"Long live the emperor" lingers on to show imperial powers.
On the way back the emperor passes by Mawei Slope* again,
The emperor must be sad as the bereaved one till all hours.

---

* Mawei Slope is a town in Xingping City, Shaanxi Province where Yang Yuhuan, the favorite concubine of Emperor Xuanzong, was driven to commit suicide on the way exiling to Sichuan.

溪上遇雨

坐看黑云衔猛雨，
喷洒前山此独晴。
忽惊云雨在头上，
却是山前晚照明。

Caught in a Shower by the Stream

Looking at the sky darkened by rainy clouds gathering,
It is pouring down in the front mountain but here it's fine.
To my surprise clouds overhead are quickly scattering,
However in front of the mountain bright is the sunshine.

西施

苎萝山下如花女，
占得姑苏台上春。
一笑不能忘敌国，
五湖何处有功臣。

To Xi Shi

At the Foot of Zhuluo Mountain Xi Shi's a great beauty,
In the Wu State she's the top one to win the king's favor.
Employed in the beauty trap she knows the enemy,
Otherwise Fan Li* can't be successful and so famous.

---

* Fan Li was a senior official of the Yue State, who designed and successfully put the beauty trap into practice. However he resigned from his post after his success and went boating on the lake for a totally carefree life.

梅

溪上寒梅初满枝，
夜来霜月透芳菲。
清光寂寞思无尽，
应待琴尊与解围。

Plum Blossoms

Along the stream are winter plums laden with fresh flowers,
Sweet smell wafts in the frosty air at the moonlit night.
Lonely in the moonlight I'm lost in thought till all hours,
Only the strings and wine can free me from fret with delight.

秋夕

自怜三十未西游，
傍水寻山过却秋。
一夜雨声多少事，
不思量尽到心头。

Autumn Night

Of rank and fame at the age of thirty I feel shame,
Across mountains and rivers I'm trudging in autumn.
Pit-a-pat the rain at night beats my window frame,
Sunk into gloom I'm laden with frets in my bosom.

溪居即事

篱外谁家不系船,
春风吹入钓鱼湾。
小童疑是有村客,
急向柴门去却关。

An Extempore Verse by the Stream

Whose boat is that beyond the fence untied alongside?
Drifting down with the spring wind into the angling inlet.
"Maybe a visitor's coming," the kid thinks, "with the tide."
Making a rush for the gate, he unlocks the wicket.

秋霁

雨霁长空荡涤清，
远山初出未知名。
夜来江上如钩月，
时有惊鱼掷浪声。

A Fine Day After Autumn Rain

Blue is the vast sky after rain clear and bright,
Faraway mountains nameless loom into sight.
The crescent on the river glisters with waves,
From time to time startled fish splashes at night.

宋　赵伯驹　《江山秋色图》(局部)

杨柳枝词

雾撚烟搓一索春,
年年长似染来新。
应须唤作风流线,
系得东西南北人。

Song of Willow Twigs

From willow twigs wrapped in mist spring can be seen,
Year after year they seem to be dyed freshly green.
In fact they are the symbol of romantic tie,
Between the friends under the heaven far or nigh.

杜 牧

杜牧(803～852),字牧之,京兆万年(今陕西西安)人。曾在朝为官,颇具名气,在诗歌造诣上与李商隐齐名。其绝句构思缜密,格调俊逸,用词洗练,意境幽远,在晚唐享有很高的地位。《全唐诗》存其诗八卷。

Du Mu(803～852), styled Muzhi, was born in Wannian, Jingzhao (Xi'an City, Shaanxi Province today). As a government official Du Mu was famous and as a poet he was on a par with Li Shangyin. His quatrains, well-knit in structure, bright and brisk in style, terse in diction with implied meaning, enjoy a high reputation in the late Tang Dynasty. There are eight volumes of his poems collected in *The Complete Collection of the Tang Poetry*.

长安秋望

楼倚霜树外,
镜天无一毫。
南山与秋色,
气势两相高。

An Autumn View from Chang'an

Above the frosty trees the tower looms high,
Cloudless and clear is the mirror-like sky.
The autumn tints over the Zhongnan Mountain,
And all their majesty seems drawing nigh.

独酌

窗外正风雪,
拥炉开酒缸。
何如钓船雨,
篷底睡秋江。

Drinking Alone

Snowstorm is now raging outside my window,
Around the warm stove I open my wine jar.
Fishing in the rain as an idle fellow,
Lying aboard in autumn my boat floats far.

醉眠

秋醪雨中熟,
寒斋落叶中。
幽人本多睡,
更酌一樽空。

Sleeping in a Drunken Stupor

Brewed in autumn the wine gets mellow in rain,
In the fallen leaves my humble house dims.
Living in seclusion I have slept on the brain,
What is more I am dead drunk always in dreams.

独柳

含烟一株柳,
拂地摇风久。
佳人不忍折,
怅望回纤手。

A Lonely Willow

Standing in mist is a lonely tree of willow,
Swaying in the wind it strokes the ground to and fro.
The beauty has no heart to pluck the willow twigs,
Drawing back her slender hand she feels very low.

盆池

凿破苍苔地，
偷他一片天。
白云生镜里，
明月落阶前。

A Pot Pond

Digging a hole on the green mossy ground,
A big pot laid on the earth is a small pond.
Mirrored on the pond the clouds are white,
By the steps the moon in the pot is bright.

江楼

独酌芳春酒,
登楼已半醺。
谁惊一行雁,
冲断过江云。

A Riverside Tower

Alone in the prime of spring I'm drinking,
Tipsy already upstairs I'm walking.
A flight of wild geese all of sudden takes fright,
Through the misty river flying out of sight.

题敬爱寺楼

暮景千山雪,
春寒百尺楼。
独登还独下,
谁会我悠悠。

To the Pagoda in Jing'ai Temple

Dim are snow-covered mountains in the gloaming,
There is a nip in spring atop the tower high.
Walking upstairs and downstairs alone I'm gloomy,
My sorrow lingers long but nobody knows why.

寄远

只影随惊雁，
单栖锁画笼。
向春罗袖薄，
谁念舞台风。

To My Darling Afar

Like a sole shadow you follow the swan in fright,
As if a lonely bird I'm caged day and night.
In early spring I feel chilly to the marrow,
Who takes pity on me a solitary shadow?

题木兰庙

弯弓征战作男儿,
梦里曾经与画眉。
几度思归还把酒,
拂云堆上祝明妃。

To Mulan Temple

Armed with a bow and arrow you fight as a male,
In your dreams you paint eyebrows as you're a female.
Several times when you're homesick you drink a toast,
Wang Zhaojun* is the great heroine you revere most.

---

* Wang Zhaojun, born in Zigui(Xinshan County, Yichang City, Hubei Province today), was a beauty who married herself to the Hun chieftain (in 33 BC) for the implementation of a policy of pacification through marriage in the West Han Dynasty(202BC~AD8).

沈下贤

斯人清唱何人和,
草径苔芜不可寻。
一夕小敷山下梦,
水如环佩月如襟。

A Visit to Shen Xiaxian's Tomb

Lucid and fresh are your poems no one writes in reply,
Deeply buried in weeds I know not "Where does your tomb lie".
I came over to Xiaofu Mountain in my dream one night,
The babbling brook was bathed in the silver moonlight.

赠别·其一

娉娉袅袅十三余，
豆蔻梢头二月初。
春风十里扬州路，
卷上珠帘总不如。

A Reluctant Parting (1)

No more than fourteen years of age you're graceful and fair,
In your early puberty you're a flower bud so rare.
Along the Yangzhou Road beauties are more than enough,
Nevertheless you're the only one beyond compare.

赠别·其二

多情却似总无情，
唯觉樽前笑不成。
蜡烛有心还惜别，
替人垂泪到天明。

A Reluctant Parting（2）

Too sentimental I am to show my love for you,
Drinking with you in joy and sorrow but I can't show.
The candle is sad at the moment of our parting,
Shedding tears for us till dawn and the sorrow would grow.

念昔游

十载飘然绳检外,
樽前自献自为酬。
秋山春雨闲吟处,
倚遍江南寺寺楼。

Recollection of the Past Tour

I'm free from the yoke of etiquette for ten years,
Drinking all by myself I am greeted with cheers.
The autumn mountains and spring rain I'd like to chant,
All temples south of the Yangtze River are my haunts.

过华清宫

长安回望绣成堆,
山顶千门次第开。
一骑红尘妃子笑,
无人知是荔枝来。

Reflection on Huaqing Palace

Viewed from afar it stands between green peaks like brocade,
The gate of the palace are opened one by one upgrade.
On seeing the steed in dust the consort smiles in delight,
Few people know lychees must be delivered day and night.

登乐游原

长空澹澹孤鸟没,
万古销沉向此中。
看取汉家何事业,
五陵无树起秋风。

In the Imperial Paradise

A lovely bird faintly vanishes from the vast skies,
Many empires and powers have faded as time flies.
So mighty was the Han Dynasty in history,
It comes to nothing but barren tombs as autumn wind sighs.

将赴吴兴登乐游原一绝

清时有味是无能，
闲爱孤云静爱僧。
欲把一麾江海去，
乐游原上望昭陵。

A Quatrain for the Sightseeing Tour of the Imperial Paradise

Indulging in leisure in peace I am incompetent,
Now floating as clouds and now calm as a monk silent.
Let my dream come true I'm to go to my post far away,
At the top of the garden to emperor's tomb I pray.

寄扬州韩绰判官

青山隐隐水迢迢，
秋尽江南草未凋。
二十四桥明月夜，
玉人何处教吹箫。

To Han Chuo a Judge in Yangzhou

Faintly in sight are green hills and water stretches far away,
Autumn's over but south of the Yangtze River still in green array.
Twenty-four bridges are bathed in the bright moonlight at night,
You must be somewhere fluting with singing girls with delight.

别家

初岁娇儿未识爷,
别爷不拜手吒叉。
捫头一别三千里,
何日迎门却到家。

Farewell to My Family

Dear to me my son is too young to know I'm his dad,
Folding his hands instead of making farewell to me.
Stroking his hair I'll start a journey three thousand Li,
I wonder when he could greet me by gate as a lad.

江南春

千里莺啼绿映红，
水村山郭酒旗风。
南朝四百八十寺，
多少楼台烟雨中。

Spring in the South of the Yangtze River

Orioles sing for miles among green trees and red flowers,
Along the river and hill path streamers wave at all hours.
So many temples built in the past still splendid and bright,
In the mist and rain many pagodas are dim in sight.

齐安郡中偶题

两竿落日溪桥上,
半缕轻烟柳影中。
多少绿荷相倚恨,
一时回首背西风。

Random Thoughts in Qi'an Prefecture

Kissing the bridge across the stream the sun is setting,
From the shade of willows a curl of smoke is rising.
Numerous lotus leaves huddle up in sorrow,
Bent with fright at the west wind they cast a long shadow.

池州清溪

弄溪终日到黄昏,
照数秋来白发根。
何物赖君千遍洗,
笔头尘土渐无痕。

Qingxi Stream in Chizhou

Enjoying the charm of the stream from dawn to dusk,
Mirrored on the stream I count my hair turning white.
Nurtured by the stream water day and night for years,
Cleansed is my mind and my poems are freshly bright.

齐安郡后池绝句

菱透浮萍绿锦池，
夏莺千啭弄蔷薇。
尽日无人看微雨，
鸳鸯相对浴红衣。

The Back Pond of Qi'an Prefecture

Water chestnut and duckweed spread a lush green on the pond,
Through rose and shrubs orioles sing again and again around.
No figure enjoys the drizzle at the end of the day,
Bathing in pairs mandarin ducks are dressed in red array.

初冬夜饮

淮阳多病偶求欢,
客袖侵霜举烛盘。
砌下梨花一堆雪,
明年谁此凭阑干?

Drinking at Night in Early Winter

Afflicted with disease I want to drink once in a while,
Frostbitten I am drinking alone by the candlelight.
By the steps like pear flowers snowflakes whirl into a pile,
In the coming year who'll come to lean on the rail at night?

兰溪（在蕲州西）

兰溪春尽碧泱泱，
映水兰花雨发香。
楚国大夫憔悴日，
应寻此路去潇湘。

Lanxi River in Qizhou

At the end of spring crystal clear is Lanxi River vast,
Fragrant are orchid flowers in the rain by waterside.
When Qu Yuan, a senior official was wan and downcast,
Along this stream to Xiangjiang River he was exiled.

清 郑燮 《兰花图》

柳绝句

数树新开翠影齐,
倚风情态被春迷。
依依故国樊川恨,
半掩村桥半掩溪。

To Willows

Fresh are a few willows and shadows vivid green,
Swaying in the wind and the charm stands out in spring.
Graceful twigs evoke my homesickness lingering,
Across the stream the village bridge can be half seen.

鹭鸶

雪衣雪发青玉嘴，
群捕鱼儿溪影中。
惊飞远映碧山去，
一树梨花落晚风。

To Egrets

With green-jade beak you're dressed in snow-white array,
On the fish in stream flying in flock you try to prey.
Suddenly startled to the green hill you fly away,
Like petals of pear flowers in the dusk wind you play.

村舍燕

汉宫一百四十五，
多下珠帘闭琐窗。
何处营巢夏将半，
茅檐烟里语双双。

To Cottage Swallows

One hundred and forty-five Han palaces are a rare sight,
But most of them have the painted windows closed tight.
Where to nest as a half of the summer has gone past,
Under the cottage eaves you twitter in pairs fast.

题禅院

觥船一棹百分空,
十岁青春不负公。
今日鬓丝禅榻畔,
茶烟轻飏落花风。

In a Buddhist Temple

In the boat loaded with wine I drink my fill,
For ten years I've behaved of my own free will.
By the meditation bed now my hair's grey,
With petals dancing round I hold a tea tray.

屏风绝句

屏风周昉画纤腰,
岁久丹青色半销。
斜倚玉窗鸾发女,
拂尘犹自妒娇娆。

The Screen

Slim and fair is the maiden painted on the screen,
But its color has faded as the years go by.
Leaning on the window with tresses like a queen,
She flicks the dust, jealous of maiden's charm with a sigh.

汉江

溶溶漾漾白鸥飞,
绿净春深好染衣。
南去北来人自老,
夕阳长送钓船归。

The Hanjiang River

Over the gentle ripples of the vast river gulls fly,
Limpid water blending with spring tint makes a strong green dye.
The hustle and bustle make you aging before you know,
The angling boat returns home in the setting sun glow.

赤壁

折戟沉沙铁未销，
自将磨洗认前朝。
东风不与周郎便，
铜雀春深锁二乔。

Meditations on the Red Cliff

Deep in sand the broken halberds are not yet worn away,
The time of the relics is told when rubbing the rusty clay.
Had the east wind refused to favor Commander Zhou*,
His wife and her sister would be locked as the caged prey.

---

* Commander Zhou here refers to Zhou Yu (175～210), the commander-in-chief of Kingdom Wu (229～280) during the period of the Three Kingdoms (220～280).

明　仇英　《赤壁图》(局部)

泊秦淮

烟笼寒水月笼沙,
夜泊秦淮近酒家。
商女不知亡国恨,
隔江犹唱后庭花。

Berthed on Qinhuai River

Cold water and sandbar are veiled in the misty moonlight,
Berthed on Qinhuai River my boat is near wineshops at night.
The singing girl knows not the insult of a conquered land,
Beyond the river she sings the decadent song with delight.

秋浦途中

萧萧山路穷秋雨,
浙浙溪风一岸蒲。
为问寒沙新到雁,
来时还下杜陵无。

On the Way to Qiupu

The rain keeps pattering the mountain path in late autumn,
Whipping the cattails on the bank the wind blows from afar.
Tell me please, the new-arrived swan geese on the sandbar,
Did you come here by way of Emperor Xuan Mausoleum?

题乌江亭

胜败兵家事不期，
包羞忍耻是男儿。
江东子弟多才俊，
卷土重来未可知。

To Wujiang Pavilion

Victory or defeat sometimes hangs in the balance,
Standing firm under the strain of failure and fame is the true man.
Most of the youth in the south the Yangtze River are men of eminence,
Gathering forces to make a comeback I think he can.

寄远

前山极远碧云合，
清夜一声白雪微。
欲寄相思千里月，
溪边残照雨霏霏。

To a Faraway Friend

Far away from the front mountain clouds gather in the sky,
At dead of night a graceful melody is drawing nigh.
I'm to entrust to the moon my missing far away,
But when the sun sets by the stream it's drizzling from on high.

南陵道中

南陵江水漫悠悠,
风紧云轻欲变秋。
正是客心孤迥处,
谁家红袖凭江楼?

On the Way to Nanling

Slowly and still the river water in Nanling flows,
Autumn's about to come, clouds float as the brisk wind blows.
Here's the very place I feel lonely away from home,
Who's the belle leaning on the rails of riverside tower, no one knows.

雨

连云接塞添迢递，
洒幕侵灯送寂寥。
一夜不眠孤客耳，
主人窗外有芭蕉。

The Rain

From the earth towering into clouds it pours from the sky,
Behind the veil of the rain the lamp is lonely in sight.
In the alien land I'm a guest lying awake all night,
Outside the window the rain patters the plantain nearby.

遣怀

落魄江湖载酒行,
楚腰纤细掌中轻。
十年一觉扬州梦,
赢得青楼薄幸名。

Giving Vent to My Feelings

Left out in the cold I've indulged myself in wine,
Abandoned to slender girls dancing on palms of mine.
Roaming in happy dreams for ten years now I'm sober,
Aware that in the brothel I'm named a fickle lover.

秋感

金风万里思何尽,
玉树一窗秋影寒。
独掩柴门明月下,
泪流香袂倚阑干。

Recollections in Late Autumn

Endless is my thought as the west wind blows from afar,
Chilly is the shadow of the green tree near the window.
Alone with the bright moon the wicket gate is left ajar,
Leaning on the rail tears wet my sleeves I'm in sorrow.

赠渔父

芦花深泽静垂纶，
月夕烟朝几十春。
自说孤舟寒水畔，
不曾逢著独醒人。

To the Fisherman

In the deep pond among the reed catkins you angle still,
From dawn to dusk for scores of years in spite of heat and chill.
A lonely angler in a lonely boat on cold water,
You have met nobody on earth that is really sober.

叹花

自恨寻芳到已迟,
往年曾见未开时。
如今风摆花狼藉,
绿叶成阴子满枝。

Regret at Fallen Flowers

Much to my regret I've missed the flowering season,
I once saw the tiny buds lovely enough in the past.
Scattering with wind there's now a mess of petals fallen,
Branches laden with fruits and a shade of green leaves cast.

山行

远上寒山石径斜，
白云生处有人家。
停车坐爱枫林晚，
霜叶红于二月花。

Along the Path Uphill

Slanting is the stony path leading far to the cold hill,
The cooking smoke curls upwards where the white clouds rise.
So charming are the maple woods I stop my cab to feel,
Redder than spring flowers are leaves tinged with rime dyes.

酬王秀才桃花园见寄

桃满西园淑景催，
几多红艳浅深开。
此花不逐溪流出，
晋客无因入洞来。

The Peach Blossom Garden

In the west garden peach blossoms are fresh with sunshine,
Shading from light to enrich the bright colors are so fine.
Smiling on the travelers they do not drift with tide,
It's the Shangri-La people of the Jin State that took as hide.

洛阳秋夕

泠泠寒水带霜风，
更在天桥夜景中。
清禁漏闲烟树寂，
月轮移在上阳宫。

An Autumn Night in Luoyang

There's a slight chill over the water and frosty wind blows,
Enjoying the night view from Tianjin Bridge the bleakness grows.
Quiet is the water clock and misty trees lonely at night,
Atop the Shangyang Palace* deserted is the moon light.

---

* The Shangyang Palace was the imperial palace during the reign of Emperor Xuanzong, where the maids banished from the court were often confined. In this poem it implies the palace maids' grievance.

秋夕

银烛秋光冷画屏,
轻罗小扇扑流萤。
天阶夜色凉如水,
坐看牵牛织女星。

An Autumn Night

Autumn night cools the painted screen in the candle light,
The palace maid runs after a firefly with a silk fan.
Wet with dew drops the steps are cold at the tender night,
Gazing at Altair and Vega in love she tries to span.

破镜

佳人失手镜初分,
何日团圆再会君?
今朝万里秋风起,
山北山南一片云。

The Broken Mirror

Losing her grip of the mirror she got it broken,
Yearning for her darling but reunion's uncertain.
Now the autumn wind starts to blow from west far away,
Drifting with the wind the clouds come apart the mountain.

清明

清明时节雨纷纷，
路上行人欲断魂。
借问酒家何处有，
牧童遥指杏花村。

The Memorial Day in Spring

Like tears the light drizzle falls on the Memorial Day,
Heart-broken is the passer-by plodding on the way.
Asking about the wineshop he wants to drown the sad hours,
A cowherd points to the Cot of Apricot Flowers.

金谷园

繁华事散逐香尘，
流水无情草自春。
日暮东风怨啼鸟，
落花犹似坠楼人。

The Deserted Jingu Garden

Splendors of the garden vanish in a puff of fragrance,
But grass grows in spring and river flows with indifference.
Soughs and sighs the east wind with birds in the evening glow,
Like Green Pearl* tumbling from the tower flowers fall and flow.

---

* Green Pearl was a ravishing prostitute kept by a rich man Shi Chong, the owner of the Jingu Garden. When she learnt that Shi Chong was going to offer her to Sun Xin, another playboy, she tumbled down from the building and killed herself.

赵 嘏

赵嘏(806~853),字承祐,楚州山阳(今江苏淮安)人。其诗语言流畅,格律工整,风格清新自然。《全唐诗》存其诗两卷。

Zhao Gu (806~853), styled Chengyou, was born in Shanyang, Chuzhou (Huai'an City, Jiangsu Province today). Smooth language, well-knit metrical pattern in fresh and natural style are characteristics of his poems, of which two volumes are collected in *The Complete Collection of the Tang Poetry*.

到家

童稚牵衣问,
归来何太迟。
共谁争岁月,
赢得鬓边丝。

Homecoming

Pulling my garment the silly lad asks,
You return home so late for what tasks?
Putting years on yourself you vie with whom?
Grey hairs on both temples quietly loom.

春酿

春酿正风流,
梨花莫问愁。
马卿思一醉,
不惜鹔鹴裘。

Wine Brewed in Spring

Wine brewed in spring is just in fashion now,
Pear-flower wine can get rid of my sorrow.
So long as I can get wine no matter how,
I'd like to get drunk at all costs as you know.

寒塘

晓发梳临水,
寒塘坐见秋。
乡心正无限,
一雁度南楼。

Cold Pond

Sitting by the pond I'm combing in the morning,
I feel chilly by water as autumn's coming.
Lost in thought of native land I am in sorrow,
A swan over the south building casts a shadow.

长信宫

君恩已尽欲何归,
犹有残香在舞衣。
自恨身轻不如燕,
春来还绕御帘飞。

Changxin Palace

Out of favor from the emperor where can I go?
The scent of dancing dress remains like evening glow.
Regretting I'm no more slim and swift as a swallow,
That dances in the court like the emperor's shadow.

商山道中

和如春色净如秋，
五月商山是胜游。
当昼火云生不得，
一溪萦作万重愁。

On the Way to Shangshan Mountain

Tender as spring scenery and clear as autumn sky,
A trip to Shangshan in May is a pleasure so high.
Scorching clouds never appear during the daytime,
But a cloud over the stream is like a shroud of rime.

广陵道

斗鸡台边花照尘，
炀帝陵下水含春。
青云回翅北归雁，
白首哭途何处人。

On the Way to Guangling

By the Cockfight Stage* flowers in dust are blooming,
Near Yang Guang's** tomb with spring tint the water's streaming.
Towards the north a flight of swans in the sky flies,
From where the hoary-headed man on the way cries?

---

* The Cockfight Stage is in the suburbs of Yangzhou City, Jiangsu Province.
** Yang Guang(569~618) is the second emperor of the Sui Dynasty(581~618) who came into power after killing his father the first emperor of the Sui Dynasty. His mausoleum is to the north of Jiangdu, Yangzhou City, Jiangsu Province.

途中

故园回首雁初来，
马上千愁付一杯。
惟有新诗似相识，
暮山吟处共徘徊。

During the Journey

Turning around I see swans fling to my native land,
Cup in hand on horseback I'm to drink down my sorrow.
It seems to me the new poem I have met before and,
Chanted with a friend wandering in the evening glow.

西江晚泊

茫茫霭霭失西东，
柳浦桑树处处同。
戍鼓一声帆影尽，
水禽飞起夕阳中。

Berthing by West River in the Evening Glow

In the vast expanse of mist nothing can be seen,
Similar in color all trees are no more green.
With a drumbeat of garrison sails fade away,
In the evening glow a few water birds play.

南池

照影池边多少愁，
往来重见此塘秋。
芙蓉苑外新经雨，
红叶相随何处流。

Qujiang Pond

Reflected in the pond is the figure deep in sorrow,
Standing by the pond again I see the autumn tints grow.
Freshly bathed in the shower is the lotus garden,
Floating are the red leaves but where for I don't know.

江楼旧感

独上江楼思渺然，
月光如水水如天。
同来望月人何处，
风景依稀似去年。

Recollection of the Past atop a Riverside Tower

Atop the tower alone I'm lost in thought of the past,
Tender are the moonbeams melted into clear water vast.
Nowhere to find my companion that shared me the moonlight,
But the landscape seems what it was last year the very night.

唐 李思训 《江帆楼阁图》

东亭柳

拂水斜烟一万条，
几随春色倚河桥。
不知别后谁攀折，
犹自风流胜舞腰。

Willows Around the East Pavilion

Stroking misty water are thousands of twigs of willow,
Leaning on the bridge you turn green with the spring coming.
Who have plucked your twigs since my parting I don't know,
Slender and slim your graceful dance is still so charming.

新月

玉钩斜傍画檐生,
云匣初开一寸明。
何事最能悲少妇,
夜来依约落边城。

The New Moon

Clinging to the painted eaves it's like a jade hook,
From behind the clouds only a sharp angle looms bright.
To a young married woman what casts a harmful blight?
Beyond the border town the moon sets at a dark nook.

池上

正怜佳月夜深坐,
池上暖回燕雁声。
犹有渔舟系江岸,
故人归尽独何情。

Sitting by the Pond

Tenderly loving the moon I sit at dead of night,
Over the warm pond float the calls of a wild goose flight.
Along the bank some fishing boats are still busy mooring,
With all friends gone back homesickness is really a blight.

春日书怀

暖莺春日舌难穷,
枕上愁生晓听中。
应袅绿窗残梦断,
杏园零落满枝风。

Pouring out My Heart in Spring

In the warmth of springtime orioles keep on singing,
When hearing on the pillow at dawn my sorrow grows.
By the window the fragments of my dream are floating,
In the apricot garden petals fly as the wind blows.

重阳

节逢重九海门外,
家在五湖烟水东。
还向秋山觅诗句,
伴僧吟对菊花风。

Double Ninth Festival

Double Ninth Festival concurs with my tour beyond the coast,
To the east of misty Taihu Lake my home is charming most.
The autumn mountain is my favorite haunt for poetic mood,
Chanting to chrysanthemums with the monk is my mental food.

遣兴

溪花入夏渐稀疏，
雨气如秋麦熟初。
终日苦吟人不会，
海边兄弟久无书。

Pouring out My Sentiment

Summer comes and flowers by the stream are fading away,
After rain it's cool as autumn and wheat starts to be ripe.
Nobody understands my poems though I work hard all day,
I miss my brothers but no news from them for a long time.

赠别

水边秋草暮萋萋,
欲驻残阳恨马蹄。
曾是管弦同醉伴,
一声歌尽各东西。

A Parting Verse to a Friend

Autumn grass grows lushly by waterside in twilight,
Halting for the setting sun but my steed's galloping.
Sharing the melody of strings we drink in delight,
Each has to go his own way after the song of parting.

陈 陶

陈陶(生卒年不详),字嵩伯,鄱阳(今江西波阳)人。屡试不第后,隐居洪州(今江西省南昌市)。《全唐诗》存其诗两卷。

Chen Tao, styled Songbo, was born in Poyang (Boyang County, Jiangxi Province today). Having failed in imperial examinations one after another, Chen Tao kept himself in seclusion in the West Mountain in Hongzhou (Nanchang City, Jiangxi Province today). Two volumes of his poems are collected in *The Complete Collection of the Tang Poetry*.

赋得古莲塘

阖闾宫娃能采莲,
明珠作佩龙为船。
三千巧笑不复见,
江头废苑花年年。

The Ancient Lotus Pond

Good at gathering lotus seeds is the king's palace maid,
The dragon boat is decorated with bright pearls and jade.
The smart smiles of the past maids are now nowhere to be seen,
But flowers in the garden bloom yearly like a routine.

江上逢故人

十年蓬转金陵道，
长哭青云身不早。
故里相逢尽白头，
清江颜色何曾老。

Meeting an Old Friend on the River

Ten years are spent wandering on the way to Jinling,
Rising to fame is my goal but it's come to nothing.
All the folks I've met in the hometown their hairs turn white,
Only the river with no change flows still day and night.

春归去

九十春光在何处，
古人今人留不住。
年年白眼向黔娄，
唯放蛴螬飞上树。

Spring on the Wane

Three months of spring have passed and where is it now?
People strive to make spring stay but they don't know how.
Year in year out of the poor spring takes no notice,
But to insects and worms so generous it is.

子规思

春山杜鹃来几日，
夜啼南家复北家。
野人听此坐惆怅，
恐畏踏落东园花。

Sad Thoughts over the Calls of Cuckoo

Cuckoo came to the spring mountain a few days ago,
Cuckoo, cuckoo, it calls here and there throughout the night.
Hearing its calls I sit up late and gloomy thoughts grow,
On the petals in the east garden treading is a blight.

竹

丘壑谁堪话碧鲜,
静寻春谱认婵娟。
会当小杀青瑶简,
图写龟鱼把上天。

To Bamboo

All over the hills and gullies what can be the bright green,
Looking high and low in springtime graceful most is bamboo.
If processed into strips for writing and painting screen,
Classics, even heavenly letters can be written too.

水调词

水阁莲开燕引雏,
朝朝攀折望金吾。
闻道碛西春不到,
花时还忆故园无。

The Song to the Tune of Water

A swallow leads a large brood and lotus flowers bloom,
Plucking flowers I'm pining for my darling with gloom.
Spring never comes to the west of vast desert I hear,
In the flowering season aren't you homesick, my dear?

陇西行

誓扫匈奴不顾身，
五千貂锦丧胡尘。
可怜无定河边骨，
犹是春闺梦里人。

A Trip to the Frontier Battlefield

Pledging their lives to put down the revolt of Huns,
Five thousand soldiers all laid down their lives.
Buried along the Wuding River they're the brave sons,
But still they haunt the spring dreams of their wives.

温庭筠

温庭筠(812~866),原名岐,字飞卿,太原(今山西祁县)人。屡试不第,长于诗词。其诗词藻华丽,多写个人遭际。《全唐诗》存其诗九卷。

Wen Tingyun (812~866), styled Feiqing, originally named Wen Qi, was born in Taiyuan (Qixian County, Shanxi Province today). As a frustrated candidate his official dream failed to come true, but his poems are famous for ornate diction and a vivid picture of his real-life experience. Nine volumes of his poems are collected in *The Complete Collection of the Tang Poetry*.

地肺山春日

冉冉花明岸,
涓涓水绕山。
几时抛俗事,
来共白云闲。

Spring in Difeishan Mountain

Bright and fresh are the flowers by waterside,
Trickling is the stream around the mountainside.
If I am free from the worldly cares one day,
I'll invite the white clouds to leisurely play.

碧涧驿晓思

香灯伴残梦，
楚国在天涯。
月落子规歇，
满庭山杏花。

Dawn at Bijian Post Station

Awake from the broken dream with the lamp alone,
Far away from the Chu State I sleep on my own.
The moon's setting and the cuckoo rests for a while,
All over the courtyard apricot blossoms smile.

嘲三月十八日雪

三月雪连夜，
未应伤物华。
只缘春欲尽，
留著伴梨花。

To Snow in the Third Lunar Month

In the third lunar month you swirl all night,
Meaning no harm to flowers but you're a blight.
Afraid of the fact spring will pass its prime,
Accompanying pear flowers for a short time.

杨柳枝

宜春苑外最长条,
闲袅春风伴舞腰。
正是玉人肠断处,
一渠春水赤栏桥。

To Willow Twigs

Long, long are the willow twigs outside the royal garden,
Swaying in the vernal breeze like dancing girls of grace.
Caged in the palace the pretty maids are grief-stricken,
Across the spring water Chilan Bridge is the very place.

赠少年

江海相逢客恨多,
秋风叶下洞庭波。
酒酣夜别淮阴市,
月照高楼一曲歌。

To a Young Friend

Running into a friend in a strange land I'm grief-stricken,
As we're both losers drifting about like leaves fallen.
Mellow with drink we have to part at the autumn night,
Atop the building we sing a farewell in the moonlight.

过分水岭

溪水无情似有情,
入山三日得同行。
岭头便是分头处,
惜别潺湲一夜声。

Crossing over the Watershed

Heartless is the stream but it seems heartwarming,
Along the mountain path it follows me walking.
At the watershed we have to say goodbye,
All the night long it sings to me from on high.

长安春晚

曲江春半日迟迟,
正是王孙怅望时。
杏花落尽不归去,
江上东风吹柳丝。

A Spring View at Dusk in Chang'an

In mid-spring the Qujiang Pond sees the sun slowly setting,
It's the very time for peers to have a wishful looking.
Apricot blossoms have all fallen but still there they stay,
Along the river with the spring breeze the willow twigs play.

瑶瑟怨

冰簟银床梦不成，
碧天如水夜云轻。
雁声远过潇湘去，
十二楼中月自明。

Sorrow of a Young Lady Playing Zither

Cold enough on the splendid bed but she has a bad night,
Vast is the blue sky at night and the white clouds freely swim.
All of a sudden come the cries of wild geese southward in flight,
In the boudoir lonely is the lady with the moonbeam.

宋　米友仁　《潇湘奇观图》

咸阳值雨

咸阳桥上雨如悬，
万点空濛隔钓船。
还似洞庭春水色，
晚云将入岳阳天。

Caught in the Rain in Xianyang

It's pouring down over Xianyang Bridge like water curtain,
Shrouded in rainy mist the fishing boat is but a blur.
Like the view of spring water in Dongting Lake for certain,
Southward to Yueyang it's drifting with clouds put on a spur.

李商隐

李商隐(812~858),字义山,号玉溪生,怀州河内(今河南沁阳)人。曾在朝为官,其诗构思缜密,清致婉曲,文采飞扬,风格独特。《全唐诗》存其诗三卷。

Li Shangyin (812~858), styled Yishan, also known as Yu Xisheng which is his alias, was born in Henei, Huaizhou (Qinyang City, Henan Province today). Li once held office in the imperial court and his poems are well-knit in structure with euphemistic language full of literary taste in unique style. Three volumes of his poems are collected in *The Complete Collection of the Tang Poetry*.

悼伤后赴东蜀辟至散关遇雪

剑外从军远,
无家与寄衣。
散关三尺雪,
回梦旧鸳机。

Caught in Snow at Sanguan Pass

On the way to join the army far away,
Bereaved of my wife no one sends me array.
Deep in snow at the pass I am caught in gloom,
Dreaming of my wife busy at the old loom.

乐游原

向晚意不适，
驱车登古原。
夕阳无限好，
只是近黄昏。

The Royal Paradise

In a bad mood in the evening glow,
I'm driving to the royal paradise.
Sublime most is the time when the sun sets low,
But in the gloaming daylight nearly dies.

忆梅

定定住天涯,
依依向物华。
寒梅最堪恨,
常作去年花。

The Memory of Plum Blossoms

Firmly fixed I'm in a faraway place,
Attached to the beauty of spring grace.
However fair the plum blossoms may be,
They bloom last winter which never delays.

天涯

春日在天涯，
天涯日又斜。
莺啼如有泪，
为湿最高花。

At the End of the Earth

In spring from home I'm far and far away,
And the sun slants at the end of the day.
Weep the orioles please if you are in tears,
Wet the flowers atop to you I say cheers.

细雨

帷飘白玉堂,
簟卷碧牙床。
楚女当时意,
萧萧发彩凉。

To the Drizzle

From the high palace it hangs like a curtain light,
Drooping from the sky it's like a bed of jade bright.
The tresses of the Goddess in the mien of grace,
Stroking her hair breeze brings a bit chill on her face.

滞雨

滞雨长安夜，
残灯独客愁。
故乡云水地，
归梦不宜秋。

A Hold-up by Rain

Held up by rain in Chang'an I stay the night,
Alone in sorrow waning is the lamplight.
The rainstorm to hometown is a disaster,
On dreaming home in autumn it is a blight.

柳枝

画屏绣步障，
物物自成双。
如何湖上望，
只是见鸳鸯。

Willow Branches

Willow branches are painted on the screen,
Creatures are extremely vivid in pairs.
Gazing far from the lake alone I've seen,
Only mandarin ducks in sight no one shares.

霜月

初闻征雁已无蝉，
百尺楼南水接天。
青女素娥俱耐冷，
月中霜里斗婵娟。

The Frosty Month

When the wild geese cry the buzzes of cicadas wither,
To the south of the tall tower rime glints in the moonlight.
The Rime Goddess and the Moon Goddess fear no cold weather,
They vie with each other for who is more fair and bright.

岳阳楼

欲为平生一散愁，
洞庭湖上岳阳楼。
可怜万里堪乘兴，
枉是蛟龙解覆舟。

Yueyang Tower

In order to dispel my sorrow all my life,
I climb the tower in Dongting Lake with delight.
Vast is the lake water with a wonderful sight,
But the evil dragon sinks the boat which is rife.

北齐

一笑相倾国便亡,
何劳荆棘始堪伤。
小莲玉体横陈夜,
已报周师入晋阳。

The Northern Qi Kingdom

Charming as Helen her smile causes the fall of a state,
Unbridled debauchery results in his dreadful fate.
The very night the concubine offers her body fair,
Jinyang* is captured and to the king it is a nightmare.

---

* Jinyang (Taiyuan City, Shanxi Province today) was a place of strategic importance of Northern Qi Kingdom, which was in the vicinity of Yecheng, the capital of Northern Qi Kingdom.

夜雨寄北

君问归期未有期,
巴山夜雨涨秋池。
何当共剪西窗烛,
却话巴山夜雨时。

A Poem to My Wife on a Rainy Night

You ask me the date of homecoming, but I don't know,
The autumn rain at night makes the rivers overflow.
Yearning for reunion near the window by candlelight,
We can chat about the mountain floods at rainy night.

齐宫词

永寿兵来夜不扃，
金莲无复印中庭。
梁台歌管三更罢，
独自风摇九子铃。

Song of the South Qi Palace

No sentry on guard when the foe seized the palace at night,
In the midcourt golden lotus flowers were not so bright.
In the dead of night the new king indulged in night life,
The jade bells of the old palace rang still with the wind light.

春光

日日春光斗日光，
山城斜路杏花香。
几时心绪浑无事，
得及游丝百尺长。

Spring Scenery

For beauty in spring scenery vies with the sunshine,
Along the slanting path apricot blossoms smell fine.
How and when can I be in a mood free from care?
Like fine gossamer light and long floating in the air.

吴宫

龙槛沉沉水殿清,
禁门深掩断人声。
吴王宴罢满宫醉,
日暮水漂花出城。

The Palace of the Wu Kingdom

The pavilion looms on the still water in the twilight,
Closed is the gate and palace calm with no figure in sight.
After the banquet drunk as lords are all those present,
Out of the city petals float and drawing nigh is night.

忆住一师

无事经年别远公，
帝城钟晓忆西峰。
炉烟消尽寒灯晦，
童子开门雪满松。

In Memory of Huiyuan*, an Eminent Monk

Being parted from you without rhyme or reason for years,
The bell from the court reminds me of the west peak in tears.
Goes out the incense in the burner and dim is the light,
A boy opens the gate and snow on pines comes into sight.

---

* Huiyuan, an eminent Buddhist monk of the Eastern Jin Dynasty, practiced Buddhism in Donglin Temple.

端居

远书归梦两悠悠，
只有空床敌素秋。
阶下青苔与红树，
雨中寥落月中愁。

An Idle Stay Far Away from Home

Far away from home I've no news and dream neither for years,
In bleak autumn my bed's empty I've no one to say cheers.
Leaves of trees turn red and along the steps mosses grow,
In the rain and mist dim is the moon and I'm in sorrow.

离亭赋得折杨柳·其一

暂凭樽酒送无憀，
莫损愁眉与细腰。
人世死前惟有别，
春风争拟惜长条。

Farewell Songs of Plucking Willow Twigs（1）

Nothing but a cup of wine for our parting pain,
Care kills a cat and your waist can't be more slender.
Beside death the saddest is to part time and again,
Oh, vernal breeze, please spare no willow twigs tender.

离亭赋得折杨柳·其二

含烟惹雾每依依,
万绪千条拂落晖。
为报行人休尽折,
半留相送半迎归。

Farewell Songs of Plucking Willow Twigs (2)

Hazed in the mist your gentle tresses sway with grace,
Thousands of twigs stroke the evening glow with breeze.
Would you be so kind to have some twigs reserved, please?
Leave some for your friends who'll come back to the old place.

咏史

北湖南埭水漫漫，
一片降旗百尺竿。
三百年间同晓梦，
钟山何处有龙盘。

An Elegy to Jinling the Capital of Six Dynasties

Buried deep is the historic site in waters vast,
A forest of towering poles of white flags stand fast.
For three hundred years six dynasties have the same dream,
But no dragon could guard Zhongshan Mountain till the last.

宫辞

君恩如水向东流,
得宠忧移失宠愁。
莫向尊前奏花落,
凉风只在殿西头。

Song of the Palace Maids

Like the stream water the king's favor is the eastward flow,
Favored by His Majesty or not the maids' sorrows grow.
Don't play the tune of "Fallen Flowers" while the king's drinking,
From the west of the court maybe the bleak wind will soon blow.

题汉祖庙

乘运应须宅八荒，
男儿安在恋池隍。
君王自起新丰后，
项羽何曾在故乡。

To the Temple of Emperor Gaozu of Han Dynasty

If you have good luck, come to power wherever you are,
To be a man bidding for power home's a fatal bar.
The Emperor could build a new hometown as he likes,
Attached to his hometown Xiang Yu's so near yet so far.

柳

曾逐东风拂舞筵，
乐游春苑断肠天。
如何肯到清秋日，
已带斜阳又带蝉。

To the Willow

Swaying with dancers at the feast you chase the wind from east,
Charmed by the belles in the garden you find paradise.
Desolate is the late autumn how can you bear the mist,
The sun sinks and cicadas cling to you with noisy cries.

夕阳楼

花明柳暗绕天愁，
上尽重城更上楼。
欲问孤鸿向何处？
不知身世自悠悠。

The Setting-Sun Tower

Bright are flowers, dim is willow but I'm in sorrow,
As I climb the gate tower my sorrows quickly grow.
I ask the lone swan flying overhead, "Where to go"?
Like a yo-yo floating about my own fate I don't know.

谒山

从来系日乏长绳,
水去云回恨不胜。
欲就麻姑买沧海,
一杯春露冷如冰。

Homage to the Mountain

There has been no rope long enough to fasten the sun,
And nobody can stop water or clouds from floating on.
With the nymph to buy the vast sea I try to bargain,
It turns to a cup of icy spring dew all of a sudden.

嫦娥

云母屏风烛影深，
长河渐落晓星沉。
嫦娥应悔偷灵药，
碧海青天夜夜心。

To the Moon Goddess

Upon mica-inlaid screen winking is the candlelight,
The Milky Way's on the wane and morning stars nearly set.
Having stolen the panacea the Goddess must regret,
Alone in the lunar palace she's a mope day and night.

残花

残花啼露莫留春，
尖发谁非怨别人。
若但掩关劳独梦，
宝钗何日不生尘。

Faded Flowers

In tears the faded flowers weep over the lost prime,
For years so many ladies grudge the parting time.
Once in bed with the door shut you've to dream alone,
Put aside the precious hairpin that's no more sublime.

暮秋独游曲江

荷叶生时春恨生，
荷叶枯时秋恨成。
深知身在情长在，
怅望江头江水声。

Touring Around Qujiang Pond Alone in Late Autumn

When lotus is in bud my gloom starts to grow,
When lotus fades away I'm deep in sorrow.
So long as I'm alive my love will last for you,
Wistfully looking by the pond I'm really low.

木兰花

洞庭波冷晓侵云,
日日征帆送远人。
几度木兰舟上望,
不知元是此花身。

To Magnolia Flower

On Dongting Lake the cold waves kiss the clouds wan,
Day by day friends are sent off by boat sailing on.
Time and again on board I see sails slowly fade,
I know not of the magnolia wood the boat's made.

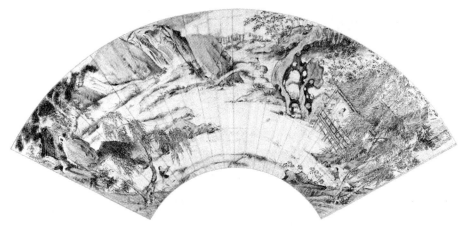

明 仇英 《兰亭图扇面》

花下醉

寻芳不觉醉流霞,
倚树沉眠日已斜。
客散酒醒深夜后,
更持红烛赏残花。

Drunk Among Flowers

Looking for flowers I'm quite drunk but I don't know,
Deep in sleep I lean on the tree and the sun sinks low.
Sobering up the visitors disperse at midnight,
I enjoy the faded flowers by the candlelight.

贾生

宣室求贤访逐臣,
贾生才调更无伦。
可怜夜半虚前席,
不问苍生问鬼神。

To Jia Yi a Talented Scholar

To seek the top talent the Emperor seems so eager,
Gifted with eminence Jia Yi was a peerless scholar.
Alas! His Majesty called him in the dead of night,
To consult about ghost and deity instead of labor.

李群玉

李群玉(813~860),字文山,澧州(今湖南澧县)人。风流旷达,不乐仕进。其诗文笔流畅,风格清丽。《全唐诗》存其诗三卷。

Li Qunyu (813~860), styled Wenshan, was born in Lizhou (Lixian County, Hunan Province today). Talented and broad-minded, Li Qunyu was not interested in official career then. His poems are smoothly written in lucid and graceful style, of which three volumes are collected in *The Complete Collection of the Tang Poetry*.

放鱼

早觅为龙去,
江湖莫漫游。
须知香饵下,
触口是铦钩。

Releasing the Captive Fish

To be an early bird for a meteoric rise,
Be careful of yourself as you roam far and wide.
The bait is sweet but it is only to entice,
Swallowing the bait you'll be a prey in the tide.

莲叶

根是泥中玉，
心承露下珠。
在君塘下种，
埋没任春蒲。

Lotus Leaves

Deep in the mud your root is a piece of jade,
Dew drops in the heart of your leaves like pearls bright.
Growing in the pond you are the best in grade,
In the shade of reed mace in spring of great height.

客愁

客愁看柳色,
日日逐春深。
荡漾春风起,
谁知历乱心。

Sorrow in a Strange Land

Gazing at willows I'm hit by dismay,
Day by day spring is fading away.
Ripples spread on the water as breeze blows,
My thoughts are tangled but no one knows.

火炉前坐

孤灯照不寐，
风雨满西林。
多少关心事，
书灰到夜深。

Sitting by the Stove

Sleepless I'm sitting by a lonely light,
Through the west woods the wind and rain sweep right.
My mind is loaded with lots of concerns,
On the stove ashes I write at midnight.

寄韦秀才

荆台兰渚客，
寥落共含情。
空馆相思夜，
孤灯照雨声。

To Mr. Wei a Talented Scholar

Both you and I roam in an alien land,
On good terms we mutually understand.
In the quiet hotel I miss you at night,
Pit-a-pat it rains in the lonely light.

赠人

曾留宋玉旧衣裳，
惹得巫山梦里香。
云雨无情难管领，
任他别嫁楚襄王。

To a Jilted Lover

Like Song Yu[*] you are gifted with literary grace,
That enchants the mountain goddess into a dreamy place.
But the floating clouds are fickle like unbridled shower,
Catering to the king of Chu State that is in power.

---

[*] Song Yu(298~222 BC), styled Ziyuan, was born in Yancheng of the Chu State (Yicheng City, Hubei Province today). Song, well gifted in classical Chinese poetry, was regarded as a great poet after Qu Yuan, the first greatest poet in China.

引水行

一条寒玉走秋泉,
引出深萝洞口烟。
十里暗流声不断,
行人头上过潺湲。

Channeling Spring Water Through a Bamboo Tube

The autumn spring flows along the bamboo tube like green jade,
From the cave hidden in grass the mist and haze never fade.
Gurgling forward the undercurrent flows far away,
Overhead the travelers it murmurs night and day.

寄友

野水晴山雪后时，
独行村路更相思。
无因一向溪桥醉，
处处寒梅映酒旗。

To a Friend

Waters and mountains loom in the open after snow,
Missing you on the way to the cot my sorrows grow.
Drinking by the stream bridge tipsy soon I don't know why,
Plum flowers bloom everywhere and tavern streamers fly.

醴陵道中

别酒离亭十里强,
半醒半醉引愁长。
无人寂寂春山路,
雪打溪梅狼藉香。

On the Way to Liling

After drinking I'm away from the post pavilion,
Half sober, half drunk on the way I'm deep in sorrow.
Walking alone on the mountain path I'm crestfallen,
Scattering by the stream are plum petals fragrant in snow.

宋 范宽 《溪山行旅图》

汉阳太白楼

江上层楼翠霭间，
满帘春水满窗山。
青枫绿草将愁去，
远入吴云暝不还。

Taibai Building in Hanyang

The building by the river towers into the mist green,
Spring water and mountains came into view from window screen.
Green maples and verdant grass divert my sorrow away,
Far into the distant clouds that is a dim sight serene.

送客

沅水罗文海燕回，
柳条牵恨到荆台。
定知行路春愁里，
故郢城边见落梅。

A Send-off to a Friend

Ripples spread on the Yuan River and return petrels,
The parting grief goes with the willow twig far away.
Pestered by spring sorrows your tour must be in dismay,
At your destination you're greeted by plum petals.

书院二小松

一双幽色出凡尘,
数粒秋烟二尺鳞。
从此静窗闻细韵,
琴声长伴读书人。

Two Small Pines by My Study

Outstanding in the mortal world are two pines of dark green,
Needle leaves like smoke atop the stems of two feet high.
Pleasant whisper in wind comes in through the window screen,
Accompanying me reading like the music from the sky.

南庄春晚

连云草映一条陂,
鸂鶒双双带水飞。
南村小路桃花落,
细雨斜风独自归。

An Evening View of the South Village in Spring

Grass-covered slope stretches to the clouds in the sky,
On the surface of water lovebirds in pairs fly.
Along the path to the South Village peach flowers fade,
In the fine rain and breeze homeward alone I wade.

秋登涔阳城

穿针楼上闭秋烟,
织女佳期又隔年。
斜笛夜深吹不落,
一条银汉挂秋天。

Atop Cenyang Building in Autumn

Closed is the Weaving Building* in the autumn mist,
The Weaving Maid's to wait a year for the date at least.
Playing the flute to the Galaxy at dead of night,
The Milky Way across the autumn sky is so bright.

---

* The Weaving Building is the abode of the Weaving Maid who has date once a year with the Herd-boy across the Galaxy on the seventh evening of the seventh month of the lunar calendar according to Chinese mythology.

题二妃庙

黄陵庙前春已空，
子规啼血滴松风。
不知精爽归何处，
疑是行云秋色中。

To the Temple of Two Concubines

In front of the Huangling Temple* spring has faded away,
Cuckoos call and blood drips to pines in the wind night and day.
"Where and when could your souls rest?" I really don't know,
Maybe the cloud and mist in autumn tint are so mellow.

---

* The Huangling Temple, located on Dongting lakeside, is said to be the temple built for E Huang and Nu Ying, the two concubines of Emperor Shun(about 2140 BC) according to Chinese legend.

北亭

斜雨飞丝织晓空,
疏帘半卷野亭风。
荷花向尽秋光晚,
零落残红绿沼中。

The North Pavilion

Drizzle weaves a curtain slanting in the morning sky,
Half rolled up is the pavilion screen by wind on high.
Fading are lotus flowers and autumn is on the wane,
Scattering on the green pond are petals of pink stain.

二辛夷

狂吟乱舞双白鹤,
霜翎玉羽纷纷落。
空庭向晚春雨微,
却敛寒香抱瑶萼。

Two Magnolias

They sing and dance like a pair of cranes wild with delight,
Plumes and feathers are the fallen petals pink and white.
Empty is the yard at dust and spring rain fades away,
Holding back their cold scent the calyxes are cupped tight.

文殊院避暑

赤日黄埃满世间，
松声入耳即心闲。
愿寻五百仙人去，
一世清凉住雪山。

Avoiding Dog Days in the *Manjusri* Temple

Dim is the blazing sun with clouds of dust over the sky,
Hearing the sough of wind in the pines I stay calm in peace.
Staying in temple with five-hundred fairies I aim high,
In the snow-capped mountain I enjoy a life of ease.

江南

鳞鳞别浦起微波，
泛泛轻舟桃叶歌。
斜雪北风何处宿，
江南一路酒旗多。

Farewell to the South of the Yangtze River

At the parting time ripples spread from the riverside light,
In the floating skiff the parting song is very touching.
In the north wind where can you stay for the snowy night?
All over the south of the Yangtze River the tavern flags are flying.

钓鱼

七尺青竿一丈丝,
菰蒲叶里逐风吹。
几回举手抛芳饵,
惊起沙滩水鸭儿。

Angling

Green is the fishing rod and fishing line long enough,
Amid paddy rice and reed mace it sways with wind sough.
Uplifting my hand many times I cast the sweet bait,
Slightly startled the wild ducks on the sands flying straight.

春晚

思乡之客空凝睇，
天边欲尽未尽春。
独攀江树深不语，
芳草落花愁杀人。

An Evening View of Spring

Suffering from homesickness I knit my brows in vain,
Gazing far I have the evening view on the brain.
Deep in silence I climb the tree by the riverside,
Gloomy about green grass and pink petals I let things slide.

卢 肇

卢肇(818~882),字子发,袁州宜春(今江西分宜)人。曾任歙州刺史。《全唐诗》存其诗一卷。

Lu Zhao(818~882), styled Zifa, was born in Yichun, Yuanzhou (Fenyi County, Jiangxi Province today). Lu was once appointed the governor of Shezhou Prefecture. There is one volume of his poems collected in *The Complete Collection of the Tang Poetry*.

杨柳枝

青鸟泉边草木春,
黄云塞上是征人。
归来若得长条赠,
不惮风霜与苦辛。

Willow Twigs

By the Qingniao Spring plants and trees are freshly green,
Beyond the frontier fort are soldiers standing guard.
If one day I can reunite with my kith and kin,
I'll be a brave soldier even if I'm hit hard.

送弟

去日家无担石储，
汝须勤苦事樵渔。
古人尽向尘中远，
白日耕田夜读书。

A Farewell Verse to My Brother

There had been a little store of food in the past,
It was an arduous task to make the living last.
Working hard like forefathers for a future bright,
Farming in the daytime you've to study at night.

牧童

谁人得似牧童心，
牛上横眠秋听深。
时复往来吹一曲，
何愁南北不知音。

To a Cowboy

None of grown-ups can be innocent as a cowboy,
Seeping on the back of the cow as autumn goes by.
Playing flute time and again it's really a great joy,
No need to worry about soul mates he's riding high.

罗 隐

罗隐(833～910),字昭谏,余杭(今浙江富阳)人。少年即负诗名,恃才傲物。绝句语言浅白,风格自然流畅。《全唐诗》存其诗十一卷。

Luo Yin (833～910), styled Zhaojian, was born in Yuhang (Fuyang County, Zhejiang Province today). Luo thought too much of his gift as a young poet. His quatrains are characterized by clear and plain language in smooth and natural style. Eleven volumes of his poems are collected in *The Complete Collection of the Tang Poetry*.

雪

尽道丰年瑞,
丰年事若何。
长安有贫者,
为瑞不宜多。

Snow

Timely snow promises a bumper year it's said,
A good year may end in disaster I'm afraid.
In the capital the poor have died of hunger,
Bumper harvest year, but more people will suffer.

蜂

不论平地与山尖，
无限春光尽被占。
采得百花成蜜后，
为谁辛苦为谁甜？

To Bees

Over the mountains and plains you fly far and wide,
Never let any charming spot slip from your side.
From flower to flower you're busy making honey,
To toil and moil for whom you are always ready?

自遣

得即高歌失却休,
多愁多恨亦悠悠。
今朝有酒今朝醉,
明日愁来明日愁。

Self-consolation

With success I'm delighted and failure, let it go,
Free from worries no sorrow to me can be a blow.
When you have wine now drink to your heart's content today,
Should sorrow come tomorrow, it'd be melted away.

鹦鹉

莫恨雕笼翠羽残，
江南地暖陇西寒。
劝君不用分明语，
语得分明出转难。

To the Parrot

Do not complain of your wings clipped in the painted cage,
It's warmer in the south of the Yangtze River than the northwest.
No need to articulate each word even though you're sage,
Clear remarks will be offensive and it's indeed a pest.

韦 庄

韦庄(836~910),字端己,京兆杜陵(今陕西西安)人。曾在朝为官。其诗多为闺情离愁之作,绝句包蕴丰满,风格清丽。《全唐诗》存其诗六卷。

Wei Zhuang (836~910), styled Duanji, was born in Duling, Jingzhao (Xi'an City, Shaanxi Province today). Wei once held office in the imperial court and his poems mainly picture parting pains and sorrows of girls and young women. His quatrains are profound in content with lucid style. Six volumes of his poems are collected in *The Complete Collection of the Tang Poetry*.

台城

江雨霏霏江草齐,
六朝如梦鸟空啼。
无情最是台城柳,
依旧烟笼十里堤。

The Imperial Citadel

Grass grows lushly and by the river rain falls thick and fast,
Birds cry in vain and like dreams six dynasties have passed.
Along the dike of citadel heartless are the willows,
Looming out of the dim mist a ten-mile shadow they cast.

江外思乡

年年春日异乡悲，
杜曲黄莺可得知。
更被夕阳江岸上，
断肠烟柳一丝丝。

Homesickness Beyond the River

Year by year in spring I am sad in the strange land,
My gloom only cuckoos and orioles understand.
Willows on the bank sway in the evening glow,
The charm of misty view makes my homesickness grow.

司空图

司空图(837～908),字表圣,自号知非子,又号耐辱居士,河中虞乡(今山西永济)人。著有诗学理论《二十四诗品》,强调注重诗歌写作中的"味外之旨"和"韵外之致"。其诗作多表现闲情逸致。《全唐诗》存其诗三卷。

Sikong Tu (837～908), styled Biaosheng, self-styled Zhi Feizi, also known as Insult-resisting Hermit, was born in Yuxiang, Hezhong (Yongji City, Shanxi Province today). His treatise *Twenty-Four Grades of Poetry* has great renown in history of Chinese literature, which reflects his theory of poetics—"the meaning beyond the rhythm" and "the appeal beyond the rhyme" should be highlighted in poem writing. Most of his poems are about the easy and carefree life, of which three volumes are collected in *The Complete Collection of the Tang Poetry*.

中秋

闲吟秋景外,
万事觉悠悠。
此夜若无月,
一年虚过秋。

The Mid-Autumn Festival

To the autumn scene I leisurely recite,
Myriads of events quickly flash through my mind.
If the moon vanishes from the sky tonight,
The autumn this year would be the worst of its kind.

宋　赵佶（宋徽宗）《溪山秋色图》

独望

绿树连村暗,
黄花出陌稀。
远陂春草绿,
犹有水禽飞。

Looking into the Distant View Alone

Blurred by green trees the village is dim in sight,
Dotting the wheat fields yellow flowers are sparse.
On the distant hill slope verdant is spring grass,
As if there are some water birds on a free flight.

即事

茶爽添诗句,
天清莹道心。
只留鹤一只,
此外是空林。

An Extempore Poem

A sip of fresh tea triggers my poetic mood,
To be a Buddhist the pure sky makes me brood.
With one and only crane flying in the sky,
Over the open forest it seems so high.

退居漫题

努力省前非，
人生上寿稀。
青云无直道，
暗室有危机。

A Poem Composed at Random After Resignation

I spare no effort to introspect my wrong,
It is rare for a person to live too long.
The route to high position is by no means straight,
In the gloomy corner danger lurks and it's great.

秋景

景物皆难驻，
伤春复怨秋。
旋书红叶落，
拟画碧云收。

The Autumn Scenery

The beautiful scenery can hardly long stay,
Pity is that spring and autumn fast fade away.
Red leaves whirling in the air, a magic theme,
The cloudscape is a painting floating in the dream.

独坐

幽径入桑麻,
坞西逢一家。
编篱新带茧,
补屋草和花。

Sitting Alone in Face of a Cottage

Through the mulberry grove is a secluded path,
To the west of the hollow there's a cottage hearth.
Clinging to the woven fences are new cocoons,
The cottage is mended with some flowers and grass.

岁尽

莫话伤心事，
投春满鬓霜。
殷勤共尊酒，
今岁只残阳。

Reflections at the End of the Year

No more talking about heart-breaking event,
I'm hoary-headed when spring is drawing nigh,
Please have a cup of wine with me on a high.
Except the sunset I've nothing to present.

鹂

不是流莺独占春，
林间彩翠四时新。
应知拟上屏风画，
偏坐横枝亦向人。

To the Oriole

The oriole sings, not that it comes out first in fresh green,
Colors of flowers in the woods change from time to time.
It is graceful enough to be painted on the screen,
But perching on the branch it yearns for the human prime.

柳

谁家按舞傍池塘，
已见繁枝嫩眼黄。
漫说早梅先得意，
不知春力暗分张。

To the Willow

Dancing to the tempo by pond who are you?
With tender buds along twigs I'm the willow.
Don't be too proud of yourself, the plum flower,
To you, to me the spring spreads the same shower.

王官

荷塘烟罩小斋虚,
景物皆宜入画图。
尽日无人只高卧,
一双白鸟隔纱厨。

Wangguan Valley

Void is my small study by the lotus pond in mist,
So pleasant is the scenery like a screen painting.
No one drops in I rest on a high pillow as I list,
Outside the screen a pair of white birds are peeping.

陆龟蒙

陆龟蒙(生卒年不详),字鲁望,姑苏(今江苏苏州)人。举进士不中,自耕乡里,游乐自适,时谓江湖散人。其诗多写景咏物。《全唐诗》存其诗十四卷。

Lu Guimeng, styled Luwang, was born in Gusu (Suzhou City, Jiangsu Province today). Failed to be a candidate of the imperial examination, he was engaged in farming and recreation by and for himself in slack season, then known as a happy-go-lucky rover. Lu was well versed in depicting scenery and varied objects. Fourteen volumes of his poems are collected in *The Complete Collection of the Tang Poetry*.

春

山连翠羽屏,
草接烟华席。
望尽南飞燕,
佳人断消息。

Spring

Range upon range of mountains are like a folding screen,
Grass and flowers stretch out far away lush and green.
Watching the swallow flying south till they vanish,
No news to me from my darling at the finish.

夕阳

渡口和帆落,
城边带角收。
如何茂陵客,
江上倚危楼。

The Setting Sun

Sailings are suspended at the ferry crossing,
Bugles outside the city wall come to ceasing.
At the riverside tower the poet heaves a sigh,
Leaning on the rail alone nobody knows why.

南塘曲

妾住东湖下，
郎居南浦边。
闲临烟水望，
认得采菱船。

Song of the South Pond

At the foot of the east lake is my abode,
To the south of the lake is yours by waterside.
Gaze into the misty lake in a good mood,
You can easily spot my boat far and wide.

秋

凉汉清泬寥,
衰林怨风雨。
愁听络纬唱,
似与羁魂语。

Autumn

Vast is the Milky Way lonely and bright,
Wailing are the woods resenting the storm.
Crickets' chirps to me are a worry slight,
It seems a caged soul murmurs off form.

芙蓉

闲吟鲍照赋,
更起屈平愁。
莫引西风动,
红衣不耐秋。

To Lotus Flowers

You are the main topic of Bao Zhao's* poetry,
And the trigger of sorrow in Qu Yuan's rhyme.
Oh, bleak west wind, it stirs up a sad story,
Your pink dress is too thin to bear autumn rime.

---

* Bao Zhao (414~466) was a literary man of the Song State during the Southern Dynasties in China.

怀宛陵旧游

陵阳佳地昔年游，
谢朓青山李白楼。
唯有日斜溪上思，
酒旗风影落春流。

Recollection of the Past Tour to Wanling

During the tour to Wanling a nice place in the past,
I visited Li and Xie's haunt* the historic site.
Never forget the slanting sun in the water vast,
And the tavern flag dancing in the ripples a charming sight.

---

* Li and Xie's haunt here refers to the favorite haunt for Xie Tiao (464~499, a famous poet) and Li Bai (701~762, a great romantic poet).

早行

水寒孤棹触天文,
直似乘槎去问津。
纵使碧虚无限好,
客星名字也愁人。

An Early Departure

A lone oar in the cold water stirs the stars and the moon,
As if looking for the crossing on a raft I'm alone.
Blue and bright is the sky even though it is very nice,
To be a new star alone I'll be put on the thin ice.

江城夜泊

漏移寒箭丁丁急,
月挂虚弓霭霭明。
此夜离魂堪射断,
更须江笛两三声。

Mooring at Night

The tick of the water clock is rapid at night,
Like a bow the moon in the sky is dim in sight.
The heavy weight on me is the pain of parting,
What is more the siren sounds sharply at its height.

冬柳

柳汀斜对野人窗,
零落衰条傍晓江。
正是霜风飘断处,
寒鸥惊起一双双。

Willows in Winter

The willow shoal faces a farmer's window on a slant,
By the riverside at dawn twigs are like wilting plants.
At the time when the bleak wind breaks a branch off the tree,
Gulls in winter would be startled in pairs from their haunt.

宋　刘松年　《四景山水图·冬》(局部)

新沙

渤澥声中涨小堤,
官家知后海鸥知。
蓬莱有路教人到,
应亦年年税紫芝。

The Newly Silted Sandbank

A newly sandbank has been silted up at the sea bay,
The government knows it earlier than the gulls in the sky.
If to Penglai Island, the fairyland there is a way,
The immortals would be taxed even on fairy pie.

晚渡

半波风雨半波晴,
渔曲飘秋野调清。
各样莲船逗村去,
笠檐蓑袂有残声。

An Evening View at a Ferry Crossing

Fine and rainy days by the river are half and half,
Fishermen sing to the autumn sky just for funfair.
All kinds of row-boats race for the cot speedy enough,
The sound of the charming songs still lingers in the air.

和袭美春夕酒醒

几年无事傍江湖，
醉倒黄公旧酒垆。
觉后不知明月上，
满身花影倩人扶。

Awaking from Drunkenness on a Spring Night with Pi Rixiu*

Wandering around the world for years I'm on a high,
Drink myself under the table like sages of the past.
Blind drunk I'm unaware of the moon bright in the sky,
A belle helps me sober up from shadows flowers cast.

---

* Pi Rixiu(838～883), styled Ximei, was a famous poet of late Tang Dynasty.

春思

江南酒熟清明天，
高高绿旆当风悬。
谁家无事少年子，
满面落花犹醉眠。

Reverie in Spring

Mellow is the wine in the south of the Yangtze River on a bright spring day,
Against the soft wind the green wine flags are fluttering high.
Who's the youngster drunk as a lord idling his time away,
With petals on his face sleeping under the open sky.

和袭美春夕陪崔谏议樱桃园宴

佳人芳树杂春蹊，
花外烟濛月渐低。
几度艳歌清欲转，
流莺惊起不成栖。

Banquet in the Cherry Orchard on a Spring Night

Along the path in spring are belles under fragrant trees,
Beyond the misty flowers nearly setting the moon is.
Time and again love songs linger sweetly in the fresh air,
Startling orioles flying who want to rest but find nowhere.

皮日休

皮日休(838～883),字逸少,后改袭美,襄阳(今湖北襄阳)人。曾任翰林学士,工诗文。在诗歌造诣上与陆龟蒙齐名。《全唐诗》存其诗九卷。

Pi Rixiu (838～883), styled Yishao, changed to Ximei later, was born in Xiangyang (Xiangyang City, Hubei Province today). Once promoted to a member of the imperial academy, Pi was well versed in poem and prose writing, enjoying equal fame with Lu Guimeng in the literary history of China. Nine volumes of his poems are collected in *The Complete Collection of the Tang Poetry*.

古宫词

玉枕寐不足,
宫花空触檐。
梁间燕不睡,
应怪夜明帘。

Song of the Ancient Palace

On the jade pillow they have no sound dream,
Flowers of the palaces touch the eaves rim.
On the roof beam swallows toss and turn all night,
Curtain is to blame because it is too bright.

聪明泉

一勺如琼液，
将愚拟望贤。
欲知心不变，
还似饮贪泉。

An Intelligent Spring

A spoon of the spring water tastes the cream of wine,
Drinking from the spring the fool desires to be a sage.
If you remain hard-hearted even though the idea is fine,
Drinking greedily from the spring still you're in the cage.

秋江晓望

万顷湖天碧，
一星飞鹭白。
此时放怀望，
不厌为浮客。

The Morning View of River in Autumn

The vast water stretches to the blue sky,
An egret like a white star flies so high.
Gazing steadily into the wide space,
Never tired of roaming I want to fly.

馆娃宫怀古

半夜娃宫作战场，
血腥犹杂宴时香。
西施不及烧残蜡，
犹为君王泣数行。

Meditations on Guanwa Palace*

Guanwa Palace was taken as the battleground at night,
Mixed with the smell of blood was that of feast for years.
Before Xi Shi lighted the waning candle for bright light,
The king was captured and for the king she burst into tears.

---

* Guanwa Palace was an ancient palace built by the king of Kingdom Wu for Xi Shi, a famous beauty presented by the king of Kingdom Yue as a trap to ensnare the king of Kingdom Wu.

雍 陶

雍陶(生卒年不详),字国钧,成都(今四川成都)人。曾在朝为官,任简州刺史。其诗文多反映山水景物,诗风清婉明丽。《全唐诗》存其诗一卷。

Yong Tao, styled Guojun, was born in Chengdu (Chengdu City, Sichuan Province today). Yong was once appointed a prefectural governor and his poems mainly picture the landscape scenery in clear and bright style, of which one volume is collected in *The Complete Collection of the Tang Poetry*.

闻子规

百鸟有啼时,
子规声不歇。
春寒四邻静,
独叫三更月。

Call of the Cuckoo

All birds in the world sing at the specific time,
But cuckoo calls from morning till night in its prime.
Chilly still in spring all neighbors are calm at night,
Only the cuckoo calls to the midnight moon bright.

送客遥望

别远心更苦,
遥将目送君。
光华不可见,
孤鹤没秋云。

Seeing a Friend Off into Distance

Parting with you on a long journey I'm in sorrow,
Gazing after you for long my eyes closely follow.
Your figure vanishes slowly as you're on your way,
Like a lonely crane in the autumn clouds fades away.

题情尽桥

从来只有情难尽，
何事名为情尽桥。
自此改名为折柳，
任他离恨一条条。

To the Bridge of Love's Ending

The true love usually lasts forever,
This bridge is called "Love's Ending" however.
Pluck a willow twig at the parting time,
"Willow Plucking" as the new name is prime.

忆江南旧居

闲思往事在湖亭，
亭上秋灯照月明。
宿客尽眠眠不得，
半窗残月带潮声。

Nostalgia for My Old Abode in the South of the Yangtze River

Around the pavilion of the lake I think of the past,
In the moonlight the autumn lamps on the lake are especially bright.
Near the window by hook or by crook I try to sleep fast,
The moon's waning and I hear the roars of the tide at night.

元　倪瓒　《秋亭嘉树图》

题君山

烟波不动影沉沉,
碧色全无翠色深。
疑是水仙梳洗处,
一螺青黛镜中心。

To Junshan Hill in Dongting Lake

Calm are the misty waves shaded by the hill of grace,
Vivid green vanishes and it gives way to the dark green.
It's said the nymph dressed herself up in the very place,
Like the hill her bun mirrors in the water clear and clean.

天津桥望春

津桥春水浸红霞，
烟柳风丝拂岸斜。
翠辇不来金殿闭，
宫莺衔出上阳花。

A Spring View at Tianjin Bridge

Under the bridge the river mirrors the rosy cloud,
Willow twigs in the mist sway along the banks in breeze.
Locked is the grand palace and peers are no more proud,
From whence warblers flying out carry petals with bliss.

韩　偓

韩偓（842～923），字致光，自号玉山樵人，京兆万年（今陕西西安）人。幼年能诗，其诗受其姨父李商隐影响，词藻华丽，风格秾艳，有"香奁体"之称。晚年作品感时伤怀，风格慷慨悲凉。《全唐诗》存其诗四卷。

Han Wo (842~923), styled Zhiguang, also known as a Woodcutter in Yushan Mountain, his literary name, was born in Wannian, Jingzhao (Xi'an City, Shaanxi Province today). Han was well versed in poem writing when he was a child. Influenced by Li Shangyin, his poems were composed with flowery language in bright style, known for the poem of "Perfume Compact", but his poems late in his life were sentimental in heroic style with desolation to some degree. Four volumes of his poems are collected in *The Complete Collection of the Tang Poetry*.

效崔国辅体

澹月照中庭，
海棠花自落。
独立俯闲阶，
风动秋千索。

Loneliness

The deep courtyard is bathed in the pale moonlight,
Falling down are petals from the crabapple tree.
Looking down at the steps she's in a trance at night,
Nothing but the swing sway in the wind she could see.

两处

楼上澹山横,
楼前沟水清。
怜山又怜水,
两处总牵情。

Two Places on My Mind

Atop the tower a quiet mountain is in sight,
In front of the tower a limpid stream flows.
Tender and loving towards them day and night,
Always concerned about them my love grows.

春闺

愿结交加梦,
因倾潋滟尊。
醒来情绪恶,
帘外正黄昏。

A Maiden in Boudoir in Spring

Longing to meet my lover in my dream,
I have my wine glass filled to the brim.
Wakened from drunkenness I'm crestfallen,
Gloom is gathering outside the curtain.

自沙县抵龙溪县,值泉州军过后,村落皆空,因有一绝

水自潺湲日自斜,
尽无鸡犬有鸣鸦。
千村万落如寒食,
不见人烟空见花。

A Postwar Village

The stream murmurs on its own and the sun's slanting,
No fowl or dogs in sight only crows are cawing.
From the deserted villages no smoke is curling,
With no figures in sight, only flowers blooming.

哭花

曾愁香结破颜迟，
今见妖红委地时。
若是有情争不哭，
夜来风雨葬西施。

Weeping over Flowers

It worried me very much buds would bloom late,
But I have seen the flowers wilting today.
Were you tender-hearted, you'd weep for their fate,
Like a belle in the night storm fading away.

新秋

一夜清风动扇愁,
背时容色入新秋。
桃花眼里汪汪泪,
忍到更深枕上流。

The Early Autumn

The cool breeze blows at night with fan in hand she's in sorrow,
Out of date at the early autumn she's lost her marrow.
Like peach blossoms swollen are her eyes brimming with tears,
In the depth of night tears run down and wet her pillow.

寒食夜

恻恻轻寒剪剪风，
杏花飘雪小桃红。
夜深斜搭秋千索，
楼阁朦胧细雨中。

On the Night of Cold-food Festival

It's chilly enough and the wind soughing at night,
Pink are peach blossoms and apricot petals white.
In the depth of night the swing moves back and forth,
I think of her boudoir dim in the drizzle light.

晓日

天际霞光入水中，
水中天际一时红。
直须日观三更后，
首送金乌上碧空。

The Sun at Dawn

Mirrored on the water are red rays on the horizon,
Both the water and the horizon are dyed rich crimson.
Atop the summit of the mountain after the midnight,
You can see the sun emerging from behind the twilight.

野塘

侵晓乘凉偶独来,
不因鱼跃见萍开。
卷荷忽被微风触,
泻下清香露一杯。

The Wild Pool

I come to the pool alone to enjoy the cool at dawn,
The duckweed is dispersing but no fish is seen jumping.
All of sudden a lotus leaf with light wind is skipping,
A cup of fragrant dew from the lotus leaf pours down.

驿楼

流云溶溶水悠悠，
故乡千里空回头。
三更犹凭阑干月，
泪满关山孤驿楼。

Atop the Post Building

Clouds are floating high and flowing is the river vast,
Turning round I cannot see my native land in sight.
In the moonlight I still lean on the rails at night,
Atop the post building in tears I think of the past.

王 驾

王驾(生卒年不详),字大用,自号守素先生,河中(今山西永济)人。曾在朝为官,后弃官归隐。其诗语言素雅,风格自然清丽。《全唐诗》存其诗六首。

Wang Jia, styled Dayong, also known as Mr. Shousu, was born in Hezhong (Yongji City, Shanxi Province today). Wang once served in the imperial court and resigned his position later for a secluded life. His poems are composed with simple but elegant language in natural and lucid style. Six of his poems are collected in *The Complete Collection of the Tang Poetry*.

社日

鹅湖山下稻粱肥,
豚栅鸡栖半掩扉。
桑柘影斜春社散,
家家扶得醉人归。

A Feast Day in Spring

At the foot of the Ehu Hill paddy crops lushly grow,
Half-closed is the coop and left ajar is the pigsty.
Feast is over, the mulberry shade slants in the dusk glow,
Helped back home are the villagers drunk still on a high.

雨晴

雨前初见花间蕊，
雨后全无叶底花。
蜂蝶纷纷过墙去，
却疑春色在邻家。

A Fine Day After Rain

Before the rain pistils first come into my sight,
After the rain no flowers but leaves shine bright.
Flying over the wall are butterflies and bees,
I wonder if in the next yard spring's at its height.

杜荀鹤

杜荀鹤(846~907),字彦之,号九华山人,池州石埭(今安徽黄山)人。早年家贫,青年时代以诗歌自负。其诗语言通俗,雅俗共赏,在晚唐时期深受欢迎。《全唐诗》存其诗三卷。

Du Xunhe (846~907), styled Yanzhi, also known as "Hermit in Jiuhua Mountain", was born in Shidai, Chizhou (Huangshan City, Anhui Province today). His family was in straitened circumstances when he was a child, but he was proud of himself as a poet when he was young. His poems were enjoyed by both highbrows and lowbrows as they are characterized by simple language in late Tang Dynasty, of which three volumes are collected in *The Complete Collection of the Tang Poetry*.

感寓

大海波涛浅,
小人方寸深。
海枯终见底,
人死不知心。

A Sentimental Sigh

The surging waves at sea may be shallow,
But deep is the mind of a mean fellow.
If the seas dry up the bed would be seen,
But as the man dies his heart's still hollow.

春闺怨

朝喜花艳春,
暮悲花委尘。
不悲花落早,
悲妾似花身。

Grievances from the Boudoir in Spring

Pleased to see spring flowers bright in the morn,
Gloomy to see flowers fade away at dusk.
Sad not because of flowers fallen like husk,
But because like flowers someday I'll be worn.

钓叟

茅屋深湾里，
钓船横竹门。
经营衣食外，
犹得弄儿孙。

To an Old Angler

The thatched cottage is located by the deep bay,
Tied to the gate is the small boat for fishing.
Besides working hard for making a living,
My family have a life happy and gay.

黄 巢

黄巢(820～884),曹州冤句(今山东曹县)人。私盐贩出身,唐末农民起义军领袖,后战败自杀。

Huang Chao (820～884), born into a family of a salt vendor in Yuanju, Caozhou (Caoxian County, Shandong Province today), was a peasant uprising leader in the last years of the Tang Dynasty. He committed suicide after his troops were defeated in 884.

题菊花

飒飒西风满院栽,
蕊寒香冷蝶难来。
他年我若为青帝,
报与桃花一处开。

To Chrysanthemums

In soughing west wind you bloom in my courtyard far and wide,
Too cold is your fragrance to keep butterflies to your side.
Some day if I am the God of Spring that is in power,
I'd like you to bloom in the same season with peach flower.

不第后赋菊

待到秋来九月八,
我花开后百花杀。
冲天香阵透长安,
满城尽带黄金甲。

To the Chrysanthemums After Failing the Imperial Examination

When autumn comes the Double Ninth Festival is nigh,
As my flower blooms the other blossoms fade away.
Wafting to the sky is the scent from a vast array,
Tinted with gold the whole capital is on a high.

译后记
Postword

  站三尺讲台,度四十春秋,其中三十载译者一直从事翻译理论与实践的教学研究。2013年退休后,译者集中精力完成了经典中国国际出版工程《元散曲英译》(1200首,五卷本)的选译,分别于2015年秋和2016年春在中国和英国出版。项目顺利结题,并荣获第十六届输出版优秀图书奖。辛劳之余,几许欣慰。

  《唐人绝句精粹》(中英文版)(以下简称为《绝句》)是《元散曲英译》的姊妹篇。两部书同时策划,只是小孙子的出世致使前者延至2016年春才动笔。唐诗总量近五万首,仅绝句就达万余首,如何选取所需的一千余首是译者面临的首要问题。迄今为止,宋人洪迈所编的《万首唐人绝句》是规模最大的唐人绝句总集。不过,其中存疑较多。明万历年间,赵宧光、黄习远对《万首唐人绝句》进行了认真的整理。然而,仍旧遗留不少问题。1991年,山西人民出版社出版了霍松林先生主编的《万首唐人绝句校注集评》,该书对前两部选集进行较为详尽的校勘,对部分难点加以注释,极大地方便了今天的读者。本书就主要参考了霍松林先生的选本,译者谨此致谢。

《绝句》选取了唐代近百位诗人的一千余首绝句,其遴选的基本原则是：初唐、盛唐、晚唐不同时期影响较大的著名诗人的代表作,如李白、杜甫、白居易、王维、刘禹锡、王建、杜牧、李商隐等,选用数量少则二十余首,多则五十余首。有的诗人就其诗歌创作而言影响并不大,但自身颇具代表性,如张九龄、薛涛等；前者官至宰相,是达官贵人的代表,后者沦为歌伎,是底层百姓的代表。这类诗人虽然作品不多,但水平较高,且为读者喜闻乐见,所以亦有作品入选。

《绝句》在遴选时常会遇到不同版本,译者通常以《全唐诗》为蓝本,并为每位入选诗人撰写了简介,包括生卒年份（生卒年不详者另外标注）、籍贯、字、号、生平事迹及作品风格,以增进读者对诗人的了解。

鉴于诗歌的特殊文体和"赋、比、兴"创作手法的要求,唐诗中常常出现文化内涵深邃的成语和典故。对身处与原文相同语境的国内读者而言,阅读不太困难,互文、关联和工具书通常可以消除理解障碍。一旦译成英文,这类文化负载词语便被置于全新的语言环境,基于同一语境而存在的互文和关联之便对译文读者而言已不复存在,这就给大多数译文读者造成了理解障碍。若采取文内释义,理解障碍便可得以解决,但释义内容往往使诗行超长,势必破坏译文的结构,"形美"则不复存在。故此,译者对较为冷僻的成语和典故（如蔡州、苍梧、临邛、斗鸡台、马嵬坡；飞燕、曹操、韩信、子猷、西施、蜀魂等）采用直译（或音译）加脚注的方法。这种文外释义的手法既保留了原诗的结构形式,又解决了译文读者的理解困难,是译者应对文化负载词的常用措施。

虽然英文诗歌中存在无韵诗,但唐诗,尤其是唐人绝句都是押韵的。如果将唐人绝句译成无韵体英文诗歌,那么翻译起来也相对容易,但诗歌三要素"意、音、形"中的"音",即大多数学者所强调的"音美"就不复存在了。为了较为全面地再现唐人绝句之美,译者将所选一千余首绝句全部译成韵体诗,采用ａｂａｂ韵、ａａｂｂ韵、ａｂｂａ韵或ａａｂａ韵。然而,诗无达诂,译无至极,《绝句》的翻译毕竟是译者一孔之见,错误与不妥之处在所难免,恳请国内外读者不吝赐教。

此外,《绝句》的出版得到了安徽大学外语学院的鼎力相助,译者谨致谢忱。安徽大学出版社的编辑为此书的出版也付出了艰辛劳动,译者深表感谢。

诗歌是民族的,但更是世界的。翻译使莎士比亚、歌德、泰戈尔跨越语言文化疆域与中国读者对话,翻译也能让李白、杜甫、白居易穿越历史时空与世界读者交流。语言是存在之家,翻译必能使中国诗歌在异国他乡找到家园。

2018 年仲夏于巴黎